FEELING
BETRAYED

FEELING BETRAYED

The Roots of Muslim Anger at America

Steven Kull

BROOKINGS INSTITUTION PRESS
Washington, D.C.

Copyright © 2011

THE BROOKINGS INSTITUTION

1775 Massachusetts Avenue, N.W., Washington, D.C. 20036

www.brookings.edu

Library of Congress Cataloging-in-Publication data
Kull, Steven.
   Feeling betrayed : the roots of Muslim anger at America / Steven Kull.
      p. cm.
   Includes bibliographical references and index.
   Summary: "Explores the depth of anti-Americanism felt by Muslim populations in the Middle East and South Asia by reporting on opinions expressed during focus group sessions and in-depth surveys over several years, complemented by data from Gallup polls, World Values Survey, and Arab Barometer"—Provided by publisher.
   ISBN 978-0-8157-0559-8 (pbk. : alk. paper)
   1. United States—Relations—Islamic countries.   2. Islamic countries—Relations—United States.   3. Anti-Americanism—Islamic countries.   I. Title.
   JZ1480.A57174 2011
   303.48'27301767—dc22   2010053915

9 8 7 6 5 4 3 2 1

Printed on acid-free paper

Typeset in Sabon and Strayhorn

Composition by R. Lynn Rivenbark
Macon, Georgia

Printed by R. R. Donnelley
Harrisonburg, Virginia

Contents

Preface

On September 11, 2001, I was in Washington just over the river from the Pentagon when it was attacked and several blocks from the White House—the apparent target of the fourth hijacked jetliner. Like most Americans I was struck by the intensity of feeling that would lead nineteen young men to immolate themselves in the effort to kill several thousand civilians going about their daily business, civilians that could have easily included me.

This led me to ask what was occurring in the larger Muslim society that could have bred this extreme hostility. Surely the feelings that were expressed that day were not developed sui generis, in complete isolation from the culture in which these young men were born. Indeed, when the 9/11 attacks were reported in some cities in the Muslim world, many people openly expressed celebratory feelings.

To understand such feelings, being a psychologist as well as an international survey researcher, I felt a need to go to the Muslim world to sit down with Muslims and let them speak. It took little prompting before they poured out their feelings, often aimed at me as the most available target and symbol of America.

These feelings turned out to be complex and layered. At the most immediate level was a narrative based on the image of America as a force that seeks to coercively dominate the Muslim world, exploit its resources, and undermine its religion. With time, though, a more subtle level of feelings emerged in which people showed a strong sense of rapport with America and the values it represents. This was coupled with a deep sense that America has betrayed the Muslim people by proffering these values as a basis for amicable and trusting relations and then failing to live up to them. It was, however, at this level of discussion that the Muslims I spoke with revealed some implicit hope that relations between America and the Muslim world could be redeemed. Out of these direct conversations in focus groups I began to develop survey questions to determine how widespread these various feelings were.

Developing these surveys was a joint venture with many other individuals who made major contributions in writing questions and analyzing the results. Particularly helpful were other staff members at the Program on International Policy Attitudes (PIPA) where we spent many hours carefully crafting questions. Most notable was Clay Ramsay, research director and cofounder of PIPA. In addition to making invaluable contributions to the questionnaire development, Stephen Weber managed the complex process of conducting the surveys in numerous countries. Evan Lewis managed the statistical data. Ebrahim Mohseni worked diligently to ensure that I understood the deepest nuances of the Muslim perspective. Melanie Ciolek coordinated the survey partners and together with Abe Medoff carried out numerous critical functions in the process of gathering and organizing the data and performing other research assistance.

A key adviser was Shibley Telhami, who cotaught seminars with me on Muslim public opinion and made many valuable contributions to the drafts of the book. Others who gave useful advice were Abdel Latif, Fares Braizat, Mathew Warshaw, Nabil Kukali, Zsolt Nyiri, Flynt Leverett, and Marina Ottaway.

The National Consortium for the Study of Terrorism and Responses to Terrorism (START) at the University of Maryland was a major source of support for the first two sets of surveys conducted in four countries and for some of the writing of the text. Scholars at START made key contributions to developing the questionnaires, especially Clark McCauley, Arie Kruglanski, Mansoor Moaddel, and Gary LaFree. Others at START who played important roles in bringing these surveys to realization were Gary Ackerman, Kathy Smarick, Victor Asal, and Laura Dugan.

The surveys for START, subsequent surveys, and the recruitment of focus group participants were conducted by survey centers that were part of the WorldPublicOpinion.org network. These included A.C. Nielsen Pakistan and SEDCO in Pakistan, Attitude Market Research and the Emac Research and Training Center in Egypt, Deka Marketing Research and Synovate in Indonesia, the Center for Strategic Studies at the University of Jordan, Leger Marketing in Morocco, the Palestinian Center for Public Opinion in the Palestinian Territories, the ARI Foundation/Infakto Research Workshop in Turkey, D3 Systems/Afghan Center for Social and Opinion Research in Afghanistan, the International Center for Social Research in Azerbaijan, Org-Quest Research Limited in Bangladesh, and the Asharq Research Center and D3 Systems/KA Research in Iraq. In many cases the researchers at these centers made important contributions to the development and refinement of the questionnaires and provided insights into the findings as well.

The first surveys for START were supported by the U.S. Department of Homeland Security through the National Consortium for the Study of Terrorism and Responses to Terrorism (START), grant number N00140510629. Any opinions, findings, and conclusions or recommendations in this document, however, are those of the author and do not necessarily reflect views of the U.S. Department of Homeland Security.

Support for surveys in additional countries, for further surveys in countries included in the first START surveys, and for the analysis and writing of this book was provided by the Rockefeller Brothers Fund, the Carnegie Corporation, and the Calvert Foundation.

The United States Institute of Peace supported some of the polling in Iran and Pakistan. Christine Fair and Paul Stares, then at the institute, made valuable contributions to questionnaire development and analysis.

Some of the polling in Iran was also conducted in conjunction with Search for Common Ground. William Miller, John Marks, and Sonya Reines contributed to the development of the questionnaires and the analysis.

My partner, Nancy Lindborg, deserves special credit. She tolerated and was an important sounding board for endless noodling about what it all meant.

Finally, I wish to express my appreciation to the people who really made this book possible—the participants in the focus groups in majority-Muslim countries who sincerely tried to communicate their feelings to a stranger from America, trusting that I would present their words fairly and with respect. I hope they feel the trust was warranted.

Introduction:
America, Radical Islamist Groups, and the Muslim People

It has been nearly a decade since the United States was attacked by a group of radical Islamists on September 11, 2001. Since then, rooting out the network of terrorists behind the attacks and related radical Islamist groups has been a major focus of American foreign and military policy. The magnitude of the American investment in this goal is extraordinary. Extensive U.S. military and intelligence resources have been directed toward fighting the central radical Islamist network al Qaeda in numerous theaters. The war in Afghanistan was waged because of al Qaeda's base of operations there under radical Islamist Taliban government protection. The war continues primarily because of fears that the Taliban, though initially defeated, could retake the country and once again provide a safe haven for al Qaeda. While the war in Iraq was initiated for a variety of reasons, it soon became a major theater for conflict with al Qaeda forces. Hundreds of thousands of U.S. troops have been rotated through these theaters, returning with mental as well as physical wounds. Hundreds of billions of dollars have been spent and, most poignantly, thousands of American lives have been lost.

Despite these massive investments, the United States has little to show for it. Al Qaeda, the Taliban, and other affiliated groups hostile to America continue to thrive. Their leaders, Osama bin Laden and Mullah Omar, have not been captured and continue to operate. More important, a surfeit of

1

young Muslim men continue to eagerly join these radical Islamist groups, ready to sacrifice their lives in the name of jihad against the United States. Attacks on U.S. targets based in the Muslim world persist. While there have been no major terrorist attacks on American soil, several terrorists have come perilously close to succeeding in what could have been highly destructive attacks.

A Systemic Problem

On the surface, it is difficult to grasp how the American military, by far the most powerful military in history, can have such trouble mastering the problem of relatively small and primitive groups such as al Qaeda. If these groups are viewed in the context of the larger system of which they are part, however, the challenge becomes clearer. While most Muslims may not support the specific terrorist acts of radical Islamist groups, the extent to which the larger Muslim society—actively or passively—supports or sympathizes with the beliefs and goals of these groups plays a key role in their survival and resiliency. As long as widespread feelings of anger and resentment provide a source of ongoing support for their cause in the form of recruits, money, and moral support, then the problem is not simply between America and radical Islamist groups, but between America and the Muslim people as a whole.

In the immediate aftermath of 9/11, while many voices in the Muslim world condemned the attacks, many Americans were shocked to hear that in some Muslim cities people had celebrated them. It was not clear, however, how widespread these feelings were. At the time, little was known about attitudes toward the United States in the Muslim world. Only a few sporadic polls (which are explored in the next chapter) had been conducted, and area specialists had to rely heavily on anecdotal evidence. Not surprisingly, this led to inconsistent conclusions about Muslim public attitudes toward the United States.

After 9/11 there was a substantial increase in polling of the Muslim world. Overall, it was not a pretty picture. As discussed in chapter 1, Muslim public views of the United States were quite negative. And while most Muslims did say they disapproved of terrorism, substantial numbers expressed some support for al Qaeda and Osama bin Laden. Later polling showed widespread support for attacks on U.S. troops and even some smaller numbers approving of attacks on U.S. civilians.

With the election of Barack Obama, polls showed substantial optimism in the Muslim world as well as in the West that this would lead to improved relations between the United States and the Muslim world. Obama's high-profile speeches addressed to the Muslim world in Ankara and Cairo were met with great anticipation. Polls taken in 2009 and 2010, however, have shown only sporadic improvement. Majorities in most majority-Muslim countries continue to have negative views of the United States, and substantial numbers express support for al Qaeda and for attacks on U.S. troops. The fundamental reality of widespread Muslim hostility toward the United States has largely persisted.

As mentioned, the context of this hostility makes it is easier to understand how al Qaeda and other groups hostile to America thrive despite the massive American military effort. When terrorist groups express feelings that are present in the larger society, it makes it easier for them to operate and to recruit new members. Thus the United States is not simply dealing with the problem of those terrorist groups, but with a larger system that encompasses the society as a whole.

A number of studies corroborate this dynamic. Alan Krueger and Jitka Maleckova studied the relationship between public attitudes and terrorist attacks using Gallup public opinion data from countries in the Middle East and North Africa and data on terrorist attacks from the National Counterterrorism Center. They found that negative attitudes toward another country's leadership (including the United States) corresponded with higher levels of terrorist attacks against that country by groups from the hostile public's country.[1] They argue that "our results are inconsistent with one hypothesis, that public opinion is irrelevant for terrorism because terrorists are extremists who act independently of their countrymen's attitudes toward the leadership of the countries they attack."[2]

Several studies have shown that public antipathy toward the United States can increase the likelihood that members of the public will be supportive of anti-American terrorist groups. A 2007 report from the United States Institute of Peace (USIP) found that one of the strongest correlates of public support for terrorism is negative attitudes toward the United States.[3] Tessler and Robbins, based on studies of public opinion in Algeria and Jordan, concluded that societal support for terrorist groups is associated with negative views of both U.S. foreign policy and their home governments, presumably due in part to their close ties with the U.S. government.[4]

Analysts of terrorism corroborate that public support for terrorist groups is critical to their operation. As the terrorism specialist Audrey Cronin comments, "Terrorist groups generally cannot survive without either active or passive support from a surrounding population."[5] The USIP study mentioned above concluded that with public support, terror groups are better able to raise funds, recruit, operate safe houses, and avoid infiltration or capture.[6] A study by the Brookings Institution reported that because of general hostility toward the United States, "al-Qaeda and like-minded groups continue to draw numerous recruits throughout the Middle East and the Islamic world more broadly."[7]

The Limits of Military Force

Viewing the problem of terrorism by radical Islamist groups as an expression of a systemic problem is key to dealing with it effectively. If hostility toward the United States were present only in a small minority of the population, it might be possible to work with the larger population to isolate and incapacitate this subculture. If there is a degree of continuity between the attitudes of the subculture and the larger culture, however, this approach may backfire. Efforts to attack the subculture may be perceived as an attack on the larger culture and may provoke an increased readiness to provide support to the subculture.

This points to the limitations of addressing the problem of terrorism through military force. Traditionally, when dealing with an opposing state, U.S. military power can play a key role because it is facing a clear target with delimited capacities, and a military attack erodes the opposing state's capacity. When dealing with a substate, terrorist actor, however, the target is not as clear because its assets can be highly dispersed throughout the host society. The threat is also hard to contain, as its magnitude lies in the capacity of terrorist organizations to mobilize recruits, which may well be virtually limitless.

Commanders of U.S. forces have recognized the limits of U.S military power and the need to view the fundamental problem as being one of America's relationship with the society as a whole. General David Petraeus, in an interview published February 2010, said of the Afghan conflict, "You can't kill or capture your way out of these endeavors."[8] General Stanley McChrystal, then commander of U.S. forces and the International Security Assistance Force (ISAF) in Afghanistan, explained,

"The biggest thing is convincing the Afghan people. This is all a war of perceptions. This is not a physical war, in terms of how many people we kill or how much ground you capture, how many bridges you blow up."[9]

Paradoxically, America's military power has not only proven to be of limited utility in fighting the terrorist threat, but in some ways has exacerbated it. As documented in the following chapters, anger at America in the Muslim world is strongly linked to a perceived military threat by the United States against Muslim people and nations. When underlying hostility is amplified by a sense of threat, it is more likely to translate into dangerously counterthreatening behavior such as terrorism. Robert Pape's study of suicide terrorism concludes that it is mainly a reaction to the threatening presence of foreign military forces in a country.[10] Further, the gains of using military force against the terrorist threat are also uncertain. Like Hercules fighting the hydra, the gains of a military attack may be superseded by the negative effects of escalating threat perceptions on both sides, and mobilizing yet more angry recruits to the terrorist cause.

As polling confirms, terrorist groups such as al Qaeda are fairly unpopular in most Muslim countries and are perceived as something of a threat. These attitudes, however, may not accrue to the benefit of the United States if the United States is perceived as an even greater threat. It is as if Muslims are living in a neighborhood with two gangs. They may not like either gang, but if the weaker gang stands up to the stronger one, this offsets the power of the stronger one. This mitigates dislike of the weaker gang and may even lead to support of the weaker gang in its struggle against the stronger one.

Because the problem of terrorism is so integrated with the society as a whole, a U.S. strategy to deal with virulent expressions of hostility toward the United States in marginal subgroups in the Muslim world must also address the attitudes of the larger society. To begin with it is essential to understand the nature of this anger in the Muslim people.

The Study

To explore the extent and roots of Muslim hostility toward America, this book includes an analysis of public opinion surveys in majority-Muslim nations conducted by a variety of organizations, focus groups in six majority-Muslim nations, and extensive new polling in eleven majority-Muslim nations.

The focus is on attitudes in majority-Muslim nations, not on Muslims who are living as minorities in other nations. There is relatively little emphasis on majority-Muslim nations in Africa, where, according to very limited data, hostility toward the United States is currently much more muted and where the populations do not appear to be highly engaged in the dominant discourse of the larger Muslim world in relation to the United States.

Focus groups were conducted by the author with representative samples in Egypt, Indonesia, Iran, Jordan, Morocco, and Pakistan. These focus groups were the basis for developing the survey questions.

The most in-depth polling was conducted from 2006 to 2007 and in 2008 in Egypt, Indonesia, Morocco, and Pakistan. Surveys were developed and carried out in conjunction with the National Consortium for the Study of Terrorism and Responses to Terrorism (START) at the University of Maryland. The nationally representative samples ranged in size from 1,000 to 1,243, giving them a margin of error of plus or minus 3 percentage points. All of the interviews were conducted face-to-face in respondents' homes.

Polling was conducted in additional countries between 2007 and 2009 in Azerbaijan, Bangladesh, Iran, Iraq, Jordan, the Palestinian Territories, and Turkey. An additional set of surveys was conducted in Egypt, Indonesia, and Pakistan separate from the START surveys. Sample sizes ranged from 583 to 1,243, giving them a margin of error of plus or minus 2.8 to 4.1 percentage points. Samples were nationally representative with the exception of Egypt, which was urban only. All of the interviews were conducted face-to-face in respondents' homes.

All of the polling was conducted with the fielding partners of WorldPublicOpinion.org, an international project managed by the Program on International Policy Attitudes (PIPA), and thus are identified as being polling of WorldPublicOpinion.org, or WPO.

Other polling data analyzed include those from surveys conducted by the World Values Survey, the Arab Barometer, the Pew Research Center, Gallup, the Sadat Chair at the University of Maryland (fielded by Zogby), GlobeScan/PIPA for the BBC World Service, ABC News, and Terror Free Tomorrow.

Chapter 1 reviews the data gleaned from other polls as well as our own, exploring the scope and depth of Muslim hostility toward the United States as it has evolved from the 1990s to the present. It explores the scope of support for al Qaeda and other violent anti-American groups, support for attacks on U.S. troops, and, finally, support for attacks on U.S. civilians.

Subsequent chapters plumb the depths and roots of this hostility. Chapter 2 introduces the central elements of a widely held overt narrative that portrays the United States as oppressing the Muslim people. It also introduces a more subtle, underlying narrative that portrays the United States as having betrayed the liberal values it has promoted and that have at times formed the basis of a trusting relationship between Muslims and America. The chapter provides evidence of how these narratives are sustained by an underlying conflict between Muslims' attraction to liberal values from outside of the Muslim culture, predominantly embodied by the United States, and the urge to resist those values so as to preserve their traditional culture.

Chapters 3 through 6 explore the four key elements of this dual narrative, in particular the beliefs among Muslims that the United States coercively dominates the Muslim world, that it seeks to undermine Islam, that it undermines democracy in the Muslim world, and that it supports Israel's victimization of the Palestinian people.

Chapter 7 explores in greater depth the complexities of how Muslims feel about radical Islamist groups such as al Qaeda in the context of their feelings toward the United States. This chapter draws heavily on the findings of the focus groups.

Chapter 8 then turns to the broader question of what kind of society Muslim publics want, exploring further the underlying tension between liberal and Islamist ideas present in Muslim society. Naturally, this has implications for U.S. policymakers who have worried about what might occur in Muslim societies if they became more democratic.

The closing chapter discusses the implications of these findings for U.S. foreign policy. The goal is not to prescribe a comprehensive U.S. foreign policy, but to consider a number of steps with the potential for mitigating Muslim anger at America, reviewing their costs and benefits in various dimensions. The likely response of the American public to such options is also considered.

Last, I offer a note about how I have gone about presenting these data in digestible form. Not all readers find it comfortable to assimilate substantial amounts of polling data, so I have made an effort, at risk of some repetition, to summarize the data at the beginning of each chapter and each section, thus giving the reader the option of skimming the more numbers-dense sections.

1 The Scope of Muslim Anger and Support for Violent Anti-American Groups

The premise of this book is that the problem of terrorism does not simply lie in the small number of people who join terrorist organizations. Rather, the existence of terrorist organizations is a symptom of tension in the larger society that finds a particularly virulent expression in certain individuals. Hostility toward the United States in the broader society plays a critical role in sustaining terrorist groups, even if most disapprove of those groups' tactics. The essential "problem," then, is one of America's relationship with Muslim societies as a whole, or an integrated system.

Clark McCauley has depicted the relationship between anti-American terrorists and their society as being like a pyramid. At the apex are the terrorists. Below them is a layer of "justifiers" who actively express support. Below them are the sympathizers who provide more passive support. At the bottom are those expressing negative views toward the United States more generally, providing the broad base from which the other groups emerge.[1]

Adapting this model (see figure 1-1), this chapter begins by exploring the broad base of those expressing negative views of the United States and its foreign policy—majorities in most cases, with some quite substantial. Next up the pyramid are those who express passive support or sympathy for al Qaeda and other anti-American groups—in some cases modest majorities, especially when those who say they have "mixed feelings" are

FIGURE 1-1. The Pyramid of Terrorist Support

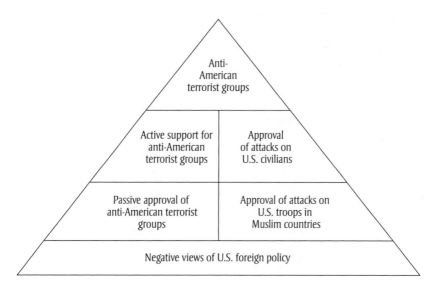

included. At a higher level are those who actively express support for anti-American groups either verbally or by approving if a child or family member were to join such a group or possibly by contributing money. This group constitutes a small but not insignificant minority.

On a parallel track up the pyramid there are those who express approval of attacks on U.S. troops, again a number that is a majority in some, but not all, nations. At a higher level of the pyramid is a considerably smaller but not insignificant minority that approves of attacks on American civilians.

Views of the United States through 2008

Before 9/11 there were very limited data available on attitudes toward the United States in the Muslim world. The U.S. Information Agency conducted some limited polling in the 1990s that showed substantially negative views toward the United States. In 1994, 61 percent of Turks said they had an "unfavorable" view of the United States, though this moderated later in the decade. In 1997 majorities with "unfavorable" views of the United States were found in Jordan (61 percent), the Palestinian Territories

(71 percent), and Lebanon (54 percent); and in 1999 only 23 percent of Pakistanis expressed "favorable" views. In Indonesia and Morocco, however, three in four expressed "favorable" views of the United States.

Shortly after the 9/11 attacks in 2001 there were a number of surveys that found largely negative views in some newly polled nations and worsening views among some of those previously polled. Negative views were particularly pronounced in countries in or around the Middle East. Gallup found that 64 percent of Saudis and 63 percent of Iranians had "unfavorable" views of the United States and that negative views were persisting in Pakistan (68 percent) and Jordan (62 percent). In the summer of 2002 Pew found 59 percent with "unfavorable" views of the United States in Egypt. In addition, views had worsened in Lebanon (59 percent, up 5 points) and in Jordan (75 percent, up 14 points). Views in Turkey, after having gradually improved during the 1990s, had turned decidedly "unfavorable" (55 percent).

Countries further away from the Middle East had milder views in the 2002 Pew poll. The biggest difference was in Uzbekistan, where 85 percent of respondents had a "favorable" view of the United States. Two majority-Muslim African nations polled also had "favorable" views— Mali (75 percent) and Senegal (61 percent). South Asians also showed less negative views of the United States than majority-Muslim countries in and around the Middle East, with a majority of Indonesians (61 percent) having a "favorable" view and Bangladeshis having divided views. In Pakistan, however, 69 percent had "unfavorable" views.

At that time, these predominantly negative views of the United States in the Muslim world in and around the Middle East were in sharp contrast to views of the United States elsewhere in the world. The 2002 Pew study found "favorable" views of the United States in thirty of the thirty-one non-majority-Muslim countries polled. On average, just 23 percent of respondents in those countries had an "unfavorable" view.

In the 2002 study Pew also asked respondents whether they favored or opposed "the U.S.-led efforts to fight terrorism." These efforts received majority approval in thirty-three of the thirty-four nations that were not majority-Muslim (Argentina was the exception). By contrast, these efforts were opposed by majorities in eight of the ten majority-Muslim nations, including those that in the same poll said they had a generally "favorable" view of the United States—Indonesia (64 percent) and Senegal (64 percent).

After the United States launched the Iraq war in March 2003, views of the United States grew more unfavorable in most corners of the world. In Pew's 2003 survey, among the ten non-majority-Muslim countries polled in 2002 as well as 2003, "unfavorable" views jumped substantially in all cases, on average 16 points from 33 to 49 percent.

Yet views grew particularly negative in the Muslim world. Even Indonesians, who had been quite positive toward the United States, grew sharply negative, with 83 percent expressing "unfavorable" views. "Unfavorable" views ballooned in Jordan (99 percent), Turkey (84 percent), Pakistan (81 percent), and Lebanon (71 percent). On average, 77 percent expressed "unfavorable" views of the United States among the eight majority-Muslim nations.

Over the next few years Pew continued to find "unfavorable" views of the United States among majority-Muslim nations. In 2007 it conducted its most complete study, which included thirteen majority-Muslim countries. Nine of them had majorities with negative views. The only country in the Middle East that was not predominantly negative was Kuwait, where views were divided. But outside of the greater Middle East region, views continued to be more mixed. In South Asia, less than half of Bangladeshis (41 percent) had "unfavorable" views, while Indonesians and Malaysians had persistently negative views. Africans in Mali and Senegal were predominantly "favorable." Nevertheless, the average across the thirteen countries was 59 percent "unfavorable."

All this was in sharp contrast to most other countries' views of the United States. Of the thirty-three non-Muslim countries polled in 2007, on average only 39 percent had "unfavorable" views of the United States, even though in some countries—especially in Argentina, China, France, and Germany—majorities had negative views.

Questions that simply ask about the United States can elicit responses based on a mix of factors such as the people, the culture, movies, and so on. Indeed, polls that ask specifically about the American people tend to be a bit less negative than views of the United States per se, which also tend to be less negative than views of U.S. influence in the world. Another series of annual surveys initiated in early 2005 by BBC/GlobeScan/PIPA sought to focus on views of U.S. foreign policy behavior, specifically asking whether the United States is having a "positive or negative influence in the world." Overall, views about U.S. influence were predominantly negative in western European, Latin American, and most Asian countries polled as well as in majority-Muslim nations. Views in African countries, however, were positive. By 2008, perhaps in anticipation of the U.S. presidential elections, non-Muslim countries around the world showed a gradual moderation in negative views of U.S. influence.

In the Muslim world, however, BBC/GlobeScan/PIPA found negative views persisting. Views worsened in several Muslim countries, including Egypt and Turkey (both reaching 73 percent negative in 2008) and Lebanon (reaching 67 percent negative in 2008). Views in Indonesia went from a plurality saying the United States was a negative influence in 2006 (47 percent) to majorities saying so in 2007 and 2008 (71 percent and 55 percent, respectively). Of the nine majority-Muslim countries surveyed at least once during this period (2005 to 2008), only in Afghanistan did a majority (72 percent in 2006, the one time it was polled) say the United States was having a positive influence in the world.

WorldPublicOpinion.org (WPO) polled five majority-Muslim nations at the end of 2006 into early 2007 and then four of the nations again in 2008, asking specifically whether respondents had a "favorable" or "unfavorable" view of "the U.S. government" rather than the United States per se. In the two waves of WPO surveys, very large majorities had "unfavorable" views of the U.S. government in Egypt (89 percent in both surveys), Indonesia (66 percent and 64 percent), and Pakistan (59 percent and 56 percent, with only 14 percent and 17 percent expressing a "favorable" view). Morocco was polled only in late 2006 and showed 76 percent with an "unfavorable" view. "Unfavorable" views declined somewhat in Iran. WPO found 93 percent with "unfavorable" views in 2006, dropping to 85 percent in 2008 and 77 percent in 2009. In a separate 2006 WPO poll, Afghanis were asked their views of "the United States." As in other polling, they stood out with a remarkable 81 percent having a "favorable" view.

Terror Free Tomorrow conducted a survey in Saudi Arabia in 2007 and found somewhat more moderate views (similar to those in Kuwait) than in other Muslim countries in the region, with a bare majority of 52 percent holding an "unfavorable" view of the United States. A plurality (44 to 36 percent) favored "Saudi Arabia restricting its supply of oil to the United States because of current American policies." Nonetheless, 69 percent still favored a close relationship with the United States.

Views of the United States under Obama

Because many unpopular policies of the United States—especially the Iraq war and the "war on terror"—were associated with the Bush administration, when Barack Obama was elected president in late 2008, there was anticipation in some circles that these negative feelings might abate. A BBC/GlobeScan/PIPA poll conducted before Obama's inauguration in January 2009 found majorities around the world thinking that Obama's election would lead to improved U.S. relations with the rest of the world. This was also true among the three majority-Muslim nations polled— Indonesia (64 percent), Egypt (58 percent), and Turkey (51 percent).

Hopes that U.S. relations with the Muslim world would improve were enhanced by Obama's much-heralded speech in Cairo in June 2009 in which he actively sought to repair the breach in relations between the United States and the Muslim world. In it he expressed respect for the Muslim civilization, even showing deference to the prophet Muhammad and implicitly expressing regret for some past U.S. policies, especially those during the Bush administration. The speech was well received in the hall where it was given and by the press.

These hopes for improved U.S. relations with the rest of the world have apparently been realized to a substantial extent in the non-Muslim world. Pew found that of the seventeen countries it polled in either or both 2009 and 2010, none showed a majority expressing an "unfavorable" view of the United States. Views in most non-Muslim countries improved or remained stable from 2009 to 2010. Views improved significantly in Russia and China, where majorities now have a positive view of the United States. In India positive views dipped somewhat, though they remain positive. Only in Argentina were views divided, which was still an improvement from 2009 when views were mostly "unfavorable." In WPO's 2009 polling of fourteen non-Muslim nations in which respondents were asked whether the United States was playing "a positive or negative role in the world," in no case did a majority say the United States was playing a negative role (though pluralities did in China, Russia, and Ukraine). Asked by BBC/GlobeScan/PIPA about America's influence in the world in early 2010, none of the twenty-three non-majority-Muslim nations in that study showed a majority saying that America's influence was "mostly negative." Obama himself also received very positive reviews in these studies in non-majority-Muslim countries. Indeed, among all major world leaders asked about by WPO in 2009 and Pew in 2009 and 2010, President Obama received the highest percentages of respondents expressing confidence in him to do the right thing in world affairs.

Several majority-Muslim nations have shown some changes in attitudes toward the United States under Obama. Most notably, Pew found that Indonesians swung from a majority "unfavorable" to a majority "favorable" view of the United States in 2009 (63 percent "favorable") and 2010 (59 percent "favorable"), and 67 percent said they have confidence in Obama in the 2010 Pew poll. However, questions that emphasized America's foreign policy had more mixed results. WPO found a plurality of Indonesians (39 to 32 percent) saying that the United States is playing a mainly negative role in the world in spring 2009, though by the fall this had become a slight plurality (43 to 39 percent) saying that the United States is playing a positive role. BBC/GlobeScan/PIPA found a plurality saying the United States is having a negative influence in the world in 2009 (43 to 33 percent), with this becoming almost evenly divided in 2010 (36 percent positive to 39 percent negative). In a 2009 Gallup poll only 35 percent of Indonesians approved of the performance of the U.S. leadership, though this is more than disapproved (23 percent), and 41 percent did not answer the question.

Attitudes among Azerbaijanis showed some signs of improvement. While a plurality of Azerbaijanis expressed a negative view of the U.S. role in the world in early 2009 WPO polling, in the 2009 Gallup poll a remarkably high 67 percent expressed a "favorable" view of the U.S. government, and 53 percent approved of the performance of the U.S. leadership. By early 2010 the BBC/GlobeScan/PIPA poll found a plurality having a positive view of U.S. influence.

Gallup also found majorities in 2009 approving of the job performance of the U.S. leadership—presumably responding to Obama—in several African countries (89 percent in Mali, 87 percent in Senegal, 86 percent in Chad, 83 percent in Niger, and 78 percent in Mauritania) as well as in Djibouti (81 percent), Turkmenistan (61 percent), and Bahrain (55 percent).

Polling that occurred after Obama's speech in Cairo showed some positive signs. WPO polling conducted in September 2009 found majorities saying that Obama does "respect Islam" in Indonesia (84 percent), Bangladesh (67 percent), Turkey (64 percent), and Egypt (65 percent), though 59 percent of Iranians disagreed. In late 2009 BBC/GlobeScan/PIPA found that among Egyptians positive views of U.S. influence reached

45 percent, while Gallup found 37 percent saying they approved of the U.S. leadership.

But by 2010 there were signs that what lift from Obama that may have occurred was fading. Gallup found that positive views of the U.S. leadership had slipped in Algeria (from 43 to 30 percent), Egypt (from 37 to 19 percent), Iraq (from 33 to 30 percent), and among Palestinians (from 20 to 16 percent).

Polling in 2010 from numerous organizations revealed predominantly negative views of the United States. Pew found large majorities saying they had an "unfavorable" view of the United States in Egypt (82 percent), Jordan (79 percent), Pakistan (68 percent), and Turkey (74 percent). BBC/GlobeScan/PIPA found majorities saying that the United States is having a negative influence in the world in Turkey (70 percent) and Pakistan (52 percent). The Sadat Chair found majorities expressing "unfavorable" views in Morocco (97 percent), Egypt (85 percent), Jordan (76 percent), Saudi Arabia (75 percent), the United Arab Emirates (75 percent), and Lebanon (61 percent). In the same poll majorities said they have no confidence in the United States in Morocco (97 percent), Egypt (87 percent), Jordan (63 percent), Saudi Arabia (63 percent), the United Arab Emirates (59 percent), and Lebanon (56 percent).

While views of Obama himself have proven to be positive in a few countries, for the most part majorities express a lack of confidence in him. Besides the majorities in Azerbaijan, Bangladesh, and Indonesia that expressed confidence in Obama in 2009 and 2010 polling by Pew and WPO, 2009 WPO polling found a lack of confidence in Obama in Iran (71 percent), the Palestinian Territories (67 percent), Pakistan (62 percent), Egypt (60 percent), and Iraq (57 percent). In 2010 Pew found a lack of confidence in Turkey (65 percent), Jordan (64 percent), Pakistan (60 percent), Egypt (59 percent), and Lebanon (56 percent). Increases over 2009 ranged from 6 points in Jordan and Lebanon to 13 points in Turkey. When the Sadat Chair asked in 2010 whether respondents' views of Obama were positive or negative, majorities expressed a negative view in Morocco (90 percent), Saudi Arabia (63 percent), Egypt (54 percent), the United Arab Emirates (54 percent), and Lebanon (53 percent), as did a plurality in Jordan (47 percent).

Asked specifically about Obama's international policies by Pew in 2010, views were also quite negative. Only in Indonesia did a majority approve of his policies in general (65 percent). Majorities disapproved in Jordan (81 percent), Egypt (72 percent), and Turkey (55 percent)—in every case up substantially from 2009. Pluralities disapproved in Lebanon (49 percent) and Pakistan (48 percent). Asked about more specific policies, majorities in Egypt, Indonesia, Jordan, Lebanon, Pakistan, and Turkey disapproved of Obama's policies on Afghanistan (ranging from 53 percent in Indonesia to 84 percent Jordan), on Iran (also ranging from 53 percent in Indonesia to 84 percent in Jordan), on the conflict between Israelis and Palestinians (ranging from 51 percent in Pakistan to 90 percent in Lebanon), and on the situation in Iraq (ranging from 52 percent in Indonesia to 79 percent in Egypt).

Regional and Demographic Variations

There are some regional variations in attitudes toward the United States among majority-Muslim nations. As mentioned, feelings in the Middle East and its surrounding area tend to be the most hostile. These hostile feelings tend to decline as one moves further away from that region. At present, the friendliest majority-Muslim countries are those in sub-Saharan Africa, followed by Southeast Asia, particularly Indonesia. Bangladeshis are quite warm toward Obama, though still moderately negative toward the United States. Azerbaijanis and Afghans also express some of the more moderate and friendly views, as do Uzbeks.

This pattern was evident prior to the Bush administration in the 1990s, and at that time Morocco was among the more friendly countries. During the Bush period this variation diminished, with even Indonesia becoming quite negative. With the Obama administration there has been a reversion to a more positive attitude in Indonesia and to some extent in Bangladesh. The most recent polling of Morocco by the Sadat Chair, however, found that Morocco has become even more negative toward the United States.

Many observers have hoped that younger or more educated Muslims would have more moderate views of the United States, as this would hold out long-term prospects for improved relations as these younger people come of age and the population overall becomes more educated. An analysis of the data from the eleven different majority-Muslim nations polled in 2009 and 2010—separately as well as in the aggregate—however, provides little to buoy such hopes. Variations by age were quite modest and in virtually no case provided support for the idea that younger people had warmer views toward the United States. There were some indications that older people were less negative, but these arose from older people failing to answer, as their positive views were lower as well. The biggest difference was that middle-aged people tended to be slightly more negative than either older or younger people. But this difference was not very robust. The effect of education also defied hopes. What little difference there was tended to be that those with less than a full high school education were slightly less negative than those with a full high school education or college. A regression analysis found no effects.

Passive and Active Support for Anti-American Groups

As discussed above, the primarily negative views of the United States in majority-Muslim countries form the broad basis of the societal pyramid in which terrorist groups emerge at the tip. Moving up the pyramid, out of the larger group with negative views of the United States and U.S. foreign policy are those who support anti-American groups passively and even actively. While these constitute smaller numbers than those who simply disapprove of the United States, they are still substantial.

To gauge support for anti-American groups, WPO asked respondents in polling from 2006 to 2009 how they feel about "groups in the Muslim world that attack Americans," without specifying whether these Americans are civilians or military personnel. (See figure 1-2.) In 2008 majorities in the Palestinian Territories (83 percent), Jordan (62 percent), and Egypt (61 percent) were supportive of at least some of these groups. Lesser numbers supported at least some of these groups in Bangladesh (49 percent in 2009), Turkey (42 percent), Pakistan (41 percent), Indonesia (33 percent), and Azerbaijan (10 percent). Only in Azerbaijan did a majority disapprove of all such groups. In late 2006, 38 percent of Moroccans approved of at least some groups.

Respondents in most majority-Muslim countries tend to have more negative than positive views of groups that attack Americans in general, but on a question in which respondents were asked to rate "groups in the Muslim world that attack Americans" on a 0 to 10 scale, with 0 meaning they feel "not at all supportive" and 10 meaning they feel "very supportive," the mean in every case reflected some positive feelings toward these

FIGURE 1-2. Groups That Attack Americans

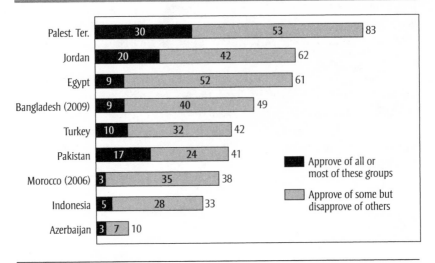

Source: WorldPublicOpinion.org, 2008.

groups. Mean scores ranged from 3.4 in Morocco to 4.3 in Indonesia, 5.0 in Pakistan, and 5.4 in Egypt. (See figure 1-3.)

WPO probed those who said they approve of at least some of the groups in the Muslim world that attack Americans to find out how many *actively* express support for them. These numbers were relatively small, but still significant. Asked whether they "speak favorably" to family or

FIGURE 1-3. Feelings toward Groups That Attack Americans

Rate your feelings about groups in the Muslim world that attack Americans on a scale from 0 (not at all supportive) to 10 (very supportive).

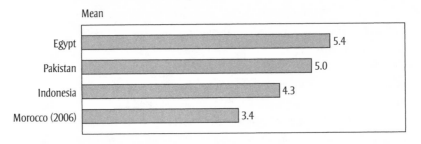

Source: WorldPublicOpinion.org, 2008.

FIGURE 1-4. Family Member Joining Groups That Attack Americans

If a member of your family were to join a group that attacks Americans, would you approve of this, disapprove of this, or have mixed feelings?

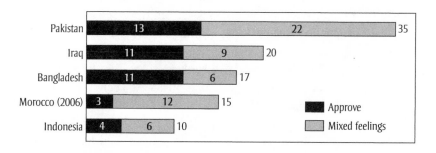

Source: WorldPublicOpinion.org, 2008–09.

friends about such groups, 25 percent said that they do in Bangladesh, as did 18 percent in Egypt and Indonesia, 14 percent in Pakistan, and 12 percent in Morocco.

Respondents in Indonesia, Morocco, and Pakistan were asked whether they "would ever consider" contributing money to "an organization that may send some of its funds to a group that attacks Americans." Very small numbers said they would do so. Substantial numbers, however, would not answer, which suggests that respondents do not clearly reject the idea. In Indonesia 7 percent said they would consider contributing money (17 percent no answer), as did 5 percent in Morocco (11 percent no answer).

Asked how they would feel "if a family member joined such a group," small but significant numbers said they would approve or at least have mixed feelings. In 2006 to 2008 polling, these numbers were 35 percent in Pakistan, 15 percent in Morocco, and 10 percent in Indonesia. Bangladeshis and Iraqis were asked this question for the first time in 2009, with 17 percent and 20 percent, respectively, having at least mixed feelings. (See figure 1-4.)

Throughout the Bush administration, large majorities in majority-Muslim countries opposed the U.S. war on terrorism. Between 2002 and 2007 Pew found large majorities opposed to "U.S.-led efforts to fight terrorism" in Jordan, Lebanon, the Palestinian Territories, and even U.S.

ally Turkey. South Asian countries—Bangladesh, Indonesia, and Pakistan—were not as overwhelmingly opposed to U.S. efforts to fight terrorism, but still had substantial majorities in opposition most years in which they were polled. Kuwait was the one country that started out in 2003 with a majority supportive of U.S.-led antiterrorism efforts, but by 2007 had a majority against such efforts. The question was asked in Malaysia only in 2007, when two-thirds were opposed.

Views of Osama bin Laden have evolved over time. In May 2003, shortly after the start of the Iraq war, majorities in the Palestinian Territories (70 percent), Indonesia (57 percent), and Jordan (55 percent) said they had confidence in Osama bin Laden to do the right thing in international affairs. Substantial numbers in Pakistan (45 percent) and Egypt (26 percent) also said this. In Lebanon (14 percent) and Turkey (15 percent) small numbers had confidence in Osama bin Laden.

In subsequent years, confidence diminished, presumably as part of a negative reaction to al Qaeda attacks on civilians, in many cases against Muslims. After the attack on a wedding party in Amman in November 2005, confidence in bin Laden fell off sharply in Jordan.

Still, when the 2006 to 2009 WPO polls asked respondents whether they had positive, negative, or mixed feelings about Osama bin Laden, only in Azerbaijan (84 percent) and Turkey (60 percent) did clear majorities express negative feelings toward him. Majorities expressed positive or mixed feelings in the Palestinian Territories (87 percent), Egypt (69 percent), Jordan (54 percent), Morocco (53 percent), and Pakistan (51 percent), with a plurality in Indonesia (35 percent) feeling this way.

As is discussed in future chapters, WPO also asked respondents whether they agree with a list of al Qaeda's goals and found majority support for nearly all of them. The goals asked about were:

—to require a strict application of sharia law in every Islamic country;

—to unify all Islamic countries into a single Islamic state or caliphate;

—to push the United States to stop providing support to such governments as Egypt, Jordan, and Saudi Arabia;

—to push the United States to remove its bases and its military forces from all Islamic countries;

—to stand up to America and affirm the dignity of the Islamic people;

—to keep Western values out of Islamic countries;

—to push the United States to stop favoring Israel in its conflict with the Palestinians.

FIGURE 1-5. Attacks on U.S. Troops in Iraq

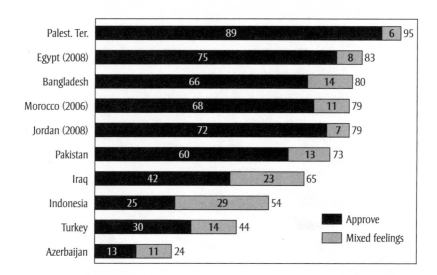

Source: WorldPublicOpinion.org, 2009.

A much more detailed analysis of attitudes toward al Qaeda and other radical Islamist groups can be found in chapter 7.

Support for Attacks on U.S. Troops

Perhaps the most startling evidence of hostility toward the United States is the widespread support for attacks on U.S. troops. WPO asked respondents whether they approve, disapprove, or have mixed feelings about attacks on U.S. military troops in Iraq, Afghanistan, and the Persian Gulf. (See figure 1-5.)

The strongest support for attacks was found among Palestinians. In 2009 WPO found overwhelming majorities of Palestinians approving of attacks on U.S. troops based in Iraq (89 percent), Afghanistan (85 percent), and the Persian Gulf (77 percent). Strong majorities approving of attacks on U.S. troops were also found in Bangladesh, Egypt, Jordan, Morocco, and Pakistan. In Azerbaijan, Indonesia, Iraq, and Turkey there were no majorities approving of attacks on U.S. troops in any of the locations, but large numbers—sometimes majorities—either approved of

FIGURE 1-6. Attacks on Civilians in the United States

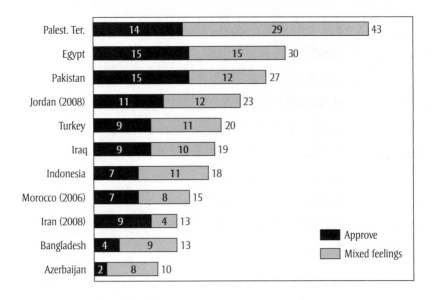

Source: WorldPublicOpinion.org, 2009.

attacks or had mixed feelings. Only the Azerbaijanis were under 3 in 10 approving or having mixed feeling about attacks in all locations.

Support for Attacks on U.S. Civilians

Support for attacks on American civilians is much lower than support for attacks on U.S. troops. Indeed, large majorities oppose them in most cases—whether these are specified as Americans working in Islamic countries or living in the United States. The numbers supporting attacks on civilians in the United States in 2009 WPO polling ranged from 2 to 15 percent (see figure 1-6). Though when it comes to attacks on U.S. civilians working in Muslim countries, approval went as high as 22 percent in Pakistan and 28 percent in the Palestinian Territories. While these numbers are low, they still represent many millions of individuals.

Furthermore, when those approving of attacks on Americans are combined with those who say they have mixed feelings about attacks either on civilians in the United States or working in Islamic countries, the numbers

FIGURE 1-7. Attacks on U.S. Civilians Working in Islamic Countries

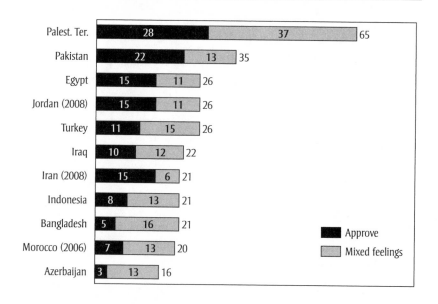

Source: WorldPublicOpinion.org, 2009.

can become quite substantial. The numbers expressing at least some degree of sympathy for attacks on American civilians working in Islamic countries reached as high as 65 percent in the Palestinian Territories, 35 percent in Pakistan, and 26 percent in Egypt, Jordan and Turkey. (See figure 1-7.)

Seven countries were polled on these questions in 2009 and in earlier years. Overall, there was very little change over this period. The numbers saying they approved or had mixed feelings about attacks on American civilians in the U.S. and Islamic countries grew among Palestinians between 2008 and 2009. Though the Indonesians generally grew more positive toward the United States during this period, the small numbers that showed sympathy for attacks did not decline.

2

The Narrative of Oppression and Betrayal and the Inner Clash of Civilizations

The polling cited in chapter 1 makes clear that negative feelings among Muslims toward the United States are widespread and enduring. The question remains, however, as to *why* these feelings are so pervasive and deep-seated. The focus groups conducted in six different majority-Muslim countries revealed the beliefs that drive Muslim anger. There was a strikingly consistent pattern when respondents discussed their views of the United States. While there were some differences of emphasis, in every case the dominant, overt theme was that the United States oppresses the Muslim people in a variety of ways. Eventually, a more subtle, underlying theme also emerged—that the United States has betrayed the Muslim people by violating its own principles of relations based on respect, tolerance, and the constraints of international law. These feelings appeared to be intensified by the inner conflicts Muslims have about entering into closer relations with the outer world.

The themes that emerged from the focus groups were developed into poll questions to test their validity, and for the most part these themes were confirmed in the polling. This chapter discusses the broad narrative of oppression and betrayal and the factors that underlie and contribute to it. The following four chapters explore the components of this readily expressed narrative, which is based on four key assertions:

—The United States seeks to and largely succeeds in coercively dominating the Muslim world, shaping it in ways that serve its interests irrespective of the wishes of the people and violating the principle of sovereign equality (chapter 3).

—The United States is hostile to Islam and seeks to undermine it and to impose a secular social order, betraying the principles of freedom of religion (chapter 4).

—Driven by anti-Islamic prejudice and seeking to use Israel as a base for regional domination, the United States supports and enables Israel in its victimization of the Palestinian people (chapter 5).

—Contrary to its democratic principles, the United States undermines democracy in the Muslim world so as to preserve its control and to ensure that Islamism is kept under wraps (chapter 6).

Some perceptions of the United States found in majority-Muslim countries, especially the view that the country is domineering and coercive, are shared by other non-Muslim nations. In the Muslim world, however, these views have a special intensity, as they form part of a larger narrative of American oppression and betrayal that combines with a long-standing and acutely felt narrative of the Islamic world being victimized by the West. For many centuries, certainly since the Crusades of the eleventh century, the West has been seen as a force seeking to occupy and subjugate Islamic peoples and undermine their religion. Interpretations of American behavior blend seamlessly into this ever-evolving story. As became clear in the polling and focus groups, the United States is seen as having added insult to injury by enticing Muslims with attractive universalist principles that imply constraint and tolerance on the part of the United States and then subsequently violating those principles and betraying the Muslim people.

For many this narrative is integrally linked to Muslims' religious identity. But this has not always been the case. Egypt's Gamal Abdel Nasser and Libya's Muammar Qaddafi, for example, have articulated the narrative of oppression in a secular vernacular, charging the United States with imperialism. Even some members of the Muslim Brotherhood, which originated in Egypt and was one of the early Islamist movements, have at times opposed the religiously based versions of the narrative.

The religious version, however, has been strongest in the context of Islamism. Islamism holds up Islam not only as a religious movement in the personal sphere, but as a political movement meant to dominate the public sphere, making Islamic law the foundation of all law. Radical Islamists, who have a fundamentalist notion of Islamic law and who are ready to use violence—even against civilians—to bring about an Islamist state, reject the language of U.S. imperialism in favor of a religious narrative that is continuous with the Crusades. As Sayyid Qutb, a radical Islamist associated with the Muslim Brotherhood who was highly influential on Osama bin Laden, wrote, "The truth of the matter is that the latter-day imperialism is nothing but the crusading spirit since it is not possible for it to appear in its true form, as was possible in the Middle Ages."[1]

In this context the struggle with the West is seen as rooted in a fundamental Manichaean conflict that leads to the inevitability of violent conflict. In the words of Osama bin Laden, "The West's occupation of our countries is old, yet new. The struggle between us and them, the confrontation and clashing, began centuries ago and will continue because the ground rules regarding the fight between right and falsehood will remain valid until Judgment Day. . . . There can be no dialogue with occupiers except through arms."[2]

Interestingly, while most Western writers reject the notion that the West oppresses the Muslim world, there are many who articulate ideas that resonate quite closely with the idea of a fundamental conflict between Islam and the West. In 1990 Bernard Lewis, in an article titled "The Roots of Muslim Rage," first proffered the idea that there is a deep-seated "clash of civilizations" between Islam and the West, which he identified as the source of Muslim anger at the West and specifically America.[3] Several years later this idea was elaborated in greater depth by Samuel Huntington.[4] While this idea has engendered much critical debate, it is implicit in many analyses of the conflict between Islam and the West.

As the coming chapters show, much that is expressed by Muslims in polls and focus groups fits into this long-standing narrative of religious and cultural polarization, which, with the West's superior military power, leads to Western oppression of the Muslim world. Yet there is more to the story of how Muslims see their relationship with the West, particularly the United States.

In fact, when given the chance, many Muslims reject the notion that the clash of civilizations is fundamental. Many express an attraction to aspects of the West, especially its liberal ideas. These include principles such as pluralism, religious tolerance, sovereign equality, and restraint on the use of military force according to international law. They also include the development of empirically based research and critical thought that has driven the success of Western science, technology, and industry and allowed the West to grow its economy at a much faster rate.

The question of how to respond to the West has created cleavages in Muslim society. Some, especially in the educated and wealthier classes, have been drawn to the idea of fully liberalizing the culture of Muslim countries, typified by Turkey's president Mustafa Kemal Atatürk, who in the 1920s and 1930s undertook a large-scale secularization of Turkish society. Others, most notably radical Islamists, have completely rejected Western culture and sought to preserve traditional Islamic ways.[5]

Few Muslims, however, are firmly in one or the other of these camps. As is explored in chapter 8, most Muslims embrace both liberal ideas and traditional Islamic ideas. Liberalism is not necessarily seen as foreign or Western. Indeed, many Islamic scholars see it as being deeply rooted in Islam. Aspects of rational and scientific thought were already well developed in Islamic society at the time of the Renaissance and the Enlightenment of the West and influenced their development. Ideas related to democracy and human rights are also present in Islamic thought.

At the same time, there are some key tensions between traditional Islam and liberalism. There is a tension between the commitment to sharia as the revealed basis of law and the notion of law as derived from the will of humans. There is a tension between the preeminent role of tradition, extending to a wide range of daily activities, and the right of the individual to make independent choices provided they do not harm others. The multitude of lifestyle options presented by Western media barrages Muslim societies in ways that make them uncomfortable.

Thus for many Muslims there is what could be called an "inner clash of civilizations" between their attraction to liberal ideas and the pluralistic world it implies, and their desire to preserve their traditional culture. The struggle between these impulses creates cultural and political instability in many Muslim countries. It leads to overt conflict between organized forces pulling in opposite directions along the lines of this polarity.

This conflict also leads to tension and conflict with the outside non-Muslim world as Muslims seek to preserve their sense of autonomy and Muslim identity. Historically this has been focused on Western European colonizers, while today the focus is more on the United States. But the feelings toward the United States are complex and not entirely negative.

There is an attraction to what America has to offer, while there is also a fear of being overwhelmed by it. This fear sometimes leads to exaggerated perceptions of American power.

In the context of this inner conflict between attraction and vulnerability to the United States, a deeper narrative emerges. This narrative has two key elements. One is that the United States puts forward liberal ideas, including religious tolerance, that are reassuring to Muslims who both wish to open to the West and to preserve their autonomy and identity. Intrinsic in such liberal principles is respect for Islam as a religion and culture, providing assurances that Muslims have the right to live as they wish without being dominated by the West despite its overwhelming military and economic superiority. These principles create in some Muslims an often unspoken sense of bonding with the West and especially America, which is seen as their leading author and proponent. This tacit bonding is, arguably, a basis for some long-term optimism about the potential for improving the relationship between the United States and the Muslim world.

This benign image of America has historical roots, and even today many Muslims imply that there was once a better time, a time when the United States fulfilled its ideals. The late nineteenth-century idealistic American missionaries who helped establish numerous universities in the Arab world that continue today are remembered favorably. Sayyid Qutb, who would later become a leading radical Islamist who inspired al Qaeda, wrote about the admiration he felt for America when he traveled there in 1948.[6] Even now, the United States is remembered as having stood by its principles in 1956 during the Suez crisis when it reversed a British, French, and Israeli invasion of Egypt.

The second element in this deeper narrative is the perception that the United States, after having disarmed Muslims with reassuring liberal principles, has violated those principles out of self-interest and religious bias at the expense of the Muslim people. This includes violating the principles of national sovereignty and equality, self-determination, religious equality, and democracy. The violation of these principles engenders a profound sense of betrayal. Because it is linked to a feeling of having been deceived, there is a sense of humiliation, which leads to an anger that can be greater than the simpler anger at an oppressive hegemon.

Ultimately, the anger derived from the underlying narrative of betrayal merges with the anger based on the more overt narrative of hegemonic oppression. Charges of hegemonic oppression are more comfortably made. But the underlying sense of betrayal, rooted in a sense of vulnerability and disappointment, lends a unique intensity to the anger.

The Implicit Attraction to the West and the Broader World

Despite the prevalence of arguments from radical Islamists that the conflict between Islam and the West arises inevitably from intrinsic features of their cultures, most Muslims reject this narrative. In 2006 and 2007 WorldPublicOpinion.org (WPO) and BBC/GlobeScan/PIPA both asked whether violent conflict is "inevitable" between Muslim and Western cultures, or whether "it is possible to find common ground." In every nation polled, a majority or a plurality endorsed the view that it is possible for Muslim and Western cultures to find common ground. This included majorities in Lebanon (68 percent), Indonesia (66 percent), Morocco (54 percent), and Egypt (54 percent) and pluralities in Turkey (49 percent), the United Arab Emirates (47 percent), and Pakistan (38 percent). Iranians were asked the same question in a February 2008 WPO poll, and nearly two-thirds (64 percent) agreed that achieving common ground is possible (see figure 2-1). Views in majority-Muslim countries were generally comparable to other countries, though more recently there has been a substantial decline in this view among Americans, with only a bare majority saying that common ground is possible.[7]

In the focus groups respondents regularly raised the notion of there being a fundamental clash of civilizations, but invariably this was done in a pejorative sense. Implicitly or explicitly, the idea was rejected and seen as a characteristic problem of Western thinkers with an anti-Islamic bias.

Muslims also tend to reject the view that their antipathy toward the United States is rooted in a rejection of American values, stressing instead that it is U.S. foreign policy that aggravates them. This was often expressed in the focus groups. The Sadat Chair has regularly asked the following question in six Arab nations: "Would you say that your attitudes toward the United States are based more on American values or on American policy in the Middle East?" In all cases large majorities said their attitudes are based more on American policy. Most recently, in 2009 majorities took this view in Jordan (91 percent), Saudi Arabia (89 percent), Lebanon (87 percent), Morocco (85 percent), Egypt (71 percent), and the United Arab Emirates (66 percent). (See figure 2-2.)

FIGURE 2-1.   Clash of Civilizations or Common Ground?

Thinking about Muslim and Western cultures, do you think that violent conflict between them is inevitable or that it is possible to find common ground?

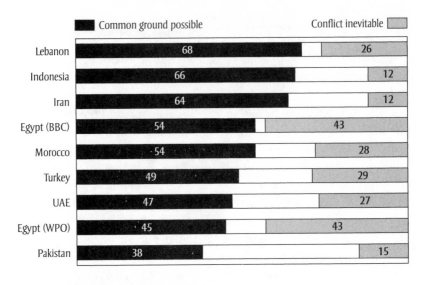

Source: WPO and BBC, 2006–08.

FIGURE 2-2.   Attitudes Based on Values or Policy?

Would you say that your attitudes toward the United States are based more on American values or on American policy in the Middle East?

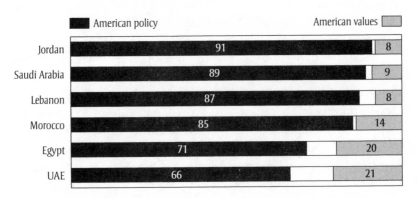

Source: Sadat Chair, 2009.

FIGURE 2-3. Attributes of U.S. and Western Culture

The culture of the United States and other Western countries has many positive attributes.

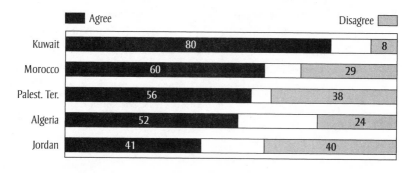

Source: Arab Barometer, 2006.

Muslims directly express positive views of various aspects of Western culture. In a 2006 Arab Barometer poll majorities in four out of five majority-Muslim nations polled agreed that "the culture of the United States and other Western countries has many positive attributes" (80 percent in Kuwait, 60 percent in Morocco, 56 percent in the Palestinian Territories, and 52 percent in Algeria). The one exception was Jordan, which was divided (41 percent agreed, 40 percent disagreed). (See figure 2-3.)

Another way that people expressed their attraction to the West in the focus groups was to differentiate between their dislike of the American government and their liking of the American people. Typical was a comment by a Jordanian woman, "When we talk about the USA we separate between the American people, their civilization, traditions, customs, and the American foreign policy." A Pakistani man complained that the American government seeks to dominate the world, but then went on to sharply differentiate this from the American people: "I have seen many Americans, and they are peaceful, and they are good, and they behave in the right way, as they have to. They even treat their pets very well. When a cat is injured they treat it so well. They want to behave in the same way with people. But not the American government."

The American people were variously characterized as "beautiful," as "helpful and appreciative," as making "sacrifices for the benefit of others," and as really wanting "the best for the world." Also in polls, views of the American people tend to be more positive than views of the U.S. government.

The process of globalization has increased the contact between Islamic cultures and the rest of the world. Increasing trade; greater travel; and especially the exposure to foreign cultural products such as movies, television programming, and music have had a major impact on Muslim society. Fundamentalist Islamists have bewailed this process and largely called for the Islamic world to stay separate from the "infidel" culture for fear that it will pollute the purity of Islamic culture. Nonetheless, Muslims largely endorse globalization and increasing economic integration with the non-Muslim world.

On the whole, Muslim publics are quite positive about economic integration with other countries. When Pew asked respondents in six majority-Muslim countries in 2010 about the "growing trade and business ties" between their country and other countries, large majorities in all six countries said these ties are good for their country. This included Lebanon (93 percent), Pakistan (86 percent), Indonesia (82 percent), Turkey (83 percent), Jordan (71 percent), and Egypt (64 percent). Ironically, publics in most Muslim nations were more positive about economic integration than the public in the United States, where a smaller majority (66 percent) said it is a good thing.

When respondents were asked in WPO polling in 2007 how they felt about "the world becoming more connected through greater economic trade and faster communication," majorities said it is either a "very good" or a "somewhat good" thing for their country, including 92 percent of Egyptians, 80 percent of Indonesians, 62 percent of Moroccans, and 56 percent of Pakistanis.

In 2009 Terror Free Tomorrow (TFT) asked about the importance of the goal of "seeking trade and political relations with Western countries" in Iran and found three in four saying this is important. On the same question asked in Pakistan in 2008, TFT found that two-thirds of Pakistanis also felt this way.

WPO found in 2009 that publics in most majority-Muslim nations were also generally positive about "globalization" defined as "especially the increasing connections of our economy with others around the world." Majorities said that globalization is "mostly good" in Azerbaijan (63 percent), Pakistan (55 percent), and Turkey (51 percent) as well as pluralities in Egypt (41 percent "mostly good" to 26 percent "mostly bad") and Iraq

(30 percent "mostly good" to 20 percent "mostly bad"). However, a majority of Palestinians (58 percent) and a plurality of Indonesians (44 percent) said it is "mostly bad." Majority-Muslim countries did not differ appreciably from the average of all twenty-two nations surveyed worldwide (52 percent had positive views and 27 percent were negative).[8]

Most Muslims also express some sense of a cosmopolitan identity. Asked in World Values Survey polling from 2005 to 2009 whether they see themselves as a citizen of the world, majorities in six of seven majority-Muslim countries said they do. Percentages ranged from 56 percent in Egypt to 90 percent in Malaysia. Only in Morocco did a plurality disagree (46 to 40 percent). The views of majority-Muslim countries on global citizenship were typical of the whole of the forty-six countries surveyed worldwide.[9]

Respondents in the focus groups were often quite comfortable in highlighting and valuing many attractive ideas that were introduced from the West. A number of focus groups respondents commented that some Islamic values such as charity for the poor and equal rights have been more fully realized in some countries with liberal governments than they have in some Muslim societies.

Muslims also express respect for the economic and scientific successes of the West. Pew has found large majorities in Bangladesh, Egypt, Indonesia, Jordan, Kuwait, Lebanon, Malaysia, and the Palestinian Territories saying that they "admire the United States for its technological and scientific advances." Focus group respondents were often not shy in saying that they had much to learn from the West. Many complained that since 9/11 it has been hard to get visas to study at American universities. When asked what they want from America in a positive sense, the most common responses were education and training.

The Tension between Western Influence and Muslim Identity

At the same time that there is attraction to Western culture, there is much that Muslims find unattractive about it. There is a strong determination to preserve key aspects of traditional Muslim culture, which Muslims see as a source of strength. They have not forgotten that for much of Islam's history, its culture was by many measures more advanced than Christian culture. Even if the West has made major gains in the last few centuries, this does not mean that most Muslims have lost faith in their own culture built on Islam. They believe it has served them well for many centuries and has taken them to great heights that may well be regained in the future.

Being a Muslim is the central identity for most Muslims. This is reflected in answers to a 2006 Arab Barometer question asking whether respondents felt that they were "above all" a citizen of their nation, a Muslim, an Arab, a Christian, or could not choose. "Above all, I am a Muslim" was the answer chosen by majorities in the Palestinian Territories (68 percent), Algeria (67 percent), and Jordan (63 percent). Half (50 percent) of Moroccans also chose this. Only in Kuwait did this drop below half (43 percent). In no case did a majority say that their identity as a citizen of their nation or as an Arab was paramount.

In a seeming contradiction of their endorsement of liberal values and increasing integration with the world, large majorities of Muslims also express a desire to protect their culture from outside influence. A Pew poll of seven majority-Muslim countries in 2009 found large majorities in every case agreeing that "our way of life needs to be protected against foreign influence," ranging from 76 percent in Lebanon to 90 percent in Pakistan. When asked by WPO between 2006 and 2009 whether they agree with the al Qaeda goal "to keep Western values out of Islamic countries," majorities in Egypt (94 percent), Indonesia (81 percent), Bangladesh (80 percent), Morocco (64 percent), Pakistan (60 percent), and Turkey (51 percent) said they do. (See figure 2-4.)

American influences tend to be seen as particularly pernicious. A 2007 Pew poll in eleven majority-Muslim nations found that in ten of them, large majorities said that it is "bad that American ideas and customs are spreading here." The majorities ranged from 69 percent in Malaysia to 90 percent in the Palestinian Territories. Majorities in all three countries polled by WPO in 2008 found unfavorable views of American culture, including Indonesia (86 percent), Egypt (60 percent), and Pakistan (55 percent). The 2006 Arab Barometer survey found majorities in all five nations it polled agreeing that "exposure to the culture of the United States and other Western countries has a harmful effect" on their country, ranging from 52 percent in Morocco to 66 percent in the Palestinian Territories.

In summary, it appears that Muslims feel their culture has been destabilized by its interface with non-Muslim, especially Western, culture. While most Muslims reject the view that there is an inevitable clash of civilizations, there does appear to be an internal clash between, on one hand, Muslims' attraction to greater engagement with the outer world and a

FIGURE 2-4. Al Qaeda Goal: Keep Western Values out of Islamic Countries

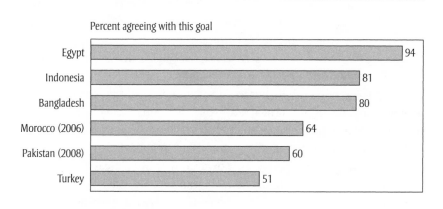

Source: WorldPublicOpinion.org, 2009.

fascination with liberal thought, and, on the other hand, anxiety that these outside influences will overwhelm the traditional Muslim culture they also wish to preserve.

The Underlying Theme of U.S. Betrayal

Despite being drawn to much that the West has to offer, the feeling of vulnerability to being overwhelmed by the West culturally, economically, and militarily leads to a great sense of trepidation in relations with the West, especially with the United States. Thus Muslims are acutely attuned to the question of whether the West, in particular the United States, will abide by its own principles and show restraint in its relation with the Muslim world.

A key attractive feature of liberal thinking is that it holds out a normative framework for dealing with such relations. Paramount is the principle embodied in the UN Charter and international law in general that military force should not be used except in self-defense. According to this principle, all nations—large and small, weak and strong—are sovereign and equal under international law, and no nation should be able to coercively impose its will on another. Naturally, such a framework is quite appealing for relatively weak Muslim nations in their dealings with the overwhelmingly more powerful United States.

In addition, liberal values point to a pluralistic order that is tolerant of all religions. For Muslims facing the United States—a cultural as well as a military superpower—it is a reassuring idea that the United States, according to the principles it proffers, would not seek to displace Islamic culture with America's preferred cultural form.

Because the United States is seen as an advocate of such liberal principles, it is seen as implicitly promising not to act like a classical imperial power imposing its hegemonic will, but to show restraint in its relations with other countries. Following the principle of sovereign equality, Muslims look to the United States to enter into noncoercive relations based on the principle of reciprocity and the recognition that all nations are autonomous.

From focus group discussions, however, it is quite clear that even as these liberal norms offer hope and reassurance, there is a widespread perception that the United States fails to consistently live up to them. A key complaint is that the United States does not abide by the international laws it urges others to follow. In WPO polling of eight majority-Muslim countries from 2008 to 2009, majorities in all of them rejected the view that "the United States has been an important leader in promoting international laws and sets a good example by following them." Instead, majorities endorsed the view that "the United States tries to promote international laws for other countries, but is hypocritical because it often does not follow these rules itself." These majorities ranged from 61 percent in the Palestinian Territories to 78 percent in Egypt (figure 2-5). Globally, such views are not unusual. Respondents in majority-Muslim nations were only slightly more likely than other countries to believe the United States is hypocritical with regard to international law.[10]

At times, it seemed that respondents in the focus groups were beseeching America to recall its higher ideals. For example, an Egyptian woman said,

> I want to give you a message to America. . . . It's that America is
> a great country, known to maintain freedoms, democracies,
> and human rights. I wish that America would respect human
> beings everywhere and try to save lost human rights all over
> the world, just as much as it is concerned about bin Laden.
> . . . We all agree that America is capable of doing this.

Similarly, an Egyptian man said, "I think it would be in America's interest and the world's as a whole if it holds to the ideals it promotes."

FIGURE 2-5. U.S. and International Law

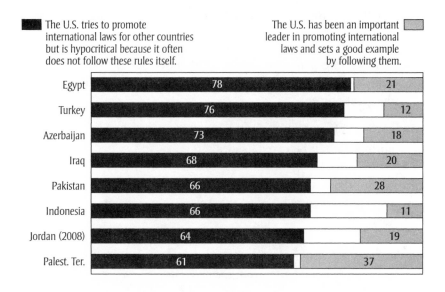

The U.S. tries to promote international laws for other countries but is hypocritical because it often does not follow these rules itself.

The U.S. has been an important leader in promoting international laws and sets a good example by following them.

Egypt	78	21
Turkey	76	12
Azerbaijan	73	18
Iraq	68	20
Pakistan	66	28
Indonesia	66	11
Jordan (2008)	64	19
Palest. Ter.	61	37

Source: WorldPublicOpinion.org, 2009.

In one unusual case, a respondent tried hard to be politely euphemistic in his criticism: "I think that the U.S. government is well respected, it has weight in the international level, but sometimes its executions are not well mastered. Sometimes in the political level they get [*pauses*]—confused."

These feelings were often presented in the form of a linear narrative, whereby the respondent initially had the experience of the United States as a beacon of laudable values and then felt let down when the United States failed to live up to them. Following are some examples from respondents in several different focus groups.

> We've always seen America as [a] source of enlightenment. . . . But what we see now makes the people have negative feelings towards the American policy.

> America represented a dream for science, freedom, enlightenment. . . . [But now] America has successfully attracted the world's hostile feelings and attitudes, especially the countries that experience unjust treatment.

Some described this change as having occurred after 9/11.

> Before 9/11, people always saw America enlightened and
> insightful. We don't see it that way anymore.

> Until [9/11] everyone thought that [the United States] is the first
> country in all aspects, but after 9/11 the U.S. lost its value as
> the great power.

> After September 11, America lost credibility; it deviated from its
> normal path; it betrayed its ideals.

Other respondents described the perceived duality in America as stemming from a disjuncture between the American people (and culture) and their government.

> What I want to say is that the America's recent destructive
> behavior is not coming from the civilians—it's the government.
> The American people are always searching for the well-being of
> everybody, they know how to help, how to implant humanistic
> principles, peace. . . . It's not the American government who
> does all [these good things]. The American government thinks
> about financing things that aren't in the benefit of the third
> world. It's selfish, capitalist, and aggressive.

> For me, I see this like a package that's sometimes black and
> sometimes pink, and that's because of the controversy happening
> inside it. [There are] two great contradictory forces. The first one
> is the civilian society, which is more cultured and more structured,
> the one who loves the good, for the good of the people. . . . The
> second force . . . is the government, who is aggressive, capitalist,
> exploiting others, trying to get the most profit.

Looking more closely at what norms respondents saw the United States as violating, a central one was that the United States, by the nature of being a superpower, is obliged to show restraint.

> America is the strongest country in the world. Any president
> should consider this fact very well, that he's the president of the

most powerful country in the world. He has to be fair, and when it comes to applying standards, he should do it from a human perspective.

This obligation was seen as derived from the fact that there are no external constraints when the United States deviates from norms, even norms the United States has promoted.

> That's power . . . even if they do something against what they say, there is no one who can penalize them.

Some respondents went out of their way to affirm the legitimacy of pursuing self-interest, while also asserting that the United States violates international norms in the process.

> No doubt that everyone and every country could pursue their interests, but there are international standards that should be respected as well as humane ones!

Particularly galling to many was the perception that the United States uses the cover of liberal principles and benign concern to pursue its narrow self-interest. Under the cover of benign intentions, the United States was portrayed as even seeking to steal Muslims' resources.

> [The United States] tends to seek its own interests and benefits under notions like democracy, justice, war on terrorism.

> If we look at the facts . . . the people dying and the resources stolen . . . the people don't benefit in any way. The final result is destruction, killing, and sabotage. If we consider all of this, then America's intention was not to protect, but to steal.

> They don't have strict principles. They act depending on what's in their profit.

Another recurring theme was that the United States fails to follow the principle of reciprocity in its relations with other countries. While this is not a norm in the sense of legal requirement, it is a natural outgrowth of a relationship that is not coercive and is based on respect for the equal sovereignty and autonomy of nations. In its surveys in 2007, 2009, and 2010, Pew asked, "In making international policy decisions, to what extent do you think the United States takes into account the interests of countries like yours?" Large majorities said "not too much" or "not at all" in Bangladesh, Egypt, Jordan, Kuwait, Lebanon, Malaysia, Morocco, Pakistan, the Palestinian Territories, and Turkey. However, a plurality of Indonesians (50 percent) in 2010 said the United States takes the interests of their country into account a "great deal" or a "fair amount," an increase from previous years (figure 2-6). Globally, many non-Muslim countries shared this view.[11]

Similarly, in the focus groups respondents regularly portrayed the United States as seeking asymmetrical and unfair advantages in its relationships, as in the following exchange in a focus group in Morocco.

> RESPONDENT 1. The United States tries in every agreement with
> any country to have more rights than obligations.
> R2. That's why . . . even the programs signed by the Moroccan
> government . . . even if it's a new imitative, people always doubt
> it because they say that it's coming from the United States, so
> it's made up to fulfill their benefits more than ours.
> R3. All they care about is their own interests.

Perhaps the most clear-cut example given in regard to the United States' failure to live up to its liberal ideals was related to human rights. The treatment of prisoners at Guantánamo and Abu Ghraib was mentioned specifically.

> [Take] the prison of Abu Ghraib. The U.S. is still a member of the
> agreement of human rights, which requires respect for human
> rights and dignity. But in the Iraq war they were the first ones
> to practice torture on civilians. This means that the government
> contradicts itself. We lately hear the words "terrorist" and
> "terror" a lot, but what we see in American prisons in Iraq, is it
> legitimate?

Others complained that the United States falls short in its external relations of the human rights standards it applies at home.

FIGURE 2-6. Taking into Account a Country's Interests

In making international policy decisions, to what extent do you think the United States takes into account the interests of countries like [survey country]?

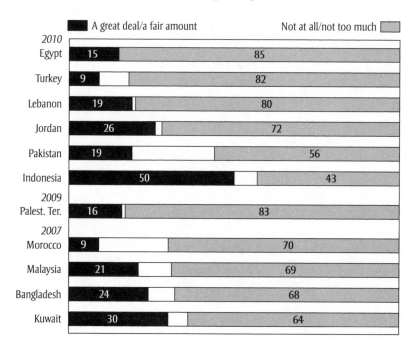

Source: Pew Global Attitudes Project.

We all know that America respects human rights when it comes to its own people. . . . Is it inherited in their religion or culture, or should it be respected in the whole world? Why doesn't America seek to establish human rights in the world?

Summing up a collective frustration with as well as underlying hope for America, an Egyptian said, "What we hope from America or from the American people is to be impartial and not have double standards according to their interests and their desires."

3 | The United States as Coercively Dominating the Muslim World

Perhaps the strongest complaint about the United States that flows from the broader narrative of American oppression is that the United States coercively dominates and exploits the Muslim world. This effort to dominate is seen as driven by specific desires to control access to oil in the Middle East as well as a broader aspiration to achieve regional hegemony and ultimately world domination. Actions by the United States to achieve these goals are seen as not only political, but also as coercive through the constant implicit and explicit threats of the use of superior military power. U.S. forces in the region are seen as key in performing this coercive function.

To a significant extent this is a reaction to the increased presence of U.S. military forces in the Muslim world. Besides the major U.S. military actions in Iraq and Afghanistan—which are widely seen as prompted by U.S. aspirations to expand its footprint in the region—during the 1990s there was a major increase in the U.S. military forces in the Persian Gulf. The U.S. Fifth Fleet commands several carrier strike groups in the region, while another carrier strike group operates at all times in the Mediterranean as part of the U.S. Sixth Fleet. The United States operates bases in Kuwait, Oman, Qatar, Saudi Arabia, and the United Arab Emirates.

Benign rationales for the presence of U.S. forces in the region—that they are a stabilizing force or that they are there to fight terrorism—are roundly dismissed. Thus there is widespread support for getting all U.S.

military forces out of Muslim countries. In this sense majorities see themselves as aligned with al Qaeda. And to this end, substantial numbers—in some nations, majorities—approve of attacks on U.S. troops operating in Muslim countries.

The perceived coercive domination by the United States is seen as objectionable from both an Islamist and a liberal perspective. As is discussed in chapter 4, a perceived goal of U.S. domination is the undermining of Islam. The U.S. military presence is seen as serving this end.

Equally potent from a liberal perspective, the U.S. efforts to dominate the Muslim world are seen as contrary to the principles of international law that the United States professes to promote. According to these principles, all nations are essentially equal and independent, and no nation should be able to coerce another with the threat of military force. International relations should be based on the principles of reciprocity and fairness.

As discussed in the previous chapter, these principles are intrinsically attractive to many Muslims, and the perception that the United States has violated these principles elicits a strong feeling of betrayal. This feeling is much more complex than simple hostility. It is premised on the perception that something attractive was originally promised—thus engendering positive feelings—but then that promise was violated, eliciting feelings of disappointment and rage that are much greater than if the promise had never been made.

Further, there is a perception that the United States has sought to seduce the Muslim world with high-minded ideas of world order, when in fact it has been using them as a cover to pursue its narrow interests. Thus Muslims tend to feel that they must be highly vigilant even when, or especially when, those ideas sound attractive.

Seeking Domination of the Muslim World

In WorldPublicOpinion.org polling conducted in 2008 and 2009, majorities in eight of nine majority-Muslim countries polled endorsed the view that "in our government's relations with the United States," the United States "abuses its greater power to make us do what the United States wants." These majorities ranged from 61 percent in Azerbaijan to 90 percent in Pakistan in 2009. Only small minorities endorsed the view that "the United States more often treats us fairly" (see figure 3-1). Respondents in

FIGURE 3-1.   Seeking Domination

In our government's relations with the U.S., do you think the U.S. more often treats us fairly, or abuses its greater power to make us do what the U.S. wants?

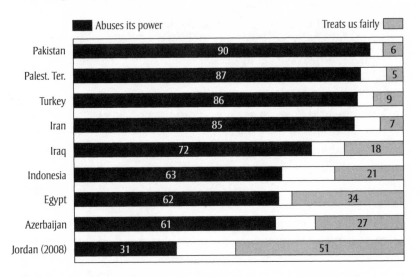

Source: WorldPublicOpinion.org, 2009.

majority-Muslim countries were a bit harsher in their assessment of U.S. foreign policy than in most other nations globally.[1]

The theme that the United States dominates other countries and pursues its interest irrespective of others' interests was echoed in the focus groups and was frequently and emotionally expressed, as represented in the following comments:

> Among the negative points about the American foreign policy is the interference in the policies of other countries with the purpose of maintaining America's internal security.

> The foreign policy of the USA is based on interference in the affairs of others, on aggression and domination.

> American policy . . . falls within what we call the absolute will of power. . . . [The United States] is pursuing a colonialism policy.

[The United States is] a big power in a way that they rule other countries.

We have become their slaves. . . . They just issue orders and we follow them.

It's the United States that kills the politics of all the others; all the underdeveloped countries are its followers. They are always dependent on the attitudes and decisions of the United States . . . not because they agree, but because they must.

Core to this thinking is the view that U.S. policy is predicated on the idea that countries with superior power can expect countries with lesser power to submit to their will. As a Moroccan man explained, "[The United States] implanted an ideology in all countries; if you are powerful on the military level . . . you can have everything you desire, everything you want because you are powerful in the military sector."

Such comments were made with bewilderment and a strong normative thrust, implying that this American position contradicts more appropriate principles for international relations that are not based on coercive power.

Besides using the threat of military force, the United States is seen as having other means of coercion such as damaging a country's image. When Iranians were asked why they thought Iran did not have a good image in the world, they insisted it was due to U.S. efforts to punish Iran—using its control over the media—for failing to submit to U.S. domination. An Iranian explained that Iran's poor image in the world was because "we do not accept going under U.S. control," and thus the United States "is doing all it can to damage our image throughout the world."

In Pakistan a number of male respondents tried to explain how the United States dominates the Pakistani political process.

RESPONDENT 1. Over here the general public has the impression that the elected leaders are just pawns . . . that whatever happens in Pakistan happens according to the wishes of America.

MODERATOR. How does the United States get such leverage and capacity to influence decisions in Pakistan?

R2. Simply because it is a superpower.

R3. Since America, which is such a big power, gives some orders,
the leaders in Pakistan agree to abide by them.

R4. We have elected the leader, but at the end of the day, the
power still lies with the United States.

These respondents were quite unequivocal that this state of affairs is
anathema to most Pakistanis, even if there are some benefits. One explained, "Even if there's forced order in your house, people won't be
happy. . . . Dictatorship leads to unhappiness."

Respondents made a direct link between resentment about U.S. domination and terrorism. A Pakistani said that U.S. domination "results in an
environment which breeds terrorism." Increased efforts to suppress terrorism through military force were seen as only exacerbating the problem.
An Egyptian explained, "The way we see it, America is going in countries
to fight terrorism in these countries. What we see happening is that it esca-
lates terrorism there."

Seeking Control of Oil

A widely repeated theme was that one of the central goals of U.S. domination is to control Middle East oil. In WPO polling of eleven majority-
Muslim countries conducted from 2006 through 2009, very large majorities said that they think it is a goal of the United States to "maintain
control over the oil resources of the Middle East" (see figure 3-2).

Such goals are attributed to President Obama as well as the United
States in general. Very large majorities in eight nations polled by WPO in
2009 perceived Obama as wanting to control Middle East oil. These percentages ranged from 78 percent in Turkey to 93 percent in the Palestinian Territories.

This effort to control oil resources is not seen as simply normal com-
mercial relations, but an illegitimate effort to steal resources. In WPO
polling in 2006 and 2007 robust majorities agreed with the statement that
"America pretends to be helpful to Muslim countries, but in fact everything it does is really part of a scheme to take advantage of people in the
Middle East and steal their oil." This position was endorsed by majorities
in Egypt (82 percent), Morocco (62 percent), and Indonesia (60 percent)
and by a plurality in Pakistan (48 percent). (See figure 3-3.)

FIGURE 3-2.   U.S. Goal: Maintain Control over Middle East
Oil Resources

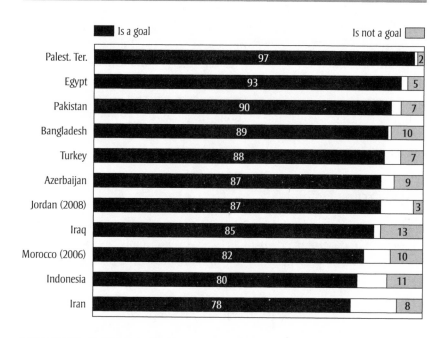

Source: WorldPublicOpinion.org, 2009.

FIGURE 3-3.   Seeking to Steal Oil

America pretends to be helpful to Muslim countries, but in fact everything it does is really
part of a scheme to take advantage of people in the Middle East and steal their oil.

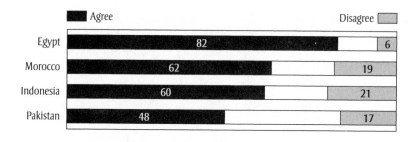

Source: WorldPublicOpinion.org, 2009.

Focus group respondents regularly spoke of America's desire to control Middle East oil. As an Iranian man said, one of the two main objectives of U.S. forces in the region is "to secure the flow of energy resources to the United States." This belief was often embedded in the larger framework of the United States illegitimately seeking total domination. As an Egyptian man said, "Every country has a right to pursue its own interests, but to control petroleum from the Qazween [Caspian] Sea to Iraq? [*shaking his head*] This is a dream of absolute domination." Another Egyptian man, when asked which international issue was of greatest concern to him, answered, "The first issue is the domination of the United States over most countries, particularly those which own oil."

Seeking World Domination

The U.S. pursuit of control over Muslim countries is seen as more than the pursuit of control over Muslim resources. For many respondents such control is seen as part of a larger United States effort to achieve world domination. This was regularly mentioned in the focus groups.

[The United States] wants to control the world.

America . . . has even gone beyond the absolute power thing, and
   it thinks it could rule the world, including Europe.

America first, and secondly Britain, want to control the world.
   They don't want peace.

This pursuit of world domination is seen as illegitimate and contrary to the liberal international order. Using liberal, normative language when asked what he would want to say to the American president, one Iranian said, "If the U.S. president were here . . . I would ask him, 'Why do you give yourself the right to make decisions on behalf of the whole world? Why don't you allow the people of other countries to make their own decisions, to choose their own government?'"

This perceived desire for domination by the United States is sometimes interpreted in psychological terms as being a collective personality trait. In the words of an Iranian, "U.S. behavior is such that it seems that it has a severe lack of self-respect and esteem. By sheer force it is trying to convey that it is powerful and just wants to show off its superiority. . . . But the more it behaves this way, its image further deteriorates." An Egyptian said, "America likes to control and dominate other countries; it is acting like a macho man."

The U.S. war against Iraq was generally seen as being part of a plan for the United States to increase its military footprint in the region. The ostensible concern about Iraq having weapons of mass destruction was largely dismissed. A 2004 Pew survey asked respondents in four majority-Muslim countries why the United States and Britain had made the claim that Iraq had weapons of mass destruction. Only small minorities said it was because the leaders were misinformed. Most said they "lied to provide a reason for invading Iraq." Thus it is not surprising that most also said that as a consequence of the war, they have less confidence that the United States is trustworthy.

Many seemed to believe that the United States has a progressive plan for dominating the world. Gaining dominance over the Muslim world was seen as the current stage in this process. A Jordanian man said, "You wiped out the U.S.S.R. The Islamic world is next, and then will come China and the others. You want a unipolar system." An Egyptian man believed that he had heard a statement by the U.S. secretary of state about this plan for world domination. He explained, "In the beginning of the Iraqi war . . . there was a statement by the American secretary of state that the next target would be Iran, then Syria, then Saudi Arabia, and finally Egypt, the grand prize." In an exchange among members of a Moroccan focus group, laced with dark humor, respondents were predicting where Morocco fit into the U.S. plan for world domination.

R1. They started with Iraq, then Iran, next Syria. It was all planned.

R2. All the Arab and Muslim countries know that. Our turn is coming, but we are not the fourth or fifth, but we are in the planning.

R3. For now [*laughter*].

R4. But it is little bit hard for the first ones.

R2. [*Sarcastically*] It will be easy for us [*laughter*].

The United States as Using the Threat of Military Force

The concern that the United States seeks to dominate Muslim countries is not simply a reaction to perceived American intentions. More importantly, it arises from a perception that the United States is implicitly or explicitly using the threat of military force to coerce Muslim nations to yield to U.S. wishes.

In the 2009 WPO survey large majorities in the six majority-Muslim countries polled said that the United States uses the threat of military force to gain advantages. These majorities ranged from 77 percent in Azerbaijan to 86 percent in Egypt and Turkey. These attitudes on the United States using the threat of military force were in keeping with attitudes globally (figure 3-4).[2]

Pew has also consistently found majorities perceiving the United States as a potential military threat. In a 2007 poll of eleven nations, majorities ranging from 57 percent in Lebanon to 93 percent in Bangladesh said they were worried "that the United States could become a military threat to our country someday." Even in Turkey—a NATO ally—76 percent had such a worry, as did 61 percent in Kuwait—a country the United States defended in the Persian Gulf War. When this question was asked by Pew in seven majority-Muslim countries in the spring of 2009 after Obama's

FIGURE 3-4. Threatening Force to Gain Advantages

Do you think [the United States] does or does not use the threat of military force to gain advantages?

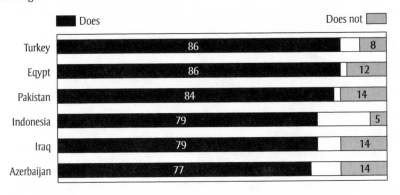

Source: WorldPublicOpinion.org, 2009.

FIGURE 3-5. Fear of U.S. Military Threat

How worried are you, if at all, that the U.S. could become a military threat to your country someday?

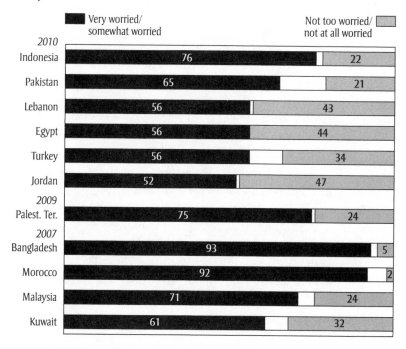

Source: Pew Global Attitudes Project.

election, the numbers fearing a military threat from the United States declined but in most cases remained majorities. In 2010 Pew found this perception edged back up in six majority-Muslim nations. Figure 3-5 shows the most recent number in each country polled.

A 2010 Sadat Chair poll of six Arab nations asked respondents to name two countries that pose the biggest threat to them. On average, 77 percent named the United States (down from 88 percent in 2008). An even larger 88 percent named Israel. No other nation was cited as a threat by substantial numbers of respondents.

In a 2008 Terror Free Tomorrow survey of Pakistanis, respondents were asked, "Which of the following countries or groups do you think pose the greatest threat to your personal safety?" Strikingly, only 14 percent said India—Pakistan's archrival and with whom it is engaged in a vigorous arms race. Far more (a 44 percent plurality) said the United States poses the greatest threat.

Characterizations of the United States as threatening were voiced regularly in the focus groups. For example, an Iranian said, "The United States shows off its power . . . threatens others and uses extortion." This threat of force is seen as a key way that the United States controls governments in the Arab world, as in the following discussion in Jordan:

> MODERATOR. You and others made some reference to how the United States controls the governments in the Arab world. How do you understand that to work? How does America gain that power?
>
> R. America was in a war with Japan. It threw an atomic bomb in Hiroshima, and Japan gave in the next day.
>
> R. We as Arab nations and governments are sure afraid of a force like the United States. We don't have the power.
>
> MODERATOR. So you think that the threat of nuclear weapons makes Arab leaders comply with the United States?
>
> R. Also, the siege imposed on Iraq for so many years and the invasion of Iraq afterwards, Arab nations are afraid to experience what happened in Iraq.

Interestingly, in some cases respondents would balk at the insinuation that their country was submitting to American threats. When a number of comments about Jordan being perceived as submissive to the United States were summarized for respondents, one of them shrugged, agreeing, and said, "Jordan is a weak country; it needs peace." But another bridled and said, "We did not say that Jordan is submissive to America." He then explained in more euphemistic language, with a touch of irony, that Jordan "is in conditions that have certain requirements."

Similarly, responses were mixed when respondents were asked in a 2008 WPO poll, "How much, if at all, do you think our government adjusts its policies out of fear that the United States might otherwise use military force against it?" Interestingly, the largest number saying that their government does make such accommodations was in Turkey, where 49 percent said it does this "some" (31 percent) or "a lot" (18 percent). Forty-seven percent in both Azerbaijan and Pakistan believed their governments change their policies "some" or "a lot" for fear of the United

States. Smaller numbers, however, said this in the Palestinian Territories (42 percent), Indonesia (41 percent), and Jordan (34 percent). At the same time, only small minorities said "not at all" in all six nations polled (ranging from 9 percent in Pakistan to 26 percent in Jordan). And, clear majorities in all cases said at least "a little."

Consistent with the perception that the U.S. stance toward Middle Eastern countries is to use military threats to force submission to the American will, U.S. military bases are seen as an instrument of such coercion. While the U.S. government has tried to make the case that people in the region benefit from the presence of U.S. troops, respondents clearly see the forces as a kind of loaded gun aimed at them. Referring to the bases, an Egyptian respondent said, "America has to put something there to scare us with." Another added that with the bases, "it is protecting itself and at the same time it is threatening other states." A Jordanian referred to the U.S. military presence as an "occupation" in a long, imperial tradition. He commented, "We are used to occupation. We have been occupied by the French and British. America has occupation goals. . . . We are used to that."

An extensive discussion in an Egyptian focus group revealed how the participants viewed the presence of military bases in the region as a means to coerce Arab countries to submit to a wide range of American goals.

MODERATOR. How do you feel about the U.S. military bases in the region, especially in the Gulf region?

R1. We don't like it. . . . The existence of U.S. military bases in any Arab country represents a threat to the Egyptian national security.

MODERATOR. Let me see a show of hands. How many people sitting here perceive the U.S. military bases as a threat to Egypt? [*most raise hands*] Why?

R1. These bases are there . . . to attack us. . . . We'll never trust the Americans.

R2. The United States is trying to influence things in Egypt. . . . The military bases represent occupation of the Arab world again.

R3. If it wants to control this area [the Arab world] . . . [the United States must] have military forces ready to take military action against any government in an Arab country that would react in a manner that is not in the U.S.'s interests.

Moderator. So the military bases of the United States are there to threaten the countries in the region that do not do what America wants them to do?

R3. Of course.

MODERATOR. Does everyone here agree with this? [*general agreement*] So what is something that Egypt might do that would prompt the United States to use military force against it?

R4. If Egypt tries to threaten Israel's security.

MODERATOR. What else?

R1. And if Egypt tries to do anything that is in contradiction with or harmful to the U.S. interests.

Moderator. Like what? Can you give an example?

R5. If there is a system in Egypt that is not loyal to the American system.

MODERATOR. What is something that Egypt could do that is so against the American system that the United States would use military forces against it? What are any other reasons aside from Egypt attacking Israel?

R4. If the United States attacks another Arab or Muslim country, Egypt would not take the U.S. side. It would support and take the side of the Arab or Muslim country.

R2. If Egypt refuses to provide facilities. If it is not a friend of the United States, it's an enemy. After the nationalization of [the] Suez Canal, England and France took it as an act against them, so they invaded Egypt.

R6. If an Islamic group, Muslim Brothers or otherwise, rises and attempts to unite the Arab world and bring together the Arab countries, especially if this group reaches the government or becomes part of the ruling regime or the regime itself.

MODERATOR. So how would those military forces be useful?

R4. It won't happen over a night, but as the idea itself begins to evolve, it would be suppressed immediately.

One Egyptian respondent tried to make the case that U.S. bases are illogically creating the problem that they are meant to address. He said, "When you put military bases everywhere, you are threatening your neighboring countries' security," which then generates hostility. This leads the United States to see the bases as necessary to "protect the U.S. troops in the Gulf." But, he counseled, "when the United States pulls out of the area, it will no longer need these bases."

Coercive Domination as Violating Liberal Principles

America's perceived coercive domination of the Muslim world is seen as particularly objectionable because it is viewed as contrary to the liberal principles that the United States professes to promote and that many Muslims find attractive. According to these principles, relations between states should not be based on relative coercive power, but the rule of international law, within which all nations have equal status irrespective of their relative military power. As was frequently cited in the focus groups, the United States is seen as using, or abusing, its superior power in its self-interest. Often such charges were made in a way that was mixed with admiration for America. For example, a Jordanian woman said, "I see that America is a very developed country from the scientific and economic aspects. If we look at it from these perspectives, it can help the countries of the world so much. But it's only applying jungle law. It likes to dominate."

A recurring theme was that the United States uses the framework of international norms as a veiled strategy for it to dominate Muslim countries. In the words of one Jordanian man, "Peace treaties, UN resolutions, international law did not achieve anything for us now. All of these are lies and efforts to mislead us. It is part of the scheme to control us. . . . Since 1948 we have tried peace, but everything turned out to be a lie. Looking to the future, we don't see anything except more wars, problems, and efforts to control our leadership. They are using force through the diplomats to control us."

Particularly infuriating was the perception that the United States, while promoting international norms, alone has the capacity to act outside of them in the pursuit of control over other countries, as noted in these comments:

> America gives itself the right to interfere in any other country and to cause damage and destruction. It granted itself this right, but no other country could grant itself this same right.

> They have a power to force underdeveloped countries to always agree with the United States. They just can't contradict it. Like

a policeman, if he tells you that you burned a red light even if you are sure that it was green, you can't say no—he's always right.

Even while complaining about U.S. noncompliance with the liberal international normative order, respondents still invoked its principles.

R. No country has a right to control another!
R. Isn't what America is doing in Iraq terrorism?
MODERATOR. How do you define terrorism?
R. Unlawful seizure of others' rights—that simple.
R. When America goes in any country, it sees that the infrastructure in this country is destroyed. The countries have to rebuild everything again from scratch. Where are human rights in all of this?

United States as Having Extraordinary Powers

Closely related to the image of the United States as seeking world domination—and an important factor in the intensity of concern about such domination—is a perception of the United States as having extraordinary powers. In the focus groups people expressed beliefs about American power that many Americans would probably find quite surprising and, at times, even seemingly paranoid.

A key belief is that the United States exerts direct control of Muslim countries. A Moroccan man said that American leaders "control every Arab and Muslim country. They know that those countries are dependant, and even those [that are] not . . . they create a problem or a way to control them." Pakistanis were especially convinced that their government is under U.S. control. As one explained, "Over here the general public has the impression that the elected leaders are just pawns. . . . Most people think that whatever happens in Pakistan happens according to the wishes of America. Americans have had complete influence over Musharraf over these past eight years." The United States is seen as having extraordinary foresight. An Iranian commented with bitterness, "I compliment the United States . . . for its ability to think ahead for some 1,000 years and for its ability to devise such scenarios as the 9/11 to secure the interests of its forthcoming generations."

A recurring theme was that the United States exerts its control in hidden ways. An Iranian said, "Whenever you see rioting, you can see the United States pulling the strings." According to a Moroccan man,

> I think there is still a hidden game . . . that is revealed afterwards in a way that's not clear enough to act about it. The United States doesn't act clearly with others; there is always a hidden idea behind what's happening. . . . There are people behind the curtains who are responsible [for] all this.

The United States is credited with manipulatively causing the conflict between and within various states. An Egyptian attributed the start of the Iran-Iraq war with the United States because it prompted Iraq to attack Iran so as to weaken both. A Pakistani noted that the United States had caused the arms race between India and Pakistan:

> R. How are we going to progress if 70 percent of our annual budget is spent on our defense sector? America has involved Pakistan and India in this arms race, and all our revenue is being wasted.
> MODERATOR. Who is putting you into this arms race?
> R. America, of course. If they are helping India develop their arsenal, and if, for instance, India makes a new missile, it becomes necessary for Pakistan to compete. This has led to an arms race between the two countries. I don't consider India as our enemy.

A 2007 Arab American Institute poll found majorities in Turkey (80 percent), Egypt (68 percent), Morocco (59 percent), Saudi Arabia (53 percent), and the United Arab Emirates (53 percent) saying that the United States was responsible for the crisis in Darfur. In some cases larger majorities blamed the United States than blamed the government of Sudan or the Sudanese rebels. Various respondents described American control as pervasive and subtle. A Jordanian man said this about the United States:

> From the economic aspect, they control the prices of oil, and the oil goes to America. In education most of the material taught now does not interfere with American policies. . . . In secondary

schools they teach them about divorce and marriage. . . . If America did not interfere, they would have included things to make people aware of the behavior of America towards other people.

A Pakistani respondent credited the United States with extraordinary powers over Pakistan. He said, "When Nawaz Sharif made Pakistan a nuclear power, Bill Clinton had his government dissolved after a few days . . . [and] . . . devalued the currency of Pakistan."

The flip side of this perception of the United States as extraordinarily powerful is the idea that the United States has the power to do many positive things as well. A Pakistani focus group in 2008 had the following exchange.

> MODERATOR. As you know, we are in the process of electing a new president in the United States. Suppose the newly elected president is here. What would you want to say to the president?
> R1. The main problem is inflation and unemployment. If this is eliminated, everything will get better. Almost everything is associated with these issues.
> MODERATOR. Do you think the United States can do something to change the unemployment condition in Pakistan?
> R2. Yes, it can.
> MODERATOR. How?
> R3. It is a superpower. If they want, they can do anything.
> MODERATOR. What would they do?
> R4. We always hear and read in the news that America has done this, America has done that. While sitting so far off, it can do so many things. Why not help us get rid of unemployment? They can make a difference.

In a seeming non sequitur, another brought up the problem of litter in the streets. When the moderator asked if America could do anything in this regard, the respondent said, "Yes, it can."

> MODERATOR. How?
> R1. The way they have done so in their own country.
> R2. There should be a law!

R1. Like the environment they have created over there, the same should be created here in Pakistan.

R3. Like they have such strict control over cleanliness, here we have trash everywhere . . . and we can throw garbage and spit out betel leaf everywhere.

R2. There they take action against such acts, here they don't care. No one cares for our country.

MODERATOR. How can America help you establish such laws here?

R1. See, if they make such laws, then people won't throw out trash.

R4. If America wants to work with the Pakistani government. . . .

R5. They should help us with these problems.

The United States is also depicted as having extraordinary powers over the world media. As mentioned previously, members of an Iranian focus group were asked why, according to international polls, Iran has a poor image in the world and responded this way:

R6. Because the United States has money and can buy mass media. World publics are not inside Iran and don't know what is going on. The perception they have has been shaped by the media. And this is the biggest problem we have with the United States. That they represent an unrealistic and false image of Iran.

R7. It is the result of negative propaganda that is made against Iran. We have no doubt that the United States is heavily invested in making Iran look bad.

MODERATOR. So you think it's entirely due to America's propaganda?

R7. 100 percent.

However, they did not seem to think that this vast power was up to the task of improving America's image.

Moderator. If America buys the media to make Iran look bad, why couldn't it buy media to make itself look good?

R7. Because the image of United States is so bad that with no amount of money it can make itself look good. It's just so obvious!

FIGURE 3-6. Controlling World Events

How much of what happens in the world today would you say is controlled by the U.S.?

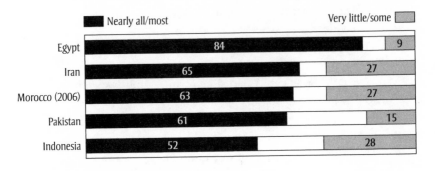

Source: WorldPublicOpinion.org, 2009.

To explore how widespread the perception of the United States as having extraordinary powers was, a WPO survey question in five majority-
Muslim countries between 2006 and 2008 asked, "How much of what
happens in the world today would you say is controlled by the United
States?" Majorities in all countries said "most" or "nearly all" is controlled by the United States. Eighty-four percent in Egypt had this view,
with 46 percent saying "nearly all" of what happens in the world is controlled by the United States. Significant majorities in Morocco (63 percent), Pakistan (61 percent), and Indonesia (52 percent) also said the
United States controls as least "most" events in the world. (See figure 3-6.)

Opposition to All U.S. Military Forces in Muslim Countries

Consistent with their perception of the U.S. military presence as threatening and coercive, polls show strong opposition to U.S. military forces in
Muslim countries. In WPO polling between 2006 and 2009 respondents
were asked whether they agreed with al Qaeda's goal of getting "the
United States to remove its bases and its military forces from all Islamic
countries." Large majorities in all countries polled agreed with this al
Qaeda goal. (See figure 3-7.)

Opposition to the U.S. military presence correlates closely with support for attacks on U.S. troops. As discussed in chapter 1, large numbers,

FIGURE 3-7. Al Qaeda Goal: Push U.S. to Remove Bases

Do you agree or disagree with the goal to push the U.S. to remove its bases and its military forces from all Islamic countries?

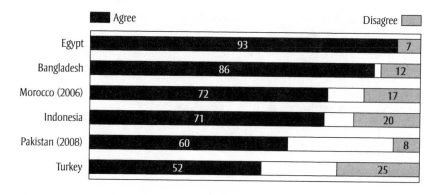

Source: WorldPublicOpinion.org, 2009.

though not always majorities, approve of attacks on U.S. troops in Afghanistan, Iraq, and the Persian Gulf. Indeed, statistical analysis reveals that those who oppose the U.S. military presence and support al Qaeda's goal of getting U.S. forces out of all Muslim countries are far more likely to approve of attacks on U.S. troops.

An Arab Barometer poll presented the bold argument that "U.S. involvement in the region justifies armed operations against the United States everywhere." Majorities in the Palestinian Territories (64 percent), Algeria (53 percent), Kuwait (51 percent), and Jordan (51 percent) agreed with this statement.

Respondents in the focus groups portrayed such attacks as natural responses to an alien occupying force, something to be distinguished from terrorism. As a Pakistani man explained,

> I think that people who resist in Iraq are not terrorists. . . . Should someone defending his country be considered a terrorist? . . . In my opinion, those who resist and defend what they own have a legitimate right to defend their land, just like America did during the British occupation of America. So why should defending a country in the Arab world be considered terrorism

and in the West be considered liberation? . . . When I'm
defending my land against occupation, that is a self-defense.

Similarly, an Egyptian man explained, "Right now Islamists are attacking
Americans in Iraq not because of Islam, but because the Americans are
occupying their land."

A 2009 Sadat Chair poll of six Arab countries asked what two steps by
the United States would most improve respondents' view of the United
States. For the weighted sample of all the countries, the most widely cited
responses were withdrawal from Iraq and withdrawal from the Arabian
Peninsula. These responses were more common than producing an Israel-
Palestine peace agreement.

Persian Gulf

In the 2008 and 2009 WPO polls of eight majority-Muslim countries,
large majorities in all eight cases said that it is a bad idea for the United
States to have naval forces in the Persian Gulf. (See figure 3-8.)

Equally large majorities also believe that the majority of people in the
Gulf region favor the withdrawal of U.S. forces (a plurality of Pakistanis
think this). Naturally, this adds to the sense that the forces there are illegitimate. (See figure 3-9.)

Respondents in the focus groups were unequivocal in saying they want
U.S. bases out of the region. Respondents said this as if it were self-
evident. When an Egyptian man was asked why he wants U.S. troops out,
he shrugged and said, "I will feel safer." A Jordanian woman commented,
"America is behind all instability and struggle in the region. . . . If they
left the world on its own, it'll do just fine."

Iraq

Support for U.S. withdrawal from Iraq is very strong. In a 2007 Pew poll,
large majorities in eleven majority-Muslim nations favored the United
States removing its troops. These majorities ranged from 56 percent in
Kuwait to 93 percent in the Palestinian Territories. Terror Free Tomorrow
also asked Saudis and Iranians whether it would improve their opinion of
the United States if it were to withdraw forces from Iraq. Sixty-seven percent of Iranians and 85 percent of Saudis said that it would.

The Pew survey of seven majority-Muslim nations in 2009 asked about
Obama's plan of "withdrawing U.S. combat forces from Iraq by December

FIGURE 3-8. U.S. Naval Forces in Persian Gulf

Do you think the U.S. having naval forces based in the Persian Gulf is a good idea or a bad idea?

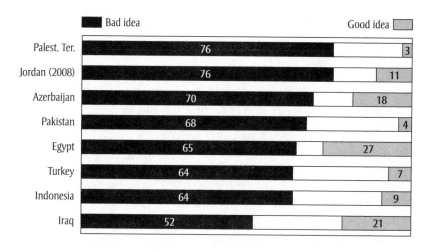

Source: WorldPublicOpinion.org, 2009.

FIGURE 3-9. Perceived Public Opposition to U.S. Bases

Do you think the majority of [people in the Middle East] approve or disapprove of the U.S. having naval forces based in the Persian Gulf?

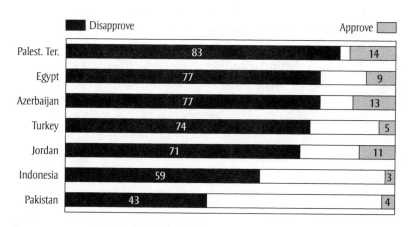

Source: WorldPublicOpinion.org, 2008.

2011." Majorities in all seven nations approved of this plan, ranging from 55 percent of Turks to 92 percent of Palestinians. This plan, however, is not enough to make most Muslims happy with Obama on this front. When Pew asked respondents in six majority-Muslim countries in 2010 about how Obama was "dealing with the situation in Iraq," majorities in all six disapproved. These majorities ranged from 52 percent in Indonesia to 79 percent in Egypt.

Afghanistan

Large majorities call for the United States to withdraw from Afghanistan. The 2010 Pew poll asked, "Do you think the United States and NATO should keep military troops in Afghanistan until the situation has stabilized, or do you think the United States and NATO should remove their troops as soon as possible?" Majorities in all six countries favored removal, including 62 percent in Indonesia, 65 percent in Pakistan, 69 percent in Lebanon, 67 percent in Turkey, and 81 percent in Egypt and Jordan.

In 2009 WPO polling of seven majority-Muslim nations, a series of questions asked about the situation in Afghanistan. Majorities or pluralities in five nations said it would be "bad" if the Taliban regained power in Afghanistan. The largest majorities were in Azerbaijan (67 percent), Pakistan (61 percent), and Turkey (61 percent) followed by Iraq (56 percent) and Indonesia (46 percent "bad," 20 percent "good"). Publics in the Palestinian Territories and Egypt dissented, however, with majorities of 68 percent and 62 percent, respectively, saying it would be "good."

Though most respondents thought it would be bad for the Taliban to regain power, majorities in Pakistan (72 percent) and Turkey (58 percent) still disapproved of the NATO mission in Afghanistan, as well as majorities in the Palestinian Territories (74 percent) and Egypt (56 percent). A majority in Azerbaijan (53 percent) and a plurality in Iraq (41 percent) approved of the mission, while Indonesians had mixed views. Similarly, majorities or pluralities in five of the seven countries said the mission should be ended (ranging from 43 percent in Indonesia to 79 percent in Pakistan). Only Azerbaijanis and Iraqis favored continuing the mission.

Large majorities in five nations said they did not approve of the Obama administration decision in February 2009 to increase the number of American troops in Afghanistan. The strongest majorities were in Pakistan (86 percent), the Palestinian Territories (83 percent), and Turkey (71 percent). Again, a plurality of Azerbaijanis approved, and Iraqis were divided on the question.

WPO also found that majorities or pluralities in five of the six nations also said they believed that the people of Afghanistan want NATO forces to leave immediately, a factor that may have influenced their attitudes about the U.S. presence. This does not appear, however, to be the case. A December 2009 ABC/BBC poll found 68 percent of Afghans approving of the presence of "U.S. military forces," an increase from 63 percent in January of that year.

This does not mean that the Afghan people have entirely positive feelings about U.S. troops. Fifty-eight percent rated the work of the United States in Afghanistan as "fair" (33 percent) or "poor" (25 percent). A similar 62 percent said the performance of NATO/International Security Assistance Force (ISAF) forces was at best "fair." In January 2009 before plans for additional troops were announced, Afghans were mixed on changing the number of U.S. and NATO/ISAF forces in the country, with 44 percent saying they should be decreased, 29 percent saying they should be kept at the current level, and 18 percent saying they should be increased. In December 2009—after the United States and its NATO allies announced plans to send a total of 38,000 more troops to the country—Afghans were generally more favorable, with 61 percent saying they supported the move and 36 percent opposing it.

Specifically on the use of air strikes in December 2009, 66 percent of Afghans said it is "unacceptable because it endangers too many innocent civilians," a decrease of 11 percentage points from earlier that year. When asked in the same poll to assign blame for civilian deaths from air strikes, views were mixed, with 36 percent blaming U.S. and NATO/ISAF forces, 35 percent blaming antigovernment forces, and 26 percent blaming both. This was a change from the January survey in which 41 percent blamed U.S. and NATO/ISAF forces, 28 percent blamed antigovernment forces, and 27 percent blamed both.

This does not mean, however, that Afghans approve of attacks on U.S. troops. Asked in December 2009, "Under current circumstances, do you think attacks against U.S. or NATO/ISAF military forces in Afghanistan can be justified?" 76 percent said they cannot be justified, an increase from 64 percent in January of that year.

Pakistan

Pakistanis, on the other hand, express clear opposition to the presence of U.S. troops in their country. A 2008 Terror Free Tomorrow poll of Pakistanis found 73 percent opposed to the presence of the U.S. military inside Pakistan, with 53 percent strongly opposed. This was a larger number than was opposed to the presence of Arab and Uzbek al Qaeda fighters, Afghan Taliban fighters, and Pakistani Taliban fighters.

Similarly, 69 percent of Pakistanis opposed "the U.S. military working with the Pakistani military to pursue Taliban and al Qaeda fighters inside Pakistan." In addition, 74 percent opposed "the U.S. military pursuing Taliban and al Qaeda fighters by itself inside Pakistan without working with the Pakistani military."

Pakistanis also see the U.S. military role in Pakistan as a destabilizing force. A 2008 Terror Free Tomorrow poll of Pakistanis asked, "Who do you consider the most responsible for the violence that is occurring in Pakistan today?" Fifty-two percent said the United States, while just 8 percent said al Qaeda and other Arab and foreign fighters, and 4 percent said the Pakistani Taliban.

This may have contributed to a lack of concern about Islamic militants operating in Pakistan that was found in polls in 2007. In 2009, however, after the Taliban's advance into the Swat Valley, WPO found a major shift in Pakistani perceptions. While in September 2007 only 34 percent thought the "activities of Islamist militants and local Taliban in Federally Administered Tribal Areas (FATA) and settled areas" were a critical threat, in 2009 this increased dramatically to 81 percent. In 2007 only 38 percent thought "the activities of religious militant groups in Pakistan" were a critical threat. In the 2009 WPO poll, however, 67 percent did. In addition, 78 percent of Pakistanis in the same study said they would support their government if it identified Afghan Taliban bases and moved to close them.

As the conflict with the Pakistani Taliban subsided to some degree in 2010, so did the levels of reported concern, though a majority continue to be worried. While in 2009 Pew found 73 percent of Pakistanis saying the Taliban was a "very serious" or a "somewhat serious" threat, this number decreased to 54 percent in 2010. Similarly, while 69 percent responded in 2009 that they were "very" or "somewhat" worried that extremist groups could take control of Pakistan, this decreased to 51 percent in 2010.

Even at the height of concern, Pakistanis have resisted the use of U.S. military power against Islamist militants in Pakistan. When asked about "the current U.S. drone aircraft attacks that strike targets in northwestern Pakistan,"82 percent in WPO's 2009 polling called these attacks unjustified; only 13 percent disagreed. Seventy-nine percent said the United States would not be justified in bombing "bases in Pakistan of Taliban groups who are trying to overthrow the Afghan government" if it identified such bases. Similarly, in WPO's 2007 polling 77 percent of Pakistanis said the government should not allow "foreign troops to pursue and capture Taliban insurgents who have crossed over from Afghanistan."

Even if the United States were to identify al Qaeda training camps operating in Pakistan, four in five Pakistanis (81 percent) said in WPO 2007 polling they did not think it would be justified for the United States to bomb such camps, with only 13 percent saying it would be justified. Similarly, 80 percent said "the Pakistan government should not allow American or other foreign troops to enter Pakistan to pursue and capture al Qaeda fighters," with only 5 percent saying their government should permit it.

Pew also asked a series of questions in 2010 on "drone attacks that target extremist leaders" in Pakistan. Thirty-five percent reported they had heard "a lot" or "a little" about such strikes. This group of 35 percent was then asked a series of follow-up questions. Of those who said they had at least some knowledge of the drone attacks, 93 percent said these attacks are a bad thing (62 percent said they were "very bad"). An overwhelmingly majority of the group (90 percent) agreed that "they kill too many innocent people." Only 32 percent agreed that "they are necessary to defend Pakistan from extremist groups." Two-thirds (66 percent) identified the U.S. government as the party behind the attacks, with a further 15 percent volunteering that both Pakistan and the U.S. government are behind them. There does not appear to be a high degree of certainty on this, however, as only 49 percent agreed that "they are being done without the approval of the Pakistani government." Pew also asked its full sample whether or not they support the United States "conducting drone attacks *in conjunction with the Pakistani government* against leaders of extremist groups" (emphasis added). In this context views were more mixed, with 32 percent opposing such attacks and 23 supporting them (45 percent did not answer).

Support for nonmilitary forms of involvement in Pakistan to fight extremism have received far more support than military forms, though support for even nonmilitary measures appears to be diminishing. In

2010, 53 percent favored the United States "providing financial and humanitarian aid to areas where extremist groups operate," a drop of 19 points from 72 percent in 2009. Similarly, support for the United States "providing intelligence and logistical support to Pakistani troops fighting extremist groups" dropped from 63 to 48 percent.

Rejection of Benign Rationales for U.S. Military Presence

Rationales for the U.S. military presence that emphasize the benefits to the people in the region—that the presence is stabilizing or protects countries from Iran—are widely dismissed. On the contrary, U.S. forces tend to be seen as contributing to instability. In a 2007 BBC/GlobeScan/PIPA poll respondents were asked, "Do you think the U.S. military presence in the Middle East is a stabilizing force or provokes more conflict than it prevents?" Large majorities in all five majority-Muslim countries polled said that the U.S. presence provokes more conflict than it prevents. Most non-Muslim nations agreed, but majority-Muslim nations took this position in larger numbers.[3] (See figure 3-10.)

When the possibility that U.S. bases provide stability was raised with respondents in the focus groups, there was recognition that some small Gulf states may find them reassuring. For example, an Egyptian man said, "Certain countries requested [U.S. forces], like Kuwait, for example. I think it was okay with Kuwait to have American troops there." Another commented, "The military bases in the Gulf were based there after the Gulf countries were convinced that these bases are there to protect them from attacks by Iraq or Iran; and this is something that concerns them. . . . If the Kuwaitis with their small population thought they needed a huge army to face the Iraqi occupation, then maybe the presence of the U.S. forces would assure them."

But this Egyptian man also said, "It doesn't concern us." When his response was repeated back to him, "It doesn't concern you?" the rest of the exchange was as follows:

> R. [*incredulously*] In Egypt? No.
> MODERATOR. Why? Well, there is Iran.
> R. [*brushing it off*] Iran? No.
> MODERATOR. Is there anybody here who has concerns about the
>   possibilities of Iran attacking?

FIGURE 3-10. U.S. Military Presence as Stabilizing

Do you think the U.S. military presence in the Middle East is a stabilizing force or provokes more conflict than it prevents?

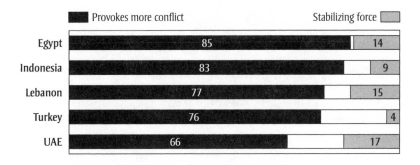

Source: BBC/GlobeScan/PIPA, 2007.

There was some concern about Egypt getting caught in the cross fire of a United States–Iran conflict, but there seemed to be consensus that Iran posed no threat to Egypt.

> MODERATOR. So you don't see Iran as a threat to Egypt?
> R. No, I don't.
> MODERATOR. So does anybody here see these bases in some way protecting you from Iran?
> R. No, a threat by Iran is not expected.

A recurring theme was that the United States uses the Iranian threat as a false pretext for its military presence. An Egyptian explained, "I think the United States is 'staging' this conflict with Iran as a country that poses a threat to the Arab countries, and thus justifies its presence in the Gulf area." Similarly, an Iranian man said, "I think the presence of U.S. forces in the Gulf is mostly to prop up Arab countries against Iran. The United States tells them that Iran is the source of all threats against you. . . . It is not really for that, but the United States is using this as a pretext for stationing its forces in the region."

WPO polls of seven Muslim countries in 2008 probed whether people would feel more positive about having bases if they were requested by a Muslim country. Respondents were presented with two statements:

(1) "When requested by the government of a Muslim country, the presence of Western troops can be helpful for security and stability," and (2) "Even when requested by the government of a Muslim country, the presence of Western troops in a Muslim country is a bad idea." A majority or plurality in every case opted for the second position, ranging from 49 percent in Azerbaijan and Pakistan to 86 percent in Egypt.

War on Terrorism as Subterfuge for Domination

Though Muslims in principle widely reject terrorism or any kind of attack on civilians, they nonetheless dismiss the U.S. "war on terrorism" in general as a rationale for U.S. intervention in Muslim countries. Few see the war on terrorism as genuinely devoted to the goal of eliminating terrorism. Focus group respondents explained that it is just an excuse for the United States to expand its presence in Muslim countries so as to dominate them.

> MODERATOR. What's the real objective of what the United States calls "war against terrorism"?
> R1. It's to exploit the Muslim world's resources indirectly.
> R2. Exactly. Just like Iraq, they pretended that the reason they went there is the Iraqi possession of weapons of mass destruction, but now it's proved to be just lies. They found nothing, they toppled Saddam, but they're still there to exploit the Iraqi resources.
> R3. They're just trying to find reasons to dominate the Middle East and use all its resources. All this started after 9/11. They found a reason to advance towards the Middle East and the Muslim countries. They have wanted to do this before, but they didn't have a solid reason to enter this part of the world. But after 9/11 they made Osama bin Laden the reason. . . . In the name of terrorism [Bush] has violated other countries.

In 2004 Pew found majorities in all four majority-Muslim countries it polled rejecting the idea that the "U.S.-led war on terrorism is a sincere effort to reduce international terrorism." These majorities were found in Morocco (66 percent), Turkey (64 percent), Pakistan (58 percent), and Jordan (51 percent).

Likewise, in a 2008 poll in Pakistan, Terror Free Tomorrow found that 72 percent opposed the U.S. war on terrorism. When asked what the war's "real purpose" was, only 14 percent said it is to defeat terrorists or al Qaeda. The majority (58 percent) said the purpose of the war on terrorism was to weaken and divide the Muslim world. Another 15 percent said it was to ensure American domination of Pakistan.

This does not mean that most think the United States has no interest in stopping terrorist attacks. In 2006–07 WPO polling, majorities or pluralities in Egypt, Indonesia, Morocco, and Pakistan agreed that the United States does have the goal "to prevent more attacks such as those on the World Trade Center."

But when asked in the same poll what the *primary* goal of the war on terrorism is, respondents saw the United States' ostensible goal ("to protect itself from terrorist attacks") as subordinate to goals of domination ("to achieve political and military domination to control Middle East resources" or "to weaken and divide the Islamic religion and it people"). Just 16 percent overall saw the goal of protection from terrorist attacks as primary, ranging from 11 percent in Egypt to 21 percent in Indonesia. The other two goals received roughly equal percentages. On average 34 percent selected the goal of achieving political and military domination, while 32 percent selected the goal of weakening and dividing the Islamic religion and its people.

Finally, Muslims show little sympathy for the argument that the United States must keep fighting terrorism in the Muslim world because if it fails to do so, terrorist groups would simply advance their front (or "follow the troops home") and conduct terrorist attacks in the United States itself. Rather, Muslims are more likely to think the opposite. In 2008 WPO asked Azerbaijanis, Egyptians, Indonesians, Jordanians, Palestinians, and Turks, "If the United States were to withdraw its military force from Iraq, do you think the likelihood that al Qaeda would commit attacks against civilians inside the United States would increase, decrease, or remain unchanged?" Only 2 to 14 percent thought attacks were more likely to increase, while the largest numbers (37 to 70 percent) thought they were more likely to decrease. Those who thought the level would remain unchanged ranged from 10 to 36 percent.

4 *The United States as Hostile to Islam*

One of the most powerful sources of anger toward the United States is the widespread perception that the United States is hostile to Islam itself. This perception is disturbing not only from an Islamic perspective in which Islam is seen as threatened, but also from a liberal perspective because the United States is seen as having failed to live up to principles of religious tolerance.

Majorities see the United States as seeking to undermine the Islamic world, undermine Islamic culture and identity, and impose American culture and even Christianity on the Muslim world. This U.S. intention is seen as being fed by an anti-Muslim bias among the American people, the acting out of American rage about the 9/11 attacks against all Muslims, and an underlying American fear of the power of a resurgent Islam.

Perceptions of a threat to Islam appear to have grown substantially in the wake of America's response to the 9/11 attacks. At the same time, the perception of the United States—and the West in general—as deeply hostile toward Islam has long-standing roots in Muslim society. One of its key articulators was Sayyid Qutb, who wrote in 1964: "The Western ways of thought . . . [have] an enmity toward all religion, and in particular with greater hostility toward Islam. This enmity toward Islam is especially pronounced and many times is the result of a well-thought-out scheme, the object of which is first to shake the foundations of Islamic beliefs and then gradually to demolish the structure of Muslim society."[1]

Many in the West hoped that with the election of Barack Obama in the United States, this view of America as hostile to Islam would change. Obama's background—his Muslim father, his middle name of Hussein, and his childhood experience living in Indonesia—seemed like promising factors in helping to change this image. Equally important, Obama's high-profile speeches in Ankara and Cairo in the first months of his tenure were widely viewed as having the potential to improve relations. Nevertheless, while Obama is viewed as having respect for Islam, the basic image of U.S. foreign policy as hostile to Islam has largely persisted.

The U.S. War against Islam

WorldPublicOpinion.org (WPO) polling from 2006 to 2009 asked respondents in ten majority-Muslim nations whether it is a U.S. goal "to weaken and divide the Islamic world." Majorities—in most cases quite large—in all ten nations said that it is. In all cases except one the majority was more than two-thirds (the exception being Indonesia at 52 percent).

Contrary to hopes, there has been little change with the election of Barack Obama. Looking at countries that were polled in both 2008 as well as in 2009—including several in the fall of 2009 after Obama's speeches in Istanbul and Cairo in which he openly sought to repair U.S. relations with the Muslim world—there was little sign of change. While the percentage saying that the United States has the goal to weaken and divide Islam did go down 11 points in Indonesia and 7 points in Turkey, there was a slight upward movement in Egypt, Pakistan, and the Palestinian Territories. There was no change in Azerbaijan and Iran. Bangladesh and Iraq, which were polled for the first time in 2009, showed very large majorities with this perception (figure 4-1).

When WPO asked about Obama himself, there were some positive signs. Asked in the fall of 2009 whether Obama respects Islam, large majorities in four out of the five majority-Muslim countries where this question was asked agreed that he does. These majorities included 84 percent in Indonesia, 67 percent in Bangladesh, 65 percent in Egypt, and 64 percent in Turkey. Iranians demurred, with 59 percent saying that Obama does not respect Islam.

FIGURE 4-1.   U.S. Goal: Weaken and Divide Islam?

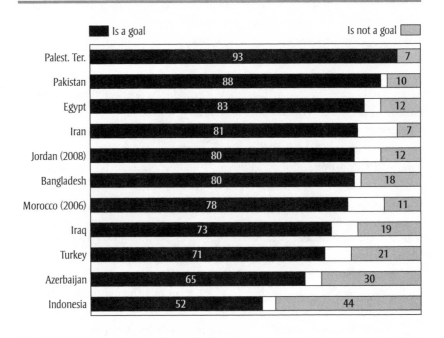

Source: WorldPublicOpinion.org, 2009.

However, when WPO asked in 2009 whether Obama has the goal to weaken and divide the Islamic world, views were more mixed. In some cases respondents made a strong differentiation between Obama and the United States. In Indonesia 61 percent said Obama does not have the goal to weaken and divide the Islamic world—even as 52 percent persisted in saying that the United States does. Similarly, in Bangladesh 54 percent said that Obama does not have this goal, while 80 percent said that the United States does. In Azerbaijan just 46 percent said that Obama has the goal of weakening and dividing Islam, while 65 percent said that the United States has this goal. Majorities in Pakistan (90 percent), the Palestinian Territories (88 percent), Egypt (73 percent), Iraq (69 percent), and Turkey (56 percent), however, did say Obama seeks to weaken and divide Islam.

The view that the United States is seeking to weaken and divide Islam may help explain the 2005 Pew findings showing that majorities of

Muslims perceive "serious threats to Islam today." These majorities were found in Jordan (82 percent), Morocco (72 percent), Lebanon (65 percent), Turkey (58 percent), and Pakistan (52 percent). In Indonesia the percentage was 46 percent. Strikingly, when three publics were asked this question in 1999—prior to the 9/11 attacks in 2001—only small minorities perceived such threats—Turkey (33 percent), Pakistan (30 percent), and Indonesia (26 percent). This strongly suggests that these increases are related to U.S. foreign policy behavior in the post-9/11 period.

The perception that the United States is effectively at war with Islam, seeking to destroy it, was elaborated at some length in an exchange during a focus group in Egypt in 2008, near the end of the George W. Bush presidency.

> RESPONDENT 1. There is the hostile tone that appears in the president's speech as he addresses Arabs or Muslims. This was obvious in his speeches after September 11, when he declared war on Muslims. He declared war between Christianity and Islam.
>
> MODERATOR. Could you be more specific about what he said that made you think that?
>
> R1. He stated this literally after September 11. He said that they have to declare a crusade against Islam, but after that, the secretary of state tried to alleviate the impact of the phrase, but the words themselves were said exactly like this.
>
> MODERATOR. This gentleman said the United States after 9/11 declared war on Islam. How many here agree with that? [*People nod.*] What does that mean?
>
> R2. This war has been there for a long time. But he declared this war after 9/11. It became very clear. Bush declared it openly.
>
> MODERATOR. What does it mean?
>
> R1. Bush said it's going to be a crusade.
>
> MODERATOR. But what does it mean?
>
> R1. It's a religious war.
>
> MODERATOR. So, the goal of that war is what?
>
> R1. The same as those of the crusades, which we encountered throughout previous centuries.
>
> MODERATOR. Which are?
>
> R2. To destroy, to eliminate the religion of Islam.

R3. If you want to support me or help me, don't come near my beliefs. You could be a friend, we can do business together, but when it comes to my religion: No!

MODERATOR. And America was trying to do this before 9/11, or only since 9/11?

MOST RESPONDENTS. After 9/11.

R3. The difference is that before 9/11 it was hidden, but after 9/11 it was declared and very obvious.

MODERATOR. Do you think with the new president it is likely to continue?

R3. Yes, 80 percent.

MODERATOR. And the others?

RESPONDENTS. [*mostly agreement*]

MODERATOR. Who has this desire to destroy Islam?

R3. It's not the American people, it's the American politics. . . . It's the government.

MODERATOR. How does America undermine Islam?

R4. It helps other people kill Muslims in wars.

MODERATOR. For example?

R4. What happened in Iraq—for no reason!

MODERATOR. So the attack on Iraq was an attack on Islam?

R4. It was a start.

R 3. Why did America go into Iraq in the first place? They said that Iraq has nuclear weapons, and as it turned out, it wasn't true.

MODERATOR. And you think America entered Iraq to fight Islam?

R3. There were other reasons, money among them. But one of the reasons was to fight Islam and to influence our own culture and traditions.

Another recurring theme in the focus groups was that the United States tries to divide the Muslim world by sowing conflict between Muslims. Here are three examples.

They know that they can't eliminate Islam from the Middle East, but they're trying to create a conflict between Muslims. They know that Muslims don't master their religion very well, so they're trying to divide us more and more.

After America came into Iraq, civil war erupted between the different sects—Sunni and Shiite. After a year, the same started in Palestine, as if whoever planned it in Iraq found it successful and implemented it in Palestine. They get Sunnis and Shiites to fight together in order to avoid conflict between them and the U.S. army. In Palestine, Hamas and Fatah are fighting against each other and forgot all about Israel, and that's it.

In the current situation there will not be an Arab unity, especially with America controlling. We are just calling for it . . . to become one people, one nation, one Arab nation. We used to be one nation, but the foreign forces came in and divided us. As soon as we get rid of the occupation, we will become one nation automatically.

The United States as Seeking to Undermine Islamic Culture and Identity

In the focus groups, while many portrayed the war against Islam in military terms, others framed it more in terms of an effort to undermine Islamic culture and identity. This was not seen as simply the side effect of America's powerful cultural presence or simply the weakness of the Muslim people in being seduced by American culture, but a purposeful effort on the part of the United States.

In the fall of 2009 WPO asked whether it is a U.S. goal to "make Muslim societies less Islamic." Majorities in Egypt (82 percent), Bangladesh (74 percent), Turkey (67 percent), and Indonesia (55 percent) said that it is. (See figure 4-2.)

In a female-only focus group in Egypt, a woman introduced the idea that there is a "war against Islam" and an effort "towards eliminating the Arab and Islamic identities." Asked, "Who wants to do that?" the discussion evolved as follows:

R1. Obviously, America and the spoiled child Israel.
MODERATOR. You think America wants to eliminate Islam?

FIGURE 4-2. U.S. Goal: Make Muslim Societies Less Islamic?

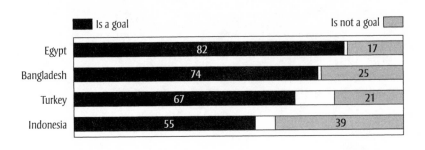

Source: WorldPublicOpinion.org, 2009.

R1. Yes, if we look at it in depth and not from an emotional perspective.
MODERATOR. What does America do to eliminate Islam?
R1. A few things together. It takes Israel's side. It kept silent while some countries attacked Islam. The matter is escalating. There are offensive Internet games on Islam and the Prophet. . . . It is also the rich countries' way to pressure the Arab world and consequently to weaken the Arab identity. . . . Children's books in America or other Western countries have this strange introduction of Muslims. In these books you'd find a Muslim is someone wearing jellabiya, has a long beard, rides on animals, and carries a weapon. This is the only image they give of a Muslim person.
MODERATOR. Why would they do that?
R2. This is a reason we don't know, and this is why we're saying that it's intentional. Let's take what happened in Denmark, for example. It is known worldwide that media is controlled by censorship. It's difficult to imagine that a supervisory authority could not have known about an article or drawings that would create public issues and affect state policies and just let it pass and be published. It doesn't happen accidentally.

Respondents described a variety of ways in which they believe their Islamic identity is under pressure. In Pakistan a number of men felt that their rights as Muslims were being denied by American sources that pressure them to cut their beards.

R. Every Muslim should get his full rights. . . . We should be allowed to live our lives. . . . [The United States is] stopping us from doing what we want, from our rights. They are stopping our women from wearing the veil and men from growing beards. If our government is not on good terms with each other, then they have the right to show disagreement, but why are they forcing us to change our religion? If we go and work at an office, which follows Western business ethics, then they want you to be clean-shaven.

R. We have been pressured by the atomic powers. We are forced not to grow beards.

MODERATOR. Who is forcing you to shave your beard?

R. Multinational companies. They kick out people from their jobs if they have beards. Even people from your country. If you want to find a job, the first thing they say is to clean your beards. Yes, in America.

R. Even in Pakistan, the multinationals operating here say that we don't want you to have a Muslim persona. And if you want to work with these companies, then you have to follow the rules such as you should not have long beards.

The United States as Seeking to Impose American Culture and Spread Christianity

Closely related to the perception that the United States is seeking to undermine Islamic culture is the perception that the United States is seeking to impose American culture on Muslim society and even to spread Christianity.

In 2009 WPO polling, large majorities in eight out of nine majority-Muslim nations had the perception that the United States is seeking to "impose American culture on Muslim society." These majorities ranged from 64 percent in Indonesia to 96 percent in the Palestinian Territories. The one exception was Azerbaijan, where only 36 percent had this perception and 51 percent did not. (See figure 4-3.)

Obama is also widely perceived as having the goal of imposing American culture. The majorities who perceived this goal were largely the same as those who viewed the United States as having such a goal. However, those majorities were lower in Bangladesh, Indonesia, and Turkey (figure 4-4).

FIGURE 4-3. U.S. Goal: Impose American Culture?

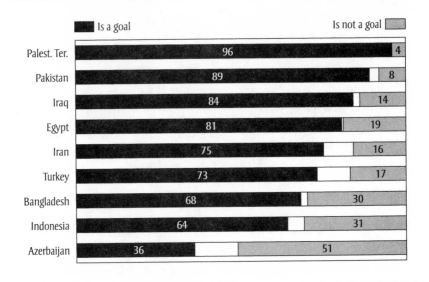

Source: WorldPublicOpinion.org, 2009.

FIGURE 4-4. Obama Goal: Impose American Culture?

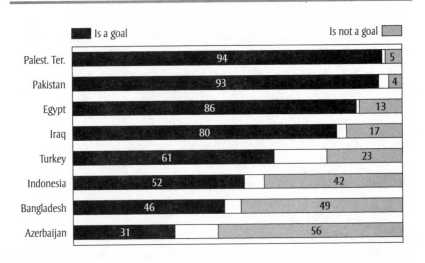

Source: WorldPublicOpinion.org, 2009.

FIGURE 4-5. U.S. Goal: Spread Christianity in the Middle East?

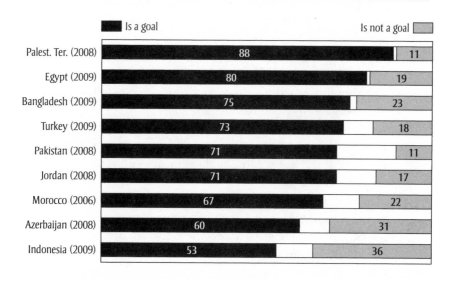

Source: WorldPublicOpinion.org.

U.S. foreign policy is even seen as having a pro-Christian agenda (figure 4-5). In the fall of 2009 WPO found large majorities saying it is a U.S. foreign policy goal "to spread Christianity in the Middle East." These majorities were found in Egypt (80 percent), Bangladesh (75 percent), Turkey (73 percent), and Indonesia (53 percent). These findings were largely the same as 2008 WPO polling in Egypt, Indonesia, and Turkey as well as in the Palestinian Territories (88 percent), Jordan (71 percent), Pakistan (71 percent), and Azerbaijan (60 percent). The same was also found in Morocco in 2006 (67 percent).

The belief that the United States is trying to impose its culture was regularly expressed in the focus groups. A Jordanian woman explained that the United States "does try to dominate the countries from the cultural and economic fields." Asked how America does that, she replied, "Through its programs on TV and the Internet. Young people look to America as a model and try to imitate it in all aspects."

An Iranian man said, "The United States in reality wants to impose its way of thinking. . . . It wants to take our hope away from us. . . . It is trying to brainwash our people so that they could not decide on their own about their future." When asked again, "How does America do that?" he replied, "Through a wide variety of mass media that they have at their disposal."

In a Pakistani focus group of females, one said, "They are trying to penetrate our society through the media and franchises like KFC." When asked to explain this American effect, they responded as follows.

R1. Everything is associated with America.

R2. There is fear of us being overwhelmed by [the United States].

R3. You look at the jeans, pants, and the media—all are influenced by America.

R4. They should not Americanize us. We should work together and not work towards becoming like Americans.

R2. Looking at how things have become modernized, it seems like they are affecting us.

R5. The youth is being influenced by such things. They have become rebellious. This is all American influence.

R1. The American society is individualistic in nature, and people in Pakistan are following suit with communities living just for themselves.

MODERATOR. And do you think that this is negative thing?

R1. Yes, it does feel bad. They are living without any real purpose to life. They steal and snatch things like mobile phones and purses, which is a bad thing.

MODERATOR. Does America *try* to do such things, or are the people of Pakistan just affected by the movies they make?

R1. [*without hesitation*] That is the objective of these movies.

Similarly, in an Egyptian focus group respondents were pressed on their assertion that the government fights Islam to spread U.S. culture. They were asked, "Is the government *actively* trying to spread its culture?" There seemed to be consensus that it is, including a man who responded, "By all means, including the media." He went on to affirm that he was not entirely negative about American culture: "I do respect and appreciate American culture and its technology, I welcome that." But he resented the American efforts to promote "the bad side of its culture . . . what contradicts my religious beliefs and Islam."

Despite the general consensus that the United States is actively trying to spread its culture, at moments in the focus groups some people would step forward and question the oft-repeated assertion that America was to blame for the Americanization of their culture. In a Moroccan group one respondent said, "Concerning the imitation, it is imposed. We don't have choice— it is globalization." Another respondent, however, said a bit sheepishly, "But we don't say no, we are accepting it." Another bobbed his head saying, "It *is* an interesting and an easy lifestyle."

American People as Having an Anti-Muslim Bias

American hostility to Islam is seen as rooted in broader anti-Muslim attitudes among the American people. Perceptions of Americans as biased against Muslims were widely expressed in the focus groups. Below are three examples, the first two from Egyptians and the third from a Jordanian.

Americans think all Muslims are terrorists.

America should be more open-minded. If a Muslim with a beard comes out and does this [terrorist attacks] . . . it doesn't mean all Muslims are bad.

Having a beard or wearing a veil is a matter of personal choice. We don't comment on people in America who are keeping their hair long or wearing torn jeans. Why don't you say that America has mafia and gangs attacking people in the streets and that there is no security? I don't speak in general terms; they too shouldn't speak in general terms. America is talking about the freedom its people have to do what they want, then it should leave the others do as they like without linking appearance to behavior. If a girl is wearing a veil, she is not necessarily a terrorist.

A May 2006 Pew poll asked respondents in five majority-Muslims countries and Muslims in Nigeria how many Americans "are hostile toward Muslims." Majorities in Turkey (61 percent), Nigeria (59 percent), Pakistan (59 percent), Egypt (57 percent), and Jordan (51 percent) said at least some Americans are hostile. Only in Indonesia did less than half (43 percent) have this view.

Asked in a 2006 Terror Free Tomorrow survey about the Danish cartoons of the Prophet Muhammad that prompted large-scale riots in the Muslim world, majorities polled in five majority-Muslim nations rejected the view that the cartoons "are an isolated example that does not reflect the overall view of the West toward Islam." Rather, majorities endorsed the view that the cartoons "reflect Western antagonism against Islam itself," including in Turkey (67 percent), Pakistan (67 percent), Saudi Arabia (65 percent), the United Arab Emirates (56 percent), and the Palestinian Territories (52 percent).

Majorities in five majority-Muslim countries polled by Pew in 2006 also said that "American opposition to a Dubai company managing several U.S. ports . . . reflect[s] prejudice against Arabs" rather then "reasonable concerns about terrorism." Majorities ranged from 58 percent in Indonesia to 72 percent in Jordan.

In some cases the hostility toward Muslims was something that respondents attributed to the U.S. government as distinct from the American people. At the same time, the American people were seen as subject to government efforts to create negative images of Muslims. This is illustrated in the following comments from a Moroccan, a Pakistani, and an Egyptian.

> The government can make them believe that terrorism equals Islam. . . . They don't take time to analyze, and they trust the prejudices that the government tries to implant in their minds.

> For the new [U.S.] government, my suggestion is that no person should be restricted because of their religion, especially Muslims. They should see everyone as a person, a soul, especially the way the American[s] care about everyone. In fact I would say that the Muslims are not as caring as Americans are. . . . [The government] should care about Muslims as well as human beings. Not hate them because they are Muslims.

> American citizens are friendly; they care about having a good job and good living and spending a nice weekend. However, the American policy feeds their mind with ideas like Islam is bad.

The American media is seen as playing a key role in creating negative images of Muslims in the minds of Americans. In the words of an Egyptian man, "The media in America . . . we've been seeing movies and TV series produced after 9/11 and showing Arabs as terrorists. . . . It is trying to lead the society towards an attitude that is against the Arabs and against the Muslims because it does give a bad image, not nice at all. . . . I think the media is creating differences between us."

The difficulties in getting visas to travel to the United States is perceived as another indication of anti-Muslim bias. For example, a Pakistani man said, "If someone wants to go [to the United States] for study, then this is not possible because he will have to apply for a visa, and being a Muslim—we have Muslim names such as Muhammad—and because of this visa requests are rejected."

American Rage about 9/11 Being Acted Out against All Muslims

A number of respondents in the focus groups expressed the view that American hostility toward the Muslim world—because of rage about the 9/11 attacks—was being unfairly generalized to all Muslims. The United States was effectively accused of engaging in collective punishment. Following are three examples.

> Those who were involved in this [9/11] incident in America, why have they not been brought forward and punished? . . . Instead of doing this, they said that al Qaeda is responsible for this, and they attacked Iraq. If a wanted man walks into the World Trade Center, would the government then say that to catch that person we should bombard the whole building? This is exactly what is going on in Iraq.

> I admit that a lot of lives were lost at the World Trade Center. . . . But does this mean that America kills every Muslim in this world?

Some respondents lamented the loss of America's liberal commitment to tolerance of diverse races and cultures in the wake of 9/11, as shown in this comment:

> After 9/11 the United States lost its value as the great power in a certain way. What's especially important is that it lost that harmony between the different races and cultures. Now if

you're not a pure American, and especially if you're an Arab, you'll find lots of difficulties to get into the society in all levels.

A small number of respondents even made statements strongly implying that in the wake of 9/11, the United States was actually behind various bombings in the Muslim world in an effort to worsen the image of Islam and associate it with terrorism. A Moroccan stated it this way:

> [The United States has tried to] convince the Muslim world that terrorism is equivalent to Islam . . . but not just with words or theories, but practically—like the bombings that happened in many Arab countries. . . . We never saw before bombings in Morocco, Tunisia, or in Saudi Arabia. It started to happen just after 9/11. It was like the United States was saying if you don't believe what I'm saying, then here you go, you can see by yourselves. So what happened in all Arab countries wasn't a work of chance. It's done and planned surely by someone.

The United States as Threatened by Resurgent Islam

Another factor seen as contributing to American hostility toward Islam is American concern that Islam, especially now that Islam is perceived as gaining strength in the world, poses a threat to the United States. WPO polling in 2006 and 2007 found majorities in four nations agreeing with the statement, "It is America's goal to weaken Islam so that it will not grow and challenge the Western way of life." This attitude was most widespread in Egypt, where 87 percent agreed with this statement, followed by Morocco (69 percent), Pakistan (62 percent), and Indonesia (57 percent).

Such ideas were also expressed in the focus groups. An Egyptian man explained that the United States dominates governments in the region because "America's main fear is the spread of Islam." A recurring theme was America's fear of the potential for Muslim nations to unite and create a powerful force, shown in these remarks.

> As Arabs . . . our goal is to unite as one nation. If we unite we will have a very great economy that will threaten any nation that wants to threaten us. Are you afraid of our economic unity?

I think America has a problem with Islam in this particular area. I think the problem is that Islam could unite this area and bring the people and countries together. Islam may lead the Middle East to become a new world power.

A well-educated Egyptian elaborated:

Some writers predicted this conflict between Islam and the West, like the one who wrote "Clash of Civilizations," and he portrayed Islam as an enemy of the Western culture. I think some scholars and some of the people in the American [Bush] administration have become convinced of this view—and that the next enemy is Islam, with its concentration in the area of the Middle East, where the most important resources to America and West Europe exist. That is why the American policy sees Islam as the eminent enemy and what threatens Western civilization, especially after 9/11.

Competing Images of Fundamental American Intentions

This chapter has shown abundant evidence that large majorities of Muslims endorse the overt narrative that the United States actively oppresses the Muslim world—that it seeks to undermine Islam and is driven by a belief in the fundamental polarization between Islam and the West. As discussed in chapter 2, however, there is also an underlying narrative that portrays the United States as a lapsed idealist that genuinely endorses principles of religious tolerance, but for a variety of reasons fails to live up to them.

WPO polling in 2008 and 2009 sought to find out how Muslims would respond when competing images of American intentions were put forward. Three different options were presented: (1) "The United States mostly shows respect to the Islamic world"; (2) "The United States is often disrespectful to the Islamic world, but out of ignorance and insensitivity"; and (3) "The United States purposely tries to humiliate the Islamic world" (figure 4-6).

Among all ten majority-Muslim nations polled, only small minorities said the United States generally shows respect (ranging from 5 percent in Iran to 29 percent in Bangladesh and Indonesia). There were divisions,

FIGURE 4-6. U.S. Relations with the Islamic World

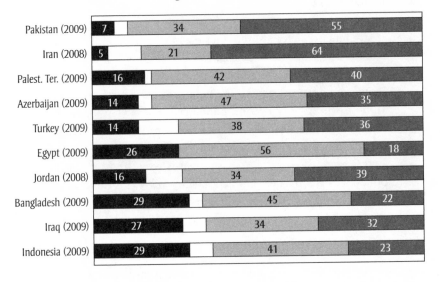

■ The U.S. mostly shows respect to the Muslim world.

☐ The U.S. is often disrespectful to the Islamic world, but out of ignorance and insensitivity.

▦ The U.S. purposely tries to humiliate the Islamic world.

	Respect	Disrespectful	Humiliate
Pakistan (2009)	7	34	55
Iran (2008)	5	21	64
Palest. Ter. (2009)	16	42	40
Azerbaijan (2009)	14	47	35
Turkey (2009)	14	38	36
Egypt (2009)	26	56	18
Jordan (2008)	16	34	39
Bangladesh (2009)	29	45	22
Iraq (2009)	27	34	32
Indonesia (2009)	29	41	23

Source: WorldPublicOpinion.org.

however, on whether the United States purposely tries to humiliate the Islamic world. Majorities in just two nations said the United States purposely tries to humiliate Muslims (64 percent in Iran and 55 percent in Pakistan). Egypt was the one country where a majority said that the United States is disrespectful out of ignorance and insensitivity (56 percent). But views in other countries were more mixed.

5 | U.S. Support for Israel

Many Muslims say that U.S. policies in relation to Israel are one of the most powerful factors impacting their views of the United States. A 2006 Sadat Chair poll asked respondents in six Arab nations to rate on a scale of 1 to 5 (5 being "extremely important") how important U.S. policy on the Arab-Israeli conflict is in developing their attitudes toward the United States. Large percentages responded with the highest rating of 5, ranging from 43 percent in Egypt to 76 percent in Jordan. Mean responses ranged from 3.79 in the United Arab Emirates to 4.56 in Jordan. A 2010 Sadat poll also asked respondents which of the policies of the Obama administration they were most disappointed with, and by far the most common response was the Israeli-Palestinian issue—on average 61 percent cited this.

American support for Israel plays into both of the dominant narratives of American relations with the Islamic world. The emergence of Israel as a non-Muslim state in the Muslim world, closely allied with and supported by America, contributes to the narrative of America as seeking to dominate the Muslim world and undermine Islam. The expansion of Israeli-held territory through successive wars, the annexation of sections of Jerusalem, and the development of settlements in Palestinian Territories are seen as a continuation of this agenda. In this context the United

FIGURE 5-1.   U.S. Policy on Arab-Israeli Conflict

In developing your attitudes toward the United States, how important is American policy toward the Arab-Israeli dispute on a scale from 1 (not important) to 5 (extremely important)?

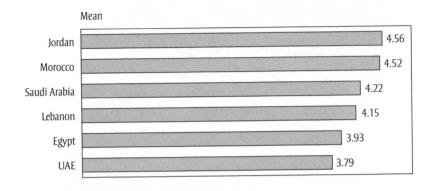

Source: Sadat Chair, 2006.

States and Israel are largely seen as a unitary actor, though there are debates about which one is more dominant.

At the same time, there is an image of the United States as being under the control of Israel and the pro-Israel lobby, failing to live up to the international norms that it has furthered—especially the expectation that as the hegemon the United States will play an impartial and evenhanded role. In this context the United States is regularly implored to waken from its torpor and assert its true self.

The United States as a Partner in Israeli Expansionism

The very existence of Israel is a major point of contention among Muslims. Large majorities reject the legitimacy of the Israeli state, which the United States played a major role in bringing into existence. In an Arab Barometer poll in 2006, majorities took the position that "the Arab world should not accept the existence of Israel as a Jewish state in the Middle East." These majorities were found in Jordan (76 percent), the Palestinian Territories (75 percent), Algeria (74 percent), Morocco (60 percent), and Kuwait (54 percent).

The existence of Israel is seen as posing an important existential threat to countries in the Arab world. Asked in a 2009 Sadat Chair poll of six

Arab nations to name two countries that pose the biggest threat to them, respondents in all six countries named Israel most often—ranging from 76 percent in the United Arab Emirates to 91 percent in Egypt. The United States was also named frequently, with numbers ranging from 49 percent in the United Arab Emirates to 82 percent in Saudi Arabia citing it as a threat. No other nation was named by significant numbers of people.

A widespread view is that the United States is complicit in the expansion of Israel's borders. In WorldPublicOpinion.org (WPO) polling of nine Muslim nations from 2006 to 2009, majorities in seven out of nine cases said it is a U.S. goal to "expand the geographic borders of Israel." This view was held by nine in ten Palestinians (90 percent) and Egyptians (89 percent) as well as by most Jordanians (84 percent), Bangladeshis (78 percent), Turks (69 percent), and Moroccans (64 percent), and Pakistanis (52 percent). Indonesians and Azerbaijanis had mixed views. (See figure 5-2.)

Israel is seen as having illegal territorial ambitions even beyond the acquisition of Palestinian Territories. As a Jordanian woman explained,

> The Israeli culture says that they should occupy lands. This is displayed in the Israeli flag—the blue colors on top and bottom indicate that Israel's borders are from water to water. They are getting there gradually. First they started with Palestine, Lebanon, and then Iraq. At the end they will reach Egypt. . . . Their goal is to occupy and to expand in order to achieve the dream of Greater Israel, which starts at the Nile and ends at the Euphrates.

But at a more fundamental level, Israel's illegal actions are seen as an extension of U.S. intentions. The United States is seen as using Israel as a kind of proxy in its effort to sustain regional hegemony as well as to weaken and undermine Islam itself. As a Moroccan man commented, "The U.S. supports Israel because it's in their interest to have a country like Israel in the Middle East." An Egyptian man explained,

> The United States is supporting Israel to become a dominating country in the Middle East. . . . America is using Israel as a military base in the Middle East. . . . If the United States wants to accomplish something in the Middle East or has certain politics it wants applied, it uses Israel as a tool to apply

FIGURE 5-2. U.S. Goal: Expand Geographic Borders of Israel?

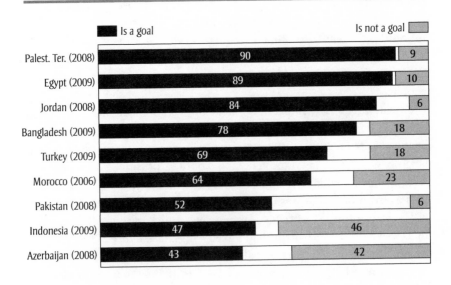

Source: WorldPublicOpinion.org.

pressure on the Arab regimes to accomplish what America wants.

The U.S. military presence in the region is not seen as a means to protect Israel, but as part of larger effort, together with the Israel-American relationship, to threaten and dominate the Arab world.

> Because of the suspicious American-Israeli relation, I don't want a military base in a neighboring country. This relation is against us. ... These bases are there not to protect Israel, but to attack us. ... Any type of relation between them [the United States and Israel] is perceived as one that is against us.

In an Egyptian focus group conducted in 2008 during the U.S. presidential campaign, respondents were quite pessimistic that a new president could augur any change on this front. For example, one respondent said,

> We don't expect anything new from the new president, whether he's a Republican or a Democrat. There are fixed ideas in the

American politics that are applied in dealing with the Arab World in general. . . . [These] state that Israel has to be the most powerful country in the Middle East."

The Palestinian Issue

While the broader Arab-Israeli conflict is of concern, Israel's treatment of the Palestinians is particularly salient. In the focus groups respondents frequently and emotionally talked about the Palestinian issue. Given how poorly many Arabs have treated Palestinians, this is somewhat surprising. It appears that Palestinians have become a symbol for the Muslim people as a whole, and Israeli actions against Palestinians have become a highly literal and visible symbol of U.S.-sponsored victimization of the Muslim people.

Polls show how much significance Muslims in the Arab world assign to the Palestinian issue. Asked in a 2009 Sadat poll of six Arab nations to rate the importance of the Palestinian issue in their priorities, large majorities rated the Palestinian issue either as more important than all other issues asked about or as one of their top three priorities. These majorities ranged from 65 percent in the United Arab Emirates to 92 percent in Saudi Arabia.

Anger about U.S. support for Israel relative to the Palestinians is also an important link to sympathy for al Qaeda, contributing to the perception that al Qaeda pursues legitimate goals, if not by legitimate means. In WPO polling done between 2006 and 2009, two-thirds or more in four of six countries polled said they support the al Qaeda goal of trying "to push the United States to stop favoring Israel in its conflict with the Palestinians." In Egypt an overwhelming 95 percent agreed (63 percent "strongly"), and in Bangladesh 78 percent agreed (36 percent "strongly"). Similarly large majorities agreed in Indonesia (77 percent, including 48 percent "strongly") and Morocco (75 percent, including 45 percent "strongly"). In Pakistan 55 percent agreed (33 percent "strongly"). Only a plurality of Turks, however, agreed (44 percent, including 26 percent "strongly"). (See figure 5-3.)

Consistent with the belief that the United States supports Israel's expansive territorial ambitions, many reject the view that the United States has genuinely sought to further the cause of establishing a Palestinian state. In polling by WPO in ten nations from 2006 to 2009, the dominant view in ten of eleven countries polled was that "the creation of an independent

FIGURE 5-3.   Al Qaeda Goal: Push U.S. to Stop Favoring Israel?

Do you agree or disagree with the goal to push the United States to stop favoring Israel in its conflict with the Palestinians?

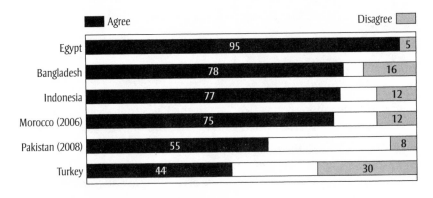

Source: WorldPublicOpinion.org, 2009.

and economically viable Palestinian state" is not a goal of the United States. The numbers asserting this is not a U.S. goal varied considerably between the countries polled, however. Bangladeshis took the strongest position, with 78 percent saying this is not a U.S. goal, followed closely by Azerbaijanis (77 percent). A majority of Pakistanis (68 percent), Moroccans (64 percent), Iraqis (63 percent), Jordanians (63 percent), Indonesians (58 percent), Egyptians (56 percent), and Turks (56 percent) also agreed that creating a Palestinian state is not a U.S. goal. Interestingly, the one nation where a majority said that it *is* a U.S. goal was in the Palestinian Territories themselves (59 percent).

Arabs report that the failure to make efforts to create a Palestinian state plays a key role in their negative views of the United States. A Sadat Chair poll presented a list of six possible actions the United States could take and asked respondents to pick two that "would improve their views of the United States the most." Majorities in the United Arab Emirates (67 percent), Lebanon (58 percent), and Saudi Arabia (52 percent) and substantial numbers in Jordan (48 percent), Egypt (38 percent), and Morocco (37 percent) selected this action as the most important: "Brokering an Israeli-Palestinian peace agreement with Israel withdrawing to 1967 borders and establishing a Palestinian state with Jerusalem as its capital."

FIGURE 5-4. U.S. Goal: Establish a Palestinian State?

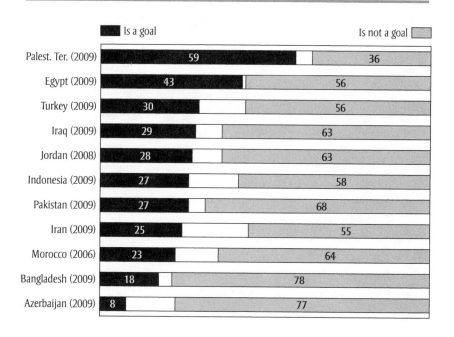

Source: WorldPublicOpinion.org.

Stopping economic and military aid to Israel was the most cited option in Saudi Arabia (57 percent) and was cited by substantial numbers of Jordanians (42 percent) and Lebanese (37 percent). For other nations, the numbers choosing this were approximately one in four.

U.S. Support Seen as Driven by Anti-Muslim Religious Bias

Consistent with the belief that the United States is hostile to Islam, many Muslims perceive U.S. support for Israel as rooted in religious bias against Islam in favor of Judaism and its common roots with Christianity. A series of comments in a Pakistani focus group reflected this view.

R1. If you pick up history you'll find that the bomb attacks on Palestine by Israel and those in Iraq were supported by the United States. When the Muslims throughout the world see this, they feel that the Americans have a very hostile attitude towards the Muslims.

R2. If you look at the oppression towards the Palestinians at the hands of the Israelites, then you as a Muslim wonder, "Why are we being targeted?" This is where the differences develop.

Respondents complained that the United States applies double standards when evaluating the actions of Israeli and Muslim actors, revealing a religious or perhaps even racial bias. A Jordanian woman explained that "Israel kills, they commit crimes," but they are not considered terrorists. However, "when we see a child carrying a small stone, and he's throwing it, or even has a Kalashnikov or a gun, he is considered as a terrorist because he is an Arab or a Palestinian." Another woman added, "America has a double standard policy. Israel kills Palestinian civilians and nobody complains. Are the Israeli civilians more valuable and more important than Palestinian ones?" Respondents pointed to other signs of what they saw as anti-Muslim or pro-Jewish bias. A Moroccan commented, "For the Jews, we can see that the United States made a law that prohibits offending or criticizing Semitism and protects it. As for Islam, there is no law protecting it in the United States."

The United States as Failing to Uphold Principles

While on one level the United States is simply denounced as unequivocally oppressing the Muslim people in concert with Israel, on another level Muslims implore the United States to uphold its liberal principles in dealing with Israel on the implicit assumption that this is something the United States can and might do.

Respondents spoke repeatedly about the United States being unfair in the way it seeks to apply international law. Asked what he would want to say to a new U.S. president, an Egyptian man said, "I want to talk about double standards in the enforcement of international law. Just as he [the president] is enforcing international law and UN Security Council decisions on the Arabs and Muslims, he should do the same with Israel."

In particular, respondents complained that the United States turns a blind eye or is silent about Israel's human rights violations against Palestinians. For example, one focus group respondent said,

America is calling for human and women's rights, but on the other side it gives Israel a green card to do everything. Why has the U.S. government been giving its support to Israel for more than fifty years? . . . Why have open-minded people inside the United States remained silent even as they see the atrocities of the Israeli government? America is using double standards, and it is supporting Israel with everything. America talks about human rights, but only with words. Where are its actions? People in Israel have all the rights, but in Palestine, no.

An Iranian man said, "Their [Palestinians'] sovereignty, freedom, and their land have been taken away from them, but no one provides them with any support," implying that the United States should provide that support.

Another Iranian man framed this reaction in the context of the world becoming more sensitive to liberal ideals, with the the United States lagging behind:

Today the whole world is more educated, and they are open minded, and they cannot tolerate this blind support that United States renders to Israel. Every day and night the Palestinians are being murdered, their women and children are indiscriminately targeted, and the United States, even the UN, have just turned a blind eye. They are humans too. They have rights too.

The United States was also portrayed as going beyond turning a blind eye and enabling Israeli violations of human rights norms by vetoing UN Security Council resolutions that criticize Israel. As an Iranian man said, "Whenever an issue is raised against Israel [inside the UN Security Council], the United States uses its veto power in support of Israel." An Egyptian man found this quite bewildering because he saw such resolutions as not affecting the interests of the United States or even Israel: "Another negative point is the use of the veto despite the fact that sometimes the resolutions vetoed don't affect America's interests . . . [or] without even harming Israel. A ceasefire in Lebanon, for example—America vetoed the resolution."

Finally, the United States providing economic and military aid to Israel is seen as helping enable Israel to carry out policies that violate Palestinian rights. As a Jordanian man commented, "[The Americans] help Israel in its domination over the Palestinians."

The United States Turning a Blind Eye to Israel's Nuclear Weapons

Another way the United States is portrayed as failing to uphold international norms is in its complicity in Israel's acquiring of nuclear weapons. Indeed, it is widely assumed in the Muslim world and elsewhere that the United States aided Israel's acquisition of nuclear weapons in the very period when the United States was actively corralling all other countries into signing the Nuclear Non-Proliferation Treaty.

This is seen as another example of the United States applying double standards. As one Jordanian woman said, "As an American, do you feel that Israel has the right to possess nuclear weapons while others are not allowed to?" This was said with a perplexed tone, apparently assuming that if Americans could grasp this inconsistency, they would act differently.

Respondents emphasized that this special treatment of Israel was discriminatory against Muslim countries such as Iran. What was striking was the extent to which respondents invoked norms for a proper international order that they assumed the United States would naturally want to abide by. For example, an exchange in an Egyptian focus group went as follows:

> R1. I am against nuclear weapons generally, but Iran has a right to own nuclear weapons as long as other countries own them.
> R2. Why didn't America argue about nuclear weapons in Israel? Prohibiting nuclear weapons should be on an equal basis with all countries.
> R3. Israel has nuclear weapons, and the power should be balanced.
> R1. With Israel, which owns nuclear power and doesn't allow international inspectors to go in, America never mentions Israel's nuclear power.

United States as an Underperforming Hegemon

In some cases respondents in focus groups, consistent with the image of the United States as an oppressive imperialist, seemed to be saying that the United States should simply stop supporting Israel and disengage from the region. However, consistent with the narrative of the United States as a lapsed idealist, a more common position was to criticize the United

FIGURE 5-5. U.S. Efforts to Resolve the Israeli-Palestinian Conflict

How well do you think the United States is doing its part in the effort to resolve the Israeli-Palestinian conflict?

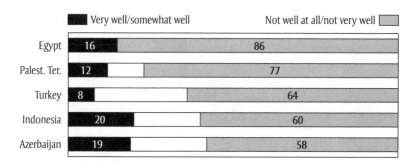

Source: WorldPublicOpinion.org, 2008.

States for failing to properly perform its role as an enlightened hegemon of the Middle East.

This view that the United States is not fulfilling its obligations in the region is widespread. Asked in 2008 WPO polling of five majority-Muslim nations how well the United States is "doing its part in the effort to resolve the Israeli-Palestinian conflict," majorities said "not very well" or "not well at all" in all five: Egypt (86 percent), the Palestinian Territories (77 percent), Turkey (64 percent), Indonesia (60 percent), and Azerbaijan (58 percent). (See figure 5-5.)

From the perspective of the United States as an oppressor, this would seem to have little meaning, as the United States would be assumed to be simply pursuing its interests. The criticism, however, appeared to be based on the assumption that the United States has an obligation to behave according to international norms and, most importantly, that the United States understands this. Comments to this effect were made with an imploring tone and an implied expectation that the United States might recover its normative compass and assume its proper role.

A recurring theme was that the United States, as the global hegemon, should play the role of an evenhanded and honest broker. As a Jordanian man explained tersely, "The Palestinian issue is an issue that concerns all Arab people and nations. . . . Since the USA is the only power in the world, they should deal with the peace issue in a more just manner." An

Egyptian man said, "It is like [the United States is] giving one person a spoon of money and another of poison at the same time."

The view that the United States fails to be evenhanded is widespread. A May 2007 Pew poll of eleven Muslim nations found majorities in ten cases saying that U.S. policies in the Middle East favor Israel too much. Respondents in all countries in the Middle East region said so by 70 to 91 percent.

Respondents did not hesitate to complain that the United States does not do enough to help the Palestinians, clearly assuming that this is a U.S. obligation. The following exchange in a Moroccan focus group illustrates this.

> R. [The United States doesn't] help [the Palestinians], though there are some civilian associations who try to help a little bit.
> R. [U.S. efforts are] just to say to the world that [the United States] support[s] human rights, but they're not really helping them.
> R. Well, we know that Palestine suffers from strict restrictions that Israel is imposing on them. They're nearly starving, and the United States does nothing to help the civilians. Even if they're against Hamas or the government, they still need to help.
> R. I think it's because Palestinians have nothing to offer to the United States, contrary to Iraq, which has oil.

When respondents were pressed with suggestions of efforts the United States has made to help the Palestinians, these were largely dismissed.

> MODERATOR. To what extent is the United States involved in the creation of an independent Palestinian state?
> R. They agree about the creation of a Palestinian state, but on the condition that Israel gets the biggest portion of the cake— 70 percent of the territory. So they're taking the Israeli side.
> MODERATOR. Do you think that the United States helps the Palestinians financially?
> R. The financial aid is not possible as long as there is no political stability.
> R. The fact that the United States is helping and supporting Israel makes all their help to the Palestinians nonsense.

MODERATOR. So you think that the United States doesn't provide
any financial aid?
R. Even if they provide financial aid, it will serve to nothing as
long as they support Israel. They need to help them politically
first.

An Egyptian echoed this expectation that the United States should do
more, complaining that the United States is preoccupied with other issues
in the region.

R. They don't solve the Palestinians' problem or the Middle East's
problems. They create a fuss about bin Laden and Iraq and
leave the Palestinian-Israeli issue unsolved. No one looks in this
direction or tries to solve the problem.

Another recurring theme was to bring up international law. UN resolutions 242 and 338 that call for Israel to withdraw from the Palestinian
Territories were stressed. Israel's occupation of the territories was described as illegal. Implicit was the idea that these legal factors should and,
indeed, might have some impact on American behavior. The dominant
tone, again, was frustration that the United States was failing to play its
proper role.

As respondents spoke about America's perceived underperformance in
the focus groups, they would sometimes become agitated and in their
frustration portray the United States as intrinsically hostile toward Palestinians and, more generally, Arab and Muslim interests. The cognitive
dissonance of believing, on the one hand, that the United States could
and might play an evenhanded role, and perceiving, on the other, that the
United States continually fails to do this, causes a high degree of stress.
Sometimes respondents would attempt to simplify their arguments by
characterizing the United States as nothing but a self-serving oppressor
that responds only to force or terrorism. But this characterization rarely
lasted very long. Soon they would revert to implicitly imploring the
United States to rediscover its higher nature.

6 | The United States as Undermining Democracy

The fourth central theme in the narrative of American oppression of the Muslim people is the claim that the United States actively undermines democracy in the Muslim world by providing critical support to authoritarian regimes that are friendly to it and that it effectively controls. Despite America's professions of support for democracy, the United States is seen as an obstacle to real democratization, and professions of support are seen as purposely misleading. Muslim governments—as well as the Muslim people—are often seen as victims of U.S. domination. From this view of the United States flows a desire for the United States to simply disengage from the region.

This perception of the United States as being an undemocratic force in the Arab world has been noted by scholars of the region. Ussama Makdisi, in his analysis of anti-Americanism in the Arab world, comments that as "the U.S. government saw itself far less as a force for liberal or democratic change than as a guarantor of the status quo," there was a "new identification of American power as a force for repression rather than liberation in the Arab world."[1] Muqtedar Khan comments, "It is not the hatred of democracy or freedom, but the desire for democracy that has made many Muslims hate the United States, which they blame for the perpetuation of undemocratic politics in their world."[2] Tessler and Robbins conclude from an analysis of surveys in Algeria and Jordan that approval of terrorist attacks against U.S. targets is not driven by religious orientations, judgments about Western culture, or economic circumstances, but by anger toward the United States as an agent that sustains support for unpopular governments.[3]

American concerns that democracy in Muslim countries could lead to the election of Islamist parties that could then impose a nondemocratic system are largely dismissed in polls and focus groups. This concern tends to be seen as either a ruse to rationalize American domination through authoritarian secular governments or an offensively dismissive belief, with racist overtones, that people in the Muslim world are not capable of democracy. The deep opposition to Islamist parties is seen as being rooted in an anti-Islamic bias.

Consistent with the view of the United States as having liberal values that it fails to fulfill, many Muslims also portray the United States as having drifted away from its underlying and real commitment to democracy. There is therefore hope that the United States could potentially change. In this context there is not a desire for the United States to withdraw from Muslim countries, but a desire for it to play an active role in pressuring autocratic governments to become more democratic.

The United States as Seeking Domination, Not Democracy

This view of the United States as not genuinely seeking to promote democracy, but to dominate governments in the service of imperial interests was regularly mentioned in the focus groups. A Jordanian woman described America as supporting dictatorships in the Middle East rather than promoting democracy in the interest of the people:

> In our region [the Americans] help the dictatorship regimes. They don't help the nations—the people—at all to practice liberation and to have free opinion. All they say are just mottos, but in practice they don't help the people of the countries. On the contrary, they help the ruling governments. . . . The American policy is not based on the liberation of people!

Another echoed her assertion, saying that America "calls for freedom and democracy, but only in America." An Egyptian man quoted Noam Chomsky: "I remind you of Chomsky's saying: 'America is the biggest terrorist country in the world.' It's not just Latin America and Chile and the massacres around the world. America has supported dictators who protect its interests." An Iranian man commented incredulously, "If they have a problem with our political system, then how is it that they accept the undemocratic political systems of regional Arab countries?!"

A recurring theme was that the United States seeks to control Muslim governments in the service of its interests. A Pakistani man said,

> [U.S. leaders] control every Arab and Muslim country. They know that those countries are dependent, and even those who are not, they create a problem or a way to control them. America's interference aims to keep these nondemocratic regimes to serve its interests. . . . In Pakistan's sixty-year history, there has been very little democracy. A country can make proper progression under democracy, but not under military rule.

By controlling Muslim governments, the United States is seen as undermining their ability to serve the people, as demonstrated in the following focus group comments.

> America is controlling the leadership [of Muslim countries] who controls the people. They use them as a tool to control the population. They would not allow any leadership that is working for the good of the people to work or exist.

> When the United States supports any government, it's to achieve its own benefits and interests and not those of the government itself. Any political system in the Arab countries is merely a doll in the hands of the United States. They know it, and we know it.

When a Jordanian man was asked, "If America did not have this power over Arab countries, what would be different?" he described in glowing terms a government that would serve the good of the people and resist domination. He cited Iran as a positive example of such an independent Muslim nation and the kind that the United States wants to prevent from recurring:

FIGURE 6-1.   U.S. Advocacy of Democracy in the Middle East

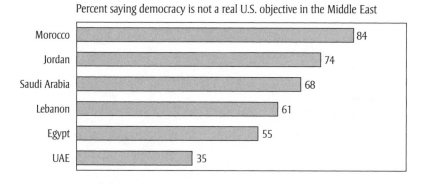

Percent saying democracy is not a real U.S. objective in the Middle East

Morocco	84
Jordan	74
Saudi Arabia	68
Lebanon	61
Egypt	55
UAE	35

Source: Sadat Chair, 2006.

There will be patriotic leadership that represents the people and
works for their benefit. It would channel the workforce and
resources towards the good of the people, so the people who
seek to occupy these countries can realize that it is not easy [to
dominate them]. Just like we see in Iran now, it has patriotic
leadership, and America . . . thinks twice before taking
measures against Iran. And it does not want any other nations
to become as powerful as Iran, so they place pressure on the
Arab and Islamic nations.

Numerous polls have also found that Muslims have little confidence
that the United States genuinely supports democracy in Muslim countries. A 2006 Sadat Chair poll of six Arab nations found that majorities
in five of them said that in the Middle East "democracy is not a real U.S.
objective." These majorities were found in Morocco (84 percent), Jordan
(74 percent), Saudi Arabia (68 percent), Lebanon (61 percent), and Egypt
(55 percent). Only in the United Arab Emirates was this not a majority
position. (See figure 6-1.)

Even as a general principle, America is seen as not supporting democracy. In a spring 2004 poll by the University of Jordan's Center for Strategic Studies, only minorities agreed that "the United States supports the

FIGURE 6-2.   The U.S. and Democracy in Islamic Countries

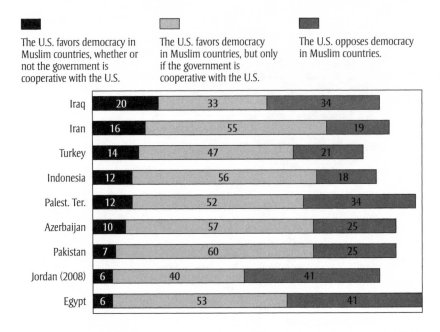

■	▢	■
The U.S. favors democracy in Muslim countries, whether or not the government is cooperative with the U.S.	The U.S. favors democracy in Muslim countries, but only if the government is cooperative with the U.S.	The U.S. opposes democracy in Muslim countries.

Iraq	20	33	34
Iran	16	55	19
Turkey	14	47	21
Indonesia	12	56	18
Palest. Ter.	12	52	34
Azerbaijan	10	57	25
Pakistan	7	60	25
Jordan (2008)	6	40	41
Egypt	6	53	41

Source: WorldPublicOpinion.org, 2009.

practice of democracy in the world." These minorities were found in Lebanon (41 percent), Jordan (35 percent), Egypt (21 percent), and the Palestinian Territories (19 percent).

A May 2005 Pew survey of six majority-Muslim nations asked respondents, "Are you more optimistic or more pessimistic these days that the Middle East region will become more democratic?" In most cases pluralities or slight majorities were pessimistic. Further, among those who were pessimistic about democracy in the Middle East, large majorities (ranging from 62 to 98 percent) said their pessimism was "at least partly due to U.S. policies." Among those who were optimistic, though, views were mixed as to whether their optimism could be attributed to U.S. influence.

WorldPublicOpinion.org (WPO) polling of nine majority-Muslim countries in 2008 and 2009 found very small numbers believing that "the United States favors democracy in Muslim countries, whether or not the government is cooperative with the United States." Rather, views were mixed between the view that "the United States favors democracy in Muslim countries, but only if the government is cooperative with the United States," and the view that "the United States opposes democracy in Muslim countries." (See figure 6-2.)

Similarly, a Pew survey in May 2007 asked respondents whether the United States "promotes democracy wherever it can" or "promotes democracy mostly where it serves its self-interest." Large majorities (ranging from 64 to 82 percent) in Bangladesh, Egypt, Kuwait, Malaysia, Turkey, and the Palestinian Territories said the latter, as did substantial majorities (from 55 to 58 percent) in Indonesia, Jordan, and Pakistan. Only in Morocco did this view fall below half (46 percent), though it was still a large plurality. Such views were also common elsewhere in the world.[4]

Apparently, the U.S. war against Iraq enhanced the image of the United States as seeking domination and diminished the image of the United States as being a force for democratization, despite American claims that this was a central motive. Pew asked in March 2004, "As a consequence of the war, do you have more confidence or less confidence that the United States wants to promote democracy all around the world?" In all four Muslim counties polled, majorities said "less confidence," including in Turkey (73 percent), Morocco (66 percent), Pakistan (57 percent), and Jordan (56 percent). Those saying "more confidence" ranged from 5 to 15 percent.

U.S. Opposition to Islamist Parties

Participants expressed particularly strong annoyance and frustration with the United States saying it supports democracy, yet when Muslims elect Islamist candidates or parties, it objects. Participants seemed to feel that the United States was putting them in a double bind—pressing Muslims to be democratic, but rejecting the choices they make. Such inconsistency was also seen as proof that U.S. democratic rhetoric is not genuine. For example, in an Egyptian focus group held in 2006, a man commented derisively, "You asked for democracy, and when democracy brought Hamas to the government, you refused to deal with them, and you severed all ties with Hamas group members. What democracy exactly are you talking about?!" Continuing, he said, "You knew that the Egyptian government interfered in the legislative elections to make sure the Muslim Brotherhood would fail in these elections." But, he complained, the United States did not really object.

America's objection to Islamist parties is seen as rooted in its anti-Islamic bias. In this context an Egyptian said, "America's main fear is the spread of Islam." The idea that the U.S. resistance to Islamist parties is for the benefit of the Muslim people is not highly persuasive. When WPO polling from 2006 to 2008 asked respondents whether it is a goal of the United States to ensure that their country "does not fall into the hands of extremist groups," only minorities in all four countries polled said that it is. The highest percentage was in Indonesia (43 percent), followed by Pakistan (40 percent) and Morocco (38 percent). Just 19 percent of Egyptians concurred.

Overall, respondents in the focus groups expressed a relatively sanguine attitude about the prospect of Islamist parties gaining political power. As is discussed in some depth in chapter 8, the dominant attitude throughout the Muslim world is that Islamist parties should be able to participate in elections. The fact that the United States is so opposed to them was viewed with some annoyance. For example, an Egyptian man commented, "What's your problem with the Muslim Brothers? We're not worried about them; it's not necessarily them who would reach the government. We're not afraid of them." The implication was that the concern was a phony rationalization for pursuing imperial objectives.

Several focus group respondents made the case that the Muslim Brotherhood is simply a reaction to political oppression and that if the United States would back off and genuine democracy were to come, they would lose their cohesion. One respondent explained,

> I think if the United States pulls out of the region, the region
> would be in a better state. The danger of the Islamist groups is
> perceived in a highly exaggerated way. The slogans that the
> Islamist groups adopt could only grow or be found in disturbed
> societies with lack of justice and freedom. But if . . . people
> could practice their rights and freedoms . . . Islamist groups or
> extremists would not exist.

The United States as a Lapsed Democratic Idealist

Many comments and poll findings on the issue of democracy point to an image of the United States as resolutely self-interested, either opposing democracy or only supportive if it serves U.S. goals of domination. Yet consistent with the image of the United States as having an underlying commitment to liberal values, America is portrayed as both supporting democracy from an idealistic perspective and as straying from these ideals.

Some participants spoke as if there was some potential for U.S. idealism to be revived and even that at moments it has been. The hope to revive it was expressed in a beseeching tone, as if it might be possible for America to respond. For example, on the question of what respondents in a 2008 focus group would want to say to a new American president, a Pakistani man said, "I would tell him that just like there is democracy in America and other countries, why can't we have something like that in Pakistan?" An Egyptian man implored the United States to try to help make the Arab regimes more democratic, with an implicit assumption that this is something that the United States might do: "Why does America support the reactionary Arab regimes despite its knowledge that these regimes are not democratic? Why not help to change these regimes for a more democratic status in the Arab region so there could be hope for the poor and vulnerable peoples who were robbed by the leadership controlling the political systems for ages now?"

Although there seemed to be some reluctance to express it directly—at least in Egypt, Jordan, and Pakistan—there was an implied desire for the United States to put more pressure on their governments to be more democratic. Presumably, the reluctance was derived from the inherent contradiction of this idea with the sweeping indictment of the United States as having no interest in democracy. Nonetheless, when respondents were asked directly, they generally agreed that they did want the United States to apply such pressure and did not indicate concern that this would be an infringement on their sovereignty.

Also, as is discussed below, Egyptians expressed enthusiasm for the pressure that the United States put on its government to undertake democratic reforms in the wake of President Bush's 2005 State of the Union speech. One respondent described a feeling of "exhilaration." Clearly, at that moment the image of the United States as genuinely supporting democracy, irrespective of its interests, was vivid and credible. Polls at that time also showed a temporary elevation of the belief that the United States supports democracy. When the United States backed away from pressing for such reforms, this image declined and was eclipsed by the image of the United States as seeking to ensure domination. The belief that democratic idealism does persist somewhere in America's heart, however, does not appear to have died completely.

This does not mean that most Muslims necessarily want the United States to take an aggressive stance in seeking to promote democracy. Indeed, the whole notion of promoting democracy has become associated with the U.S. invasion of Iraq, as the invasion was rationalized in such terms. Thus polls have found low enthusiasm for the United States assertively seeking to promote democracy. A Terror Free Tomorrow poll in December 2007 asked in Saudi Arabia how much the "United States pushing to spread democracy in the Middle East" would improve respondents' opinion of the United States. A slight majority said "not at all" (38 percent) or "not significantly" (13 percent), while 37 percent said "somewhat" (20 percent) or a "great deal" (17 percent). Also, Terror Free Tomorrow found a majority of Iranians saying that the United States working to spread democracy inside Iran would improve their opinion "not at all" (47 percent) or "not significantly" (12 percent), while minorities said it would "somewhat" (14 percent) or a "great deal" (12 percent).

Shifts in Response to American Actions

There is striking evidence in the polls and in the focus groups that images of U.S. intentions in regard to democracy can shift quite substantially in response to changed actions on the part of the United States. One of these changes occurred under the George W. Bush administration. As mentioned, in Bush's January 2005 State of the Union speech, he announced that the United States was making a greater commitment to democracy in the Muslim world. Subsequently, the United States did indeed put greater pressure on some Muslim countries, especially Egypt, to make some democratic reforms.

Polling conducted by Pew before and after President Bush's January 2005 State of the Union address suggests that it and the subsequent shifts in U.S. policy did have some effect on perceptions of U.S. intentions regarding democracy promotion. Pew asked respondents in three countries in both March 2004 and May 2005 and in two countries in May 2005 only whether the U.S. government favored or opposed "democracy in our country." In the 2004 poll 51 percent of Moroccans said that the United States favored democracy, rising to 62 percent in 2005. Pakistan flipped from a plurality (36 percent) saying the United States opposed democracy in 2004 to a plurality saying it favored democracy (39 per-

cent). Majorities of Lebanese (54 percent) and Indonesians (65 percent)—
polled in 2005 for the first time—also said that the United States favored
democracy in their country.

Later in the year, in response to electoral gains by Egyptian parliamentary candidates associated with the Muslim Brotherhood and the victory of Hamas in the Palestinian elections, the Bush administration
backed away from its support for democratic reforms. Subsequently,
Muslim governments, especially in Egypt, reversed the emerging reforms.

Polls conducted in late 2005 seemed to detect this change. Asked in an
October 2005 Gallup poll whether they agreed that "the United States is
serious about . . . the establishment of democratic systems in this region,"
majorities disagreed in Jordan (66 percent), Egypt (64 percent), Turkey
(59 percent), Lebanon (58 percent), Iran (56 percent), Pakistan (54 percent), and Indonesia (52 percent). Only in Morocco did a majority agree
(65 percent), while views were divided in Bangladesh.

The conflicting images of U.S. intentions regarding democracy were
also quite clear in an Egyptian focus group conducted in 2007 in which
the events of 2005 were discussed. One man started by unequivocally
portraying the United States as opposed to democracy. Asked what he
would like to say to a new president, he said angrily, "Support democracy in Egypt!" When asked, "You feel that the United States now does
not support democracy in Egypt?" he responded sharply, "Not at all!"
But then he paused and gave a much more nuanced account, detailing
how his views shifted in response to changes in the Bush administration
positions.

R. Sometimes we feel that the United States *is* supporting the
government and sometimes it . . . [acts] on the account of the
people. The current President [Bush], earlier in his term, said
that he supported democracy in the Middle East. There was a
pressure on all the current governments to support human
rights in the Middle East, and especially Egypt. Right now we
don't see this. Right now we feel that they're against democracy
in the Middle East. . . . When America first started putting
pressure on the government to ensure democracy, it started to
change its tone—the way it talks—and started considering
making amendments to the constitution.

MODERATOR. When did this happen?

R. Three years ago with the change of Article 76 of the Egyptian Constitution. The government started talking about making a change, and the people started feeling more secure and that change will happen in terms of democracy and human rights.

MODERATOR. Because of the U.S. pressure?

R. Yes, and once the U.S. pressure stopped, the situation became worse and worse. . . . The pressure helped the people. Applying pressure on the government made it apply less pressure itself on the people.

This respondent expressed support for the United States applying such pressure, though he did so abashedly, with an apparent recognition that this was somewhat at odds with his earlier bombastic statements that the United States simply opposes democracy in Egypt.

MODERATOR. So would you like the United States to put more pressure on the government?

R. I'm afraid to say it, but yes. Today, we need human rights, we need democracy, and we need to fight corruption. Once the system feels it is supported by the United States, it doesn't care to do anything.

Another respondent joined in making a similar analysis of the change that occurred 2005.

When Condoleezza Rice said that the United States will apply pressure on the government in Egypt to effectuate democracy, the American pressure really started then to promote practicing more freedoms and making a change. . . . [But] when Hamas and Islamic groups appeared in the big picture—it first appeared in Palestine—with their honest and straightforward elections, the Egyptian regime feared that if democracy was practiced in the same way in Egypt, it could lead to the rise of the Islamic groups like the Muslim Brothers, just like Hamas did. And that is the reason why America was reluctant to help the system recently in supporting the democracy and started to overlook what the regime is doing.

This led other respondents to revert to a portrayal of the United States as intrinsically unconcerned about democracy. One said, "I don't think the United States is interested in or concerned with democracy in the Arab world." Yet another said that the 2005 push for democracy was another effort at seeking control. Because the United States was having trouble in Iraq, he said, "the United States thought of trying a different 'pressure' tool, which is democracy."

7 | *Views of Al Qaeda and Other Radical Islamists*

S ome of the most prominent articulators of the narrative of U.S. oppression of the Muslim people are al Qaeda and other radical Islamist groups who espouse violence against America. Given the widespread anger at America in the Muslim world, it would not seem surprising if there were significant support for such groups. But feelings toward such groups are complex and replete with ambivalence.

Attitudes toward radical Islamists are influenced by much more than the Islamists' approach to the United States. Radical Islamism has been the counterpoint to liberalism in the Muslim-world discourse. It has rejected the democratic process as the basis for governance, universally based principles of human rights, and an international order based on international law and international institutions. Radical Islamists see these as departing from the Islamic basis for order and as derived from cooperation with infidels.

The goal of al Qaeda, the Taliban, and other radical Islamist groups to create a purely Islamist society and reject liberal values elicits a complex response. In principle there is support for the goal of increasing the role of sharia in the governing of society. Most Muslims, however, also endorse liberal ideas such as democracy and international law—which are rejected by radical Islamists—and they are generally wary of Islamic extremism.

This tension overlaps with the polarized feelings Muslims have toward the United States. On the one hand Muslims are drawn to the liberal ideals that the United States professes, yet they fear American domination and perceive it as hostile to Islam.

Al Qaeda is perceived as a threat, as most Muslims do not want al Qaeda to have the power to impose their fundamentalist system. But the United States is perceived as a greater threat, not only because its perceived goals of domination are anathema, but because it has such overwhelming military and economic power. Thus al Qaeda is perceived as something of a bulwark against the United States, even if it is also somewhat of a threat.

As we have seen, majorities agree with nearly all of al Qaeda's goals to change U.S. behavior in the Muslim world and to defend Islam from American domination. And there is significant support for attacks on U.S. troops in Afghanistan, Iraq, and the Persian Gulf, many of which are conducted by al Qaeda and related groups.

On the other hand, there is unequivocal opposition to attacks on civilians, which al Qaeda conducts. This applies to attacks on American civilians as part of an effort to change American behavior as well as attacks on Muslim civilians in support of the goals of making society purely Islamic. Terrorism per se is roundly rejected.

With these competing responses, the subject of al Qaeda and other radical Islamist groups elicits substantial conflict and even cognitive dissonance. In the focus groups it was quite clear that people often found the subject discomfiting.

As is demonstrated below, this ambivalence can result in a variety of defensive responses. One of the most simple is to deny that al Qaeda or other radical Islamist groups engage in attacks on civilians, even denying their involvement in the 9/11 attacks. Another more subtle response is to frame al Qaeda as a creation of the United States and thus characteristic of its progenitor rather than being truly Muslim.

Some Muslims have more complex ways of rationalizing their support for al Qaeda by creating special provisos that justify violence against civilians. This is particularly important, as it is an indicator of the success of al Qaeda and others to redefine Islamic norms.

Many Muslims, though, are able to differentiate their responses, agreeing with many of al Qaeda's goals, but not its methods. However, while many people make this differentiation in response to separate questions on goals and methods, when presented directly with the idea of supporting al Qaeda's goals but opposing its methods as a single response option, majorities do not endorse this. Apparently, it is not easy to simultaneously think about two attitudes that are at odds with each other. This creates a certain instability in responses.

The net effect of these dynamics is that in the Muslim world as a whole, there is not a clear majority taking a positive or negative position on al Qaeda, Osama bin laden, or other radical Islamist groups per se. When given the option, many say they have mixed feelings.

What is most significant from an American perspective is that most Muslims see the United States as a greater threat than radical Islamists, even when they are actively conducting terrorist attacks against citizens in their own country. The narrative of oppression by the United States, within which al Qaeda is something of a hero for standing up to America, supersedes the narrative of threat from radical Islamism. Thus many Muslims feel ambivalence about fighting radical Islamists. It is not as simple as saying that the enemy of my enemy is my friend, but the extent of Muslim anger toward America does diminish the motivation of Muslims to criticize groups perceived as lesser enemies.

A key example of this ambivalence is the initial reluctance of Pakistanis to support the fight against the Taliban operating in Pakistan. It was only when the Taliban attacks on Pakistani civilians became highly egregious that they overcame their resistance to being aligned with American goals and supported concerted military action against the Taliban.

Support for al Qaeda's Goals

When asked a series of questions about al Qaeda's goals by WorldPublic Opinion.org (WPO), majorities in five countries polled consistently expressed support for them. Egypt and Indonesia were polled in 2007, 2008, and 2009 (2009 numbers are cited below). Pakistan was polled in 2007 and 2008 (2008 numbers are cited below). Morocco was polled in late 2006 and Bangladesh in 2009. In Turkey, polled in 2009, pluralities or modest majorities also supported such goals.

Al Qaeda's goals of acting to defend Islam from the United States were widely supported. Majorities in virtually all cases agreed with the goals to
  —"stand up to America and affirm the dignity of the Islamic people" (94 percent in Egypt, 81 percent in Bangladesh, 72 percent in Indonesia,

69 percent in Morocco, 56 percent in Pakistan, and 47 percent in Turkey);

—"keep Western values out of Islamic countries" (94 percent in Egypt, 81 percent in Indonesia, 80 percent in Bangladesh, 64 percent in Morocco, 60 percent in Pakistan, and 51 percent in Turkey); and

—"push the United States to remove its bases and its military forces from all Islamic countries" (93 percent in Egypt, 86 percent in Bangladesh, 72 percent in Morocco, 71 percent in Indonesia, 60 percent in Pakistan, and 52 percent in Turkey).

The theme of al Qaeda defending Islam from the United States was also expressed in the focus groups. Sometimes this was accompanied by implied criticism of al Qaeda's methods, but such criticism was overridden by the imperative of defending Islam. For example, an exchange in a Pakistani focus group went as follows.

> MODERATOR. Let's talk about al Qaeda. What do you feel about al Qaeda?
> RESPONDENT. I think al Qaeda is good. Al Qaeda wants what is in Islam and wants to work on the basis of Islam.
> MODERATOR. What are they doing?
> R. They are fighting for Islam, for its safety. . . . I am not saying that everything they are doing is right, but they are working towards the safety of Islam.
> MODERATOR. Are they achieving that?
> R Not at the moment, but they will, and gradually things will be better.

In some cases, though, the emphasis was more on al Qaeda defending Muslim countries from economic exploitation by the United States. For example, another Pakistani focus group went this way.

> R1. The reason why al Qaeda came into being was that in countries such as Sudan and Algeria, if you analyze, then you'll see that [the United States has] this point of view that the oil and gas is ours. . . . So in countries like Sudan and Algeria there are people who are ready to give up their lives to defend their natural resources, which they feel are being exploited by these foreign companies.

R2. You see that al Qaeda is only in countries like Afghanistan, Iraq, etc., which have natural resources. . . . This is the reason that al Qaeda was formed.

In other cases, however, al Qaeda and other radical Islamists were portrayed as playing a role in balancing American power globally. In a discussion of terrorist attacks against Americans, a Jordanian man said, "America does not want al Qaeda, Hamas, or Hezbollah, or Iran! Then who will create balance in the world?" When this man was asked if force is important in facing America, in creating a balance, he replied, "America did not face anyone except with force."

There was also strong support for the al Qaeda goal to "push the United States to stop favoring Israel in its conflict with the Palestinians." As mentioned in chapter 5, majorities agreed with this goal in Egypt (95 percent), Bangladesh (78 percent), Indonesia (77 percent), Morocco (75 percent), and Pakistan (55 percent). A plurality agreed in Turkey (44 percent).

The one al Qaeda goal directed at the United States that was not as strongly supported was "to push the United States to stop providing support to such governments as Egypt, Saudi Arabia, and Jordan." Only pluralities of Pakistanis (46 percent) and Moroccans (42 percent) agreed, as did a modest majority of Indonesians (53 percent). A modest majority of Egyptians (56 percent) also agreed, but in this case the question only mentioned support for Saudi Arabia and Jordan.

Majorities also supported al Qaeda goals to achieve a more Islamist society. For example, the goal "to require a strict application of sharia law in every Islamic country" was supported in Bangladesh (81 percent), Morocco (76 percent), Pakistan (76 percent), Egypt (71 percent), and Indonesia (56 percent). In Turkey, however, only a plurality of 46 percent supported the goal, while 32 percent disagreed with it.

The goal "to unify all Islamic countries into a single Islamic state or caliphate" elicited support among Moroccans (71 percent), Bangladeshis (69 percent), Pakistanis (69 percent), Egyptians (63 percent), and Indonesians (51 percent). Only a plurality of Turks agreed (40 percent).

Aversion to Extremism

Concurrent with majority support for most of al Qaeda's goals is majority concern about Islamic extremism. For example, Pew's 2010 survey asked, "How concerned, if at all, are you about the rise of Islamic extremism in our country these days?" Majorities said they are at least "somewhat" concerned in Lebanon (80 percent), Pakistan (65 percent), Egypt (61 percent), and Indonesia (59 percent). However, a majority of Jordanians (55 percent) said they were not concerned and Turks were divided. When asked in the same poll about Islamic extremism around the world, majorities expressed concern in Indonesia (72 percent), Egypt (70 percent), Jordan (70 percent), Lebanon (69 percent), and Pakistan (63 percent). Turks, though, leaned toward not being concerned. In a 2009 International Republican Institute (IRI) poll, 90 percent of Pakistanis agreed that "religious extremism is a serious problem in Pakistan."

While some who support al Qaeda's goals may believe it is not extremist—a subject that is explored below—in the focus groups al Qaeda was often framed as extremist. For example, in Pakistan several respondents complained about al Qaeda.

> R1. Actually, al Qaeda wants everyone to be completely in accordance with the Quran and sunnah and everyone should be burqa-clad. Like the Taliban, they beat up any woman who does not wear a burqa.
> R2. This is not the true Islam.
> R3. Yes, we know what al Qaeda wants, but we have complete faith in our army and our countrymen.

Pakistani respondents denounced the Taliban similarly.

> MODERATOR. Would you like Pakistan to be more like what the Taliban wants?
> R1. No, we don't believe in what the Taliban wants the world to see as Islam. That is not the true image of Islam. Islam doesn't promote terrorism. We don't want the Islam that the Taliban are portraying.
> R2. Islam is a religion of virtues, peace, and tolerance, and in Islam you are even taught to befriend your enemy and live in total harmony.
> R3. In Islam you impress others with your character. This is what we need. We don't need any wars.

In both cases, when these sentiments were expressed, no one in the focus groups spoke up in defense of either al Qaeda or the Taliban.

Rejection of the View of Moderate Governments as Illegitimate

A central pillar in al Qaeda ideology is that the moderate governments of majority-Muslim countries, especially Saudi Arabia and Egypt, are not legitimate because they are not adequately committed to a pure Islamist model and are too friendly with the United States. Al Qaeda leaders chide the United States for supporting leaders who are not democratically elected, strongly implying that their governments are not seen by their own people as legitimate.

The idea that the people in moderate Muslim countries do not regard their governments as legitimate gets only minority agreement. WPO asked respondents in three nations in 2008 whether the majority of people in Egypt, Indonesia, Pakistan, and Saudi Arabia see their governments as legitimate. Though Saudi Arabia is held up by al Qaeda as particularly illegitimate, only small minorities thought that Saudis see their government as illegitimate, including 25 percent of Turks, 11 percent of Jordanians, and 9 percent of Palestinians. Slightly larger minorities (especially among Palestinians) thought most Egyptians, Indonesians, and Pakistanis view their governments as illegitimate, but in no case did a majority have such an assumption. On the other hand, in some cases only a plurality thought the publics do view their governments as legitimate.

Rejection of Attacks on Civilians, Terrorism, and Suicide Bombing

The strongest rebuff of radical Islamist ideology is in Muslims' rejection of bin Laden's call for attacks on American and other Western civilians such as in his statement, "To kill Americans and their allies—civilian and military—is an individual duty for every Muslim."[1] As discussed in chapter 1, asked by WPO in 2006 to 2009 polling whether they approve, disapprove, or have mixed feelings about attacks on civilians in the United States, large majorities said they disapprove in Bangladesh (87 percent), Azerbaijan (82 percent), Indonesia (80 percent), Morocco (78 percent), Iran (73 percent), Egypt (70 percent), Jordan (68 percent), Pakistan (66 percent), Turkey (65 percent), and the Palestinian Territories (57 per-

FIGURE 7-1. Attacks on Civilians in the U.S.

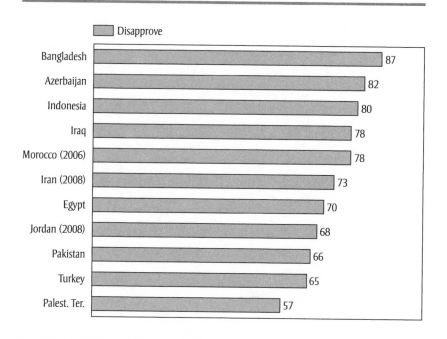

Source: WorldPublicOpinion.org, 2009.

cent) (see figure 7-1). In only four nations did approval rise above single digits—in Egypt and Pakistan (both 15 percent), the Palestinian Territories (14 percent), and Jordan (11 percent).

Attacks on "U.S. civilians working for U.S. companies in Islamic countries" were also rejected, as discussed in chapter 1, though by a slightly lower margin (79 percent of Bangladeshis, 78 percent of Indonesians, 76 percent of Azerbaijanis, 74 percent of Egyptians, 73 percent of Moroccans, 68 percent of Turks, 67 percent of Iraqis, 64 percent of Iranians and Jordanians, and 60 percent of Pakistanis). Palestinians were an exception, with only 34 percent disapproving and 37 percent saying they have mixed feelings (see figure 7-2). The highest numbers approving of attacks on civilians working in Islamic countries were in the Palestinian Territories (28 percent), Pakistan (22 percent), and Egypt, Iran, and Jordan (all 15 percent).

Terror Free Tomorrow also asked Saudis in 2007 whether they favor or oppose "Osama bin Laden's fatwa calling on all Muslims to attack the

FIGURE 7-2.   Attacks on U.S. Civilians Working in Islamic Countries

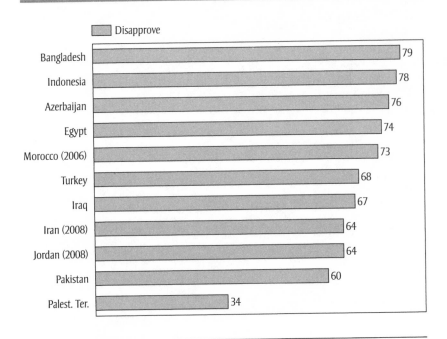

■ Disapprove

Bangladesh	79
Indonesia	78
Azerbaijan	76
Egypt	74
Morocco (2006)	73
Turkey	68
Iraq	67
Iran (2008)	64
Jordan (2008)	64
Pakistan	60
Palest. Ter.	34

Source: WorldPublicOpinion.org, 2009.

United States and Americans wherever they are." Two-thirds said they oppose this, with just 16 percent favoring it.

The 9/11 attacks have been widely denounced in the Muslim world as morally wrong. In 2001 and again in 2005, Gallup asked in Indonesia, Iran, Lebanon, Morocco, Turkey, and Pakistan how justified the attacks were. The numbers saying that the attacks were "completely" or "mostly" justified were in every case less than one in five and in half the cases were one in ten or less.

The 9/11 attacks are also seen as negative for the Muslim people—a view that has grown with time. Asked by WPO in 2008 what the effect of 9/11 has been for the people of the Islamic world, 74 percent of Egyptians called it negative (61 percent "very"), up 14 points from 2007. Fifty-eight percent of Indonesians agreed, up 2 points from 2006. In Pakistan a more modest 46 percent said it has been negative, but only 11 percent called it positive (roughly the same as 2007). In Morocco in late 2006, 62 percent called the effect negative (39 percent "very").

Attacks on European civilians are not viewed differently from attacks on Americans. In 2008 WPO polling large majorities in Egypt (85 percent) and Indonesia (72 percent) rejected attacks on Europeans, as did a modest majority in Pakistan (51 percent, with many not answering). In 2006, 82 percent of Moroccans disapproved of such attacks.

When presented with arguments justifying attacks on civilians, respondents roundly reject them. In 2006 Arab Barometer presented the argument that "armed groups are justified in attacking civilians in Iraq in order to resist the American occupation," without specifying the nationality of the victims. Large majorities rejected this argument in Kuwait (83 percent), the Palestinian Territories (83 percent), Morocco (76 percent), Algeria (72 percent), and Jordan (69 percent). Agreement ranged from 12 percent in Algeria to 18 percent in Jordan.

In the focus groups Islam was often invoked as a basis for rejecting attacks on civilians. For example, when the question of attacks on civilians was raised in a focus group in Morocco, it elicited a torrent of denunciations based on Islamic principles.

MODERATOR. What do you think of the attacks on Americans in general?

R. It is against our Islamic sharia.

R. These people that did these attacks are criminals, and Islam definitely does not approve these attacks.

MODERATOR. What do you think of the attacks in Bali?

R. Killing innocent people, innocent families, kids—I think that there is no religion in the world that approves that. These people are crazy, and they lost their minds. Maybe these people were only drinking or doing adultery, but only God knows if these people can go to hell or heaven. So we as people cannot make a verdict on them and kill them because they are drinking or committing bad deeds.

R. Islam first, forbids killing kids, women, and old people.

R. OK, Islam allowed the jihad, but jihad has laws and limits, and it was first allowed in order to restore the Islam in earth. But now Islam is very well restored all over the world, not only in the Arab world.

R. Jihad nowadays should be used to defend yourself, but not going to somebody's land and make it.

R. When an American comes to me and tells me that Muslims did these attacks, I know that this American guy doesn't have any idea about the principles of Islam.

R. Islam is a religion of tolerance.

R. These attacks are against Islam then.

Similarly, in a Pakistani group attacks on civilians were roundly denounced, though attacks on British soldiers were endorsed.

R. [Al Qaeda] has misused Islam. . . . If America and British government is killing innocent people in Afghanistan and Iraq, then you will also become like them? Will you also become a tyrant?

R. Let me tell you, about six months ago a female worker of al Qaeda committed suicide through bombing a place. In this attack only eight Americans died, and in total forty civilians died in which there were children, old and young people. You say that she is doing jihad. That woman was pregnant, and she is destroying the next generation. This is not jihad. If you talk about Islam, then let's talk about what our Holy Prophet said— that old people, children, and the innocents, and those who have laid down their weapons, should be absolved. I have seen good things that al Qaeda has done, like to the British soldier who raped women and made children homeless. What al Qaeda did to them was fine.

R. I have read an article on the Internet in which I saw photographs which showed that they (British soldiers) have disrespected women and treated children very badly. So what al Qaeda did against them is a little bit justifiable. But normally, what they (al Qaeda) are doing disrespects Islam. Our religion does not teach us this.

R. Our Prophet never told anyone to act like this. He has said that Islam is a religion of conscience.

There also seems to be a growing belief that attacks on civilians are ineffective. In 2007 and 2008 WPO asked in three countries how effective attacks against civilians, as a tactic in conflict, are in changing the situation. In Egypt the number saying such attacks are "hardly ever" effective rose from 35 to 52 percent, with just 16 percent saying they are "often" effective and 26 percent saying "only sometimes." Similarly, in Indonesia those saying they are "hardly ever" effective rose from 42 to 50 percent, with 5 percent saying they are "often" effective and 14 percent saying "only sometimes." Pakistanis were unchanged across the years, with 49 percent saying such attacks are "hardly ever" effective, 11 percent calling them "often" effective, and 13 percent saying "only sometimes."

As a general principle, majorities take a negative view of the use of violence to achieve political ends, even when attacks on civilians are not highlighted (though it is likely that respondents were still thinking in terms of attacks on civilians because attacks on U.S. military forces are much more widely endorsed). WPO asked in 2007 and 2008 a broad and explicit question: "In general, how justified are violent attacks such as bombings and assassinations that are carried out in order to achieve political or religious goals?" The response options were "strongly justified," "justified," "weakly justified," or "not justified at all." Eighty-three percent in Egypt and 89 percent in Indonesia said these methods were "not justified at all." Only 2 percent in Egypt and less than 1 percent in Indonesia called them "strongly justified." In Pakistan 67 percent said these methods are "not justified at all," with 12 percent calling them "weakly justified" (6 percent) or "justified" (6 percent) and 13 percent calling them "strongly justified."

Few think attacks on civilian infrastructure, even if no civilians are killed, can be justified. WPO asked in 2006 to 2007 about "politically motivated attacks" that do not inflict casualties such as "destroying a pipeline or bombing a radio transmitting tower." Majorities said that such attacks are "not justified at all" (rather than "strongly justified," "justified," or "weakly justified"), including 80 percent of Indonesians, 72 percent of Pakistanis, 70 percent of Egyptians, and 56 percent of Moroccans.

Terrorism per se is seen in a negative light. Asked in 2006 to 2008 WPO polling to say to what extent they see terrorism as a problem in their country—a "very big problem," a "moderate problem," a "small problem," or "not a problem"—large majorities of Egyptians and Indonesians and an overwhelming majority of Pakistanis called terrorism a "very big problem." In Egypt 57 percent said terrorism is a "very big problem," while an additional 9 percent called it a "moderate problem." In Indonesia nearly three in four (72 percent) called terrorism a "very big

FIGURE 7-3. Views of Terrorism

To what extent do you perceive terrorism to be a problem in [country]?

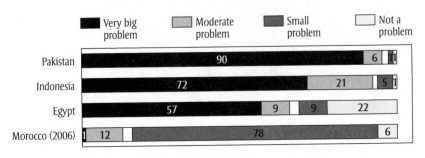

Source: WorldPublicOpinion.org, 2008.

problem," with 21 percent saying it is a "moderate problem." In Pakistan a striking 90 percent said terrorism is a "very big problem," with 6 percent saying "moderate." In Morocco, however, views diverged dramatically. When Moroccans were asked this question in late 2006, more than four-fifths (84 percent) said terrorism is either only a "small problem" (78 percent) or "not a problem" (6 percent). Only 13 percent of Moroccans called it either a "very big problem" (1 percent) or a "moderate problem" (12 percent). (See figure 7-3.)

When Terror Free Tomorrow asked Saudis in December 2007 to assess the importance of "addressing the problem of terrorism" (as "very important," "somewhat important," "somewhat unimportant," or "not at all important"), 88 percent said it is important, with 75 percent saying it is "very important." Six in ten said it is important to defeat "al Qaeda and other jihadi groups" (42 percent said "very important").

Attitudes about suicide attacks are more complex. Suicide attacks, for example, do not necessarily target civilians; many are against military targets. In any case, majorities in three of the four countries polled by WPO from 2006 to 2009 said that suicide attacks are "rarely" or "never" justified. Egyptians, though, tended to believe they are justified "sometimes" or "often."

Respondents were asked what they think when they hear or read about "an attack in which a Muslim blows himself up while attacking an enemy." In two countries majorities said such suicide bombings are "never justified" (69 percent in Indonesia and 60 percent in Pakistan). An additional

13 percent of Indonesians and 9 percent of Pakistanis said suicide bombings are "rarely" justified.

Moroccans also tended to think such attacks are unjustified, though less emphatically. A slight majority said they are "never" (34 percent) or "rarely" (19 percent). Thirty-six percent said they were justified at least "sometimes."

Three in five Egyptians (59 percent), however, considered suicide bombings to be "often" (40 percent) or "sometimes" (19 percent) justified. About a quarter (28 percent) said they are "never" justified, and 7 percent called such actions "rarely" justified. This is in contrast to Egyptian responses to poll questions that asked specifically about attacks on civilians, which Egyptians strongly opposed. This suggests that Egyptians may think of suicide attacks as being against noncivilian targets.

Terror Free Tomorrow also found in June 2008 a large majority of Pakistanis (73 percent) saying that suicide bombings are "never" justified. Furthermore, in a separate question that asked whether Islam permits suicide bombing attacks against civilians, an even larger 81 percent said suicide bombing is "never permitted." In the focus groups suicide bombing was regularly denounced as being contrary to Islam. For example, a Jordanian man said, "I would not term blowing oneself up as Islamic. Islam doesn't give permission to persecute others and has taught us to live in complete harmony and brotherhood."

Differentiating Goals and Methods of al Qaeda

Given that large majorities of Muslims share al Qaeda's hostility toward the United States and approve of many of its goals, yet also largely disapprove of attacks on civilians, one might expect Muslims to simply differentiate between support for al Qaeda's goals and opposition to its methods. It appears, however, that doing so is not easy. When directly offered this option, less than a majority of respondents endorse it.

In WPO polling from 2006 to 2009 respondents in eight different nations were presented a question by that offered three alternatives for characterizing their views of al Qaeda:

—"I support al Qaeda's attacks on Americans and share its attitudes toward the United States."

—"I oppose al Qaeda's attacks on Americans but share many of its attitudes toward the United States."

FIGURE 7-4. Views of al Qaeda

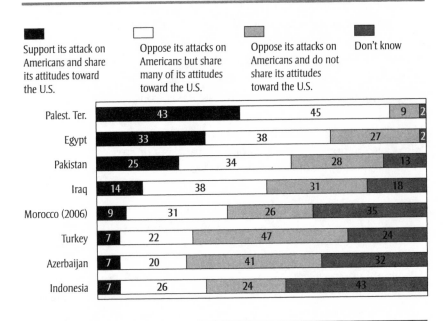

Source: WorldPublicOpinion.org, 2009.

—"I oppose al Qaeda's attacks on Americans and do not share its attitudes toward the United States."

In no country did a majority choose the differentiated position of opposing the attacks but sharing al Qaeda's attitudes toward the United States. But in no case did a majority endorse the other positions either. In fact, substantial numbers declined to answer the question, including a third of Azerbaijanis and 43 percent of Indonesians. (See figure 7-4.) This suggests that many Muslims have difficulty sorting out their feelings toward al Qaeda.

Dealing with Dissonance through Denial and Avoidance

There is ample evidence of the difficulty among many Muslims in resolving the cognitive dissonance between sympathizing with al Qaeda's goals and not wanting to accept violence. Because such dissonance is an unpleasant experience, it is normal for people to use various defense mechanisms to avoid the experience. In the focus groups people used a variety of means to avoid dealing with the subject of al Qaeda.

Some questioned whether al Qaeda or bin Laden even existed. For example, when a Moroccan focus group was asked, "What do you think of al Qaeda?" one respondent answered, "I'm not sure it even exists." Another chimed in, "Sometimes I think it's just an American movie." A common way of supporting this idea was to claim that the United States controls the media. The following exchange in an Egyptian focus group regarding the 9/11 attacks illustrates this.

> R. I hate anyone who kills innocent human beings, regardless of their religion.
> MODERATOR. Did al Qaeda do that?
> R. My information comes from the media that USA controls. . . . I don't have any proof that there is such a thing as al Qaeda and that it destroyed the twin towers in America. All we saw was a Hollywood movie.

Despite the abundant evidence to the contrary, including videotapes of Osama bin Laden and other al Qaeda leaders claiming responsibility for the 9/11 attacks, polls have found that many Muslims strongly resist accepting this. In Pew's 2006 survey respondents were asked whether they believed that "groups of Arabs carried out the attacks against the United States on September 11." Majorities said they did not believe this in Indonesia (65 percent), Egypt (59 percent), Turkey (59 percent), and Jordan (53 percent) as well as a plurality in Pakistan (41 percent). The numbers saying they did believe it ranged from 15 percent in Pakistan to 39 percent in Jordan. Large numbers did not provide an answer either way, especially in Pakistan (44 percent), Turkey (25 percent), and Indonesia (20 percent).

WPO asked in 2007 and 2008, "Who do you think was behind the 9/11 attacks?" in an open-ended question (no response options were provided). Out of seven nations polled in those years, a majority in only one—69 percent in Azerbaijan—gave a response that either named al Qaeda or alluded to it (such as referring to Islamic extremists or militants). In some nations only very small numbers gave such an answer. In 2008 the lowest numbers identifying Islamic extremists as behind 9/11 were in Pakistan, with just 4 percent. This was followed by Jordan (11 percent), Egypt (23 percent), Indonesia (30 percent), Turkey (39 percent), and the Palestinian Territories (42 percent). In Morocco, polled in late 2006, 45 percent

FIGURE 7-5. Identity of 9/11 Perpetrators

Who do you think was behind the 9/11 attacks? [*Open-ended question*]

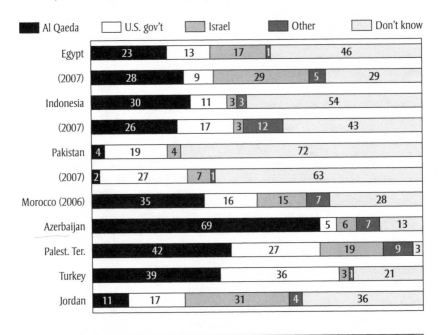

Source: WorldPublicOpinion.org, 2008.

thought Islamic extremists were behind the 9/11 attacks. (See figure 7-5.) This is in sharp contrast to views in non-Muslim countries in the 2008 WPO polls. Among twelve non-Muslim countries polled and Taiwan, ten identified al Qaeda or Islamic extremists as the perpetrators, as did pluralities in another two. Only in Mexico were views mixed.

The low numbers among Muslims citing al Qaeda as behind 9/11 does not mean, though, that there is consensus about who was behind it. Significant minorities in Turkey (36 percent) and Palestinian Territories (27 percent) cited the U.S. government, but quite small numbers did so in Jordan (17 percent), Egypt (13 percent), Indonesia (11 percent), and Azerbaijan (5 percent). In late 2006, 30 percent of Moroccans thought the U.S. government was behind the attacks. Israel was cited by minorities of Jordanians (31 percent), Palestinians (19 percent), and Egyptians (17 percent) as well as by small numbers of Azerbaijanis (6 percent), Pakistanis

(4 percent), Indonesians (3 percent), and Turks (3 percent). In 2006, 7 percent of Moroccans gave this answer.

Another possible indicator of inner conflict and avoidance in regard to al Qaeda is the failure to answer the question at all. Across the two years of polling, the failure to answer the question of who was behind the 9/11 attacks reached as high as 72 percent in Pakistan, 54 percent in Indonesia, and 46 percent in Egypt. Large percentages of nonresponses were also found in Jordan (36 percent) and Turkey (21 percent).

Remarkably, in all three countries in which the question was asked in both 2007 and 2008, there was an extraordinary increase in the numbers declining to say who they thought was responsible for 9/11—something not seen on other trend questions. Nonresponses rose 17 points in Egypt, 11 points in Indonesia, and 9 points in Pakistan. On many other quite controversial questions, however, Pakistanis were more forthcoming in 2008 than in 2007. This suggests that rather than the passage of time allowing greater distance and deliberation, avoidance and denial may have increased.

A related question about 9/11 in 2007 WPO polling asked how confident respondents were that they knew who was behind the September 11 attacks. Majorities in all four countries polled either said they were "not at all confident" or declined to answer. In Egypt 44 percent were "not at all confident" and an additional 24 percent declined to answer; in Morocco 31 percent were "not at all confident" and 21 percent declined; in Indonesia 23 percent were "not at all confident" and 42 percent declined. Pakistan had the lowest percentage saying they were "not at all confident" (14 percent), but a majority (56 percent) would not answer.

It is possible that people are genuinely confused and have grown more confused over time. Based on observations in the focus groups, however, it appears that, for the most part, people are defensive.

In some cases this effort to defend against the idea that Muslims were behind 9/11 took a rather extreme form. Some respondents not only said that al Qaeda was not behind 9/11, but said flatly that al Qaeda had never engaged in any attacks on civilians. All evidence to the contrary was dismissed as having been fabricated by Western sources to discredit Islam. Some argued that the United States itself was surreptitiously undertaking major terrorist attacks in an effort to make people believe that the attacks were being committed by Muslims and thus discredit Islam.

Yet another approach was to portray al Qaeda as mercenarily working for outside forces that want to discredit Arabs and Islam. A Jordanian man explained this as follows.

MODERATOR. What are your feelings about al Qaeda?

R. It does not relate to Islam at all. It is an extremist group that aims to divide nations.

MODERATOR. Why does it want to do that?

R. Maybe the leadership gets money and encourages people who work for them to do this.

MODERATOR. Why do you think the leadership wants to divide nations?

R. Their main objective is to get money.

MODERATOR. And who gives the money?

R. I don't know, but it is any nation that hates the Arabs, so they can drive the whole world to hate the Arabs and Islam.

MODERATOR. So the whole goal of al Qaeda is to provoke hostility towards the Arab and Islamic world?

R. Yes.

In some cases respondents portrayed al Qaeda as not truly Muslim, but as a creation of the United States. This was seen as starting in the 1980s when the United States provided support to radical fundamentalists to fight the Soviets. Thus their violent nature was portrayed as being largely derived from the United States. For example, an Egyptian said that "America fed [al Qaeda] with violence and stimulated anger." Another explained, "We all agree, of course, that al Qaeda was created by USA to fight the former Soviet Union. . . . Al Qaeda became an addict to America's resources, money, and weapons. . . . Then America suddenly withdrew. . . . America stopped supporting al Qaeda and the mujahedin. . . . So America becomes the number one enemy of al Qaeda."

America was portrayed as being a kind of victim of its creation. In the words of one respondent, "America encourages some movements and helps them. It uses them to achieve certain purposes. Then [those movements] turn back on [the United States] to destroy it, just like magic turns on the magician."

In some cases this line of thinking would blur into the implication that al Qaeda is still working for the United States. For example, a Pakistani explained that al Qaeda "is based in America." Another added as evidence of this that bin Laden's niece is working as a model in America.

Related to this is the view that al Qaeda exists only as a reaction to the United States. For example, a Jordanian woman avoided saying explicitly that al Qaeda exists, but raised it hypothetically: "If we suppose that the al Qaeda is based in Afghanistan, [then] America should not interfere. Countries should not interfere in the internal affairs of each other. . . . This way wars will not erupt. This way neither al Qaeda nor any other similar group will emerge."

On the question of who was responsible for 9/11, many in the focus groups cited evidence that the United States or Israel was responsible, sometimes in significant detail. Some stressed that the United States had a clear motive for the attacks—to create a basis for going to war with Iraq.

Perhaps most striking, even direct claims of responsibility from al Qaeda were discounted as being possibly created by the United States. When respondents were asked whether they had seen the videos of Osama bin Laden and Ayman al-Zawahiri claiming responsibility for the attacks, respondents shrugged this off with comments like, "Hollywood can produce anything." When asked whether they had seen al Qaeda's websites, these were also dismissed with comments like, "Who can prove that the website is actually owned by them? Disinformation is also a strategy of war."

The most common response in the focus groups, though, was not denial that al Qaeda was behind the 9/11 attacks, but a resistance to dealing with the question. Many said they simply did not know, showing an apparent lack of interest in the question. Others angrily insisted that Muslims were being unfairly fingered without proof. The theories of American or Israeli complicity created enough ambiguity so as to make it impossible to resolve the question.

When respondents avoided the question by throwing out various possibilities, they were sometimes pressed to take a position. Sometimes this elicited an angry response. For example, in a group of Egyptian females, they were shifting between saying that it would be impossible for Muslims to kill civilians and insisting that there was no proof that Muslims had done so. They were pressed to give their opinion, but responded angrily.

MODERATOR. So what do you think happened? Do you think civilians were killed by al Qaeda or by Muslims?

> R. We don't have any proof, and let's not talk about this matter
> any more! We don't have any proof. It's an international issue;
> it's not our business. Dr. Kull insists on talking about al Qaeda.
> We don't have any proof that it happened. Islam prohibits
> killing of civilians.
> RESPONDENTS. [*variously*] We don't know. God only knows.

Another respondent, speaking for the group, described an unwilling-
ness to take as evidence essentially any source of information on the question, including bin Laden himself. This respondent asserted that such a
stance was typical of Arab intellectuals.

> If it did happen, we're against it. You're asking if it happened or
> not, and we don't know. But if it happened, we're against it.
> There are highly intellectual people in the Arab world, and they
> are well aware of what is going on. They wouldn't believe
> anyone who shows up on TV and says I did such and such. We
> believe only in God and the Prophet. We will not believe just
> anyone, not bin Laden, and not anyone else from America.

Perhaps the strongest indication of defensiveness was when respondents spoke animatedly about al Qaeda and Osama bin Laden, regularly
praising them for standing up to America. It seemed that the 9/11 attacks
were implicit in their comments. But when asked specifically how al
Qaeda stood up to America, they suddenly became uncomfortable and
could not or would not point to any specific instances other than al
Qaeda's general stance against America.

In a few cases people seemed genuinely uncertain about al Qaeda—
something that is not hard to understand given the highly conflicting
messages they appear to be getting from various news sources and from
various friends and acquaintances. Some respondents seemed to have
absorbed seemingly contradictory positions that they had failed to integrate. When a Moroccan man's contradictory views were pointed out to
him, interestingly, he did not react defensively, but openly expressed his
frustration in reconciling his different perspectives. Initially, he had
made the statement that the United States had suffered from 9/11,
implying that it should feel chastised. Later, though, he changed his
position.

R. Personally, I think that 9/11 is the work of the United States.

MODERATOR. You say that 9/11 is the work of the United States, but didn't you also say they suffered from it?

R. [*throws up hands*] That's what I was saying! There is nothing clear! Maybe it's the United States who's responsible of 9/11, or maybe it's bin Laden. There is always that ambiguity!!

An IRI poll conducted in Pakistan in October 2008 shortly after the suicide attack on the Marriott Hotel in Islamabad also showed confusion or avoidance on the issue of who was responsible. Pakistani officials at the time said the leads pointed to the Taliban and al Qaeda as responsible for the attack. Yet when respondents were asked, "Who do you think is responsible for the recent suicide attack on the Marriott Hotel in Islamabad?" half declined to answer. The largest number (one in five) said America, and 13 percent said the government of Pakistan. Just 5 percent said the Taliban, and 2 percent said terrorists.

In focus groups respondents made it clear that they heard the official explanations tying al Qaeda and other radical Islamist groups to bombings. And yet they clearly neither believed nor disbelieved these explanations, strangely accepting both sides without actually reconciling them. For example, in an exchange with Pakistani women, at first they implicitly questioned the government position and media reporting that al Qaeda was behind various bombings.

MODERATOR. What is your opinion of al Qaeda?

R1. We tend to associate everything with al Qaeda.

R2. We have a very negative attitude of al Qaeda because of the media.

MODERATOR. Do you think that what it is saying is not true?

R3. See, there have been many suicide attacks, but nobody knows who was behind them.

R4. We have been exposed to lies for so long that we can't differentiate the truth from the lies.

R5. Whenever there is a bomb blast or any other act of terrorism, the government blames it on al Qaeda. Even the news channels on television concur with the government's point of view. Our minds are brainwashed to believe that al Qaeda is behind all the violence.

When this respondent was pressed to come to closure with the question of whether she believed the government and the media, her tone changed from one of animated complaining to one that was thoughtful but somewhat dissociated.

> R5. Yes. If you read it in the papers and see it in the news, then you tend to believe it.

It seemed that she was saying that at moments she did believe it, but that she also had mental constructs that allowed her not to believe it.

Another example is a Jordanian woman who was able to describe her inner conflict rather lucidly.

> R. I want to say something. We are facing two facts. One of them says that al Qaeda is Islamic and is working to liberate the other countries, while the other says that America made al Qaeda. It is impossible that America with all its power and technology is not able to control al Qaeda; it is not possible. This means that America has created al Qaeda.
>
> MODERATOR. Are you saying that this is a point of view or your point of view?
>
> R. It is the point of view of most of the people who live around us. They say al Qaeda was created by America.
>
> MODERATOR. Do you believe that?
>
> R. I believe up to 70 percent that this is true.

Rationalization of Radical Islamist Attacks on Civilians

Even though majorities consistently reject attacks on civilians, significant minorities in polls have endorsed them. More important, when presented with arguments that rationalize attacks on civilians, substantial numbers have said they agree with them, or at least do not reject them by simply not answering. Though these numbers are minorities in most cases, they do represent large numbers of people and are quite significant to our analysis, as they are an important part of the societal support structure for radical Islamist groups.

In 2009 WPO polling respondents in four countries were asked whether they agreed or disagreed with the argument that "groups in the

FIGURE 7-6. Terrorist Groups as Defending Islam

Groups in the Muslim world that attack American civilians are defending Islam against America's efforts to divide and dominate the Islamic world.

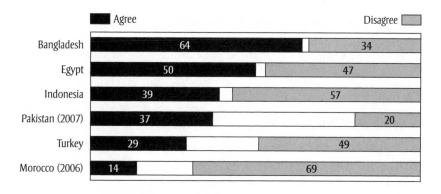

Source: WorldPublicOpinion.org, 2009.

Muslim world that attack American civilians are defending Islam against America's efforts to divide and dominate the Islamic world." In Bangladesh a majority of 64 percent agreed, with another 3 percent not answering. In Egypt 50 percent agreed, and 3 percent did not answer. In Indonesia a substantial minority (39 percent) agreed, and 5 percent declined to answer. Even in America's ally Turkey, 29 percent agreed, and a remarkable 22 percent failed to answer. (See figure 7-6.) To be sure, the statement did not explicitly endorse such attacks, but laid out a rationale for them. It is unclear whether respondents actually supported such attacks or were simply agreeing or disagreeing with the perceived intent.

In 2008 WPO presented the more unequivocal statement, "Though it is generally wrong to attack civilians, attacks against U.S. civilians are sometimes justified because it is the only way to get the American government to stop and listen to the concerns of the Islamic people." Among Egyptians, 22 percent said they agreed (14 percent) or did not answer (8 percent). Among Indonesians, 36 percent agreed (17 percent) or did not answer (19 percent). The response options were a bit different for Pakistanis, with 28 percent agreeing, 23 percent having "mixed feelings," and another 25 percent not answering. Only 24 percent disagreed.

In the focus groups some respondents also effectively rationalized the use of terrorist attacks. A Jordanian man said,

We do not have hope in the future, and we do not see any solution
except in using force. We heard a lot and took part in many
peace conferences, but they did not achieve any results.
Nothing affects the West except terrorist operations, or what
you call in the U.S. terrorist operations.

When respondents rationalized such attacks, in virtually every case
they sought to maintain the basic norm against such attacks, while specifying particular conditions under which they would be acceptable. The
most obvious form of this was to discount attacks on civilians as unin-
tended collateral damage. For example, a Jordanian man said, "You can't
control war the way you want. Al Qaeda has an objective to fight for the
good of the Islamic world and people. Sometimes people who implement
plans, they make mistakes and kill innocent people."

One of the most common defenses was that attacks on civilians would
be acceptable in an effort to defend one's country against an occupier. Terrorist attacks in Iraq were justified as a defense against the American
occupation, though this argument seemed to be applied to attacks on
Iraqi civilians as well as U.S. troops. This principle was applied in defense
of Palestinian attacks on Israelis. For example, a focus group with Jordanian women went as follows.

MODERATOR. Do you think that the attacks on civilians can ever
be justified?

R. No, there is no justification. We also don't like the American
people to be harmed. At the end they are also human beings.
We don't want them to be harmed, and we don't want that for
ourselves too.

MODERATOR. What about when Palestinians attack Israeli civilians?

R. I think the situation here is different. Palestine is an occupied
country, and the Palestinian people want to liberate their
country and resist occupation by all means. They have been
suffering for sixty years, and nobody is helping them. The
Israelis are picking up the crops they planted. Even if civilians
are killed, they are settlers.

MODERATOR. So you think this morally justifies the attacks on
Israeli civilians?

R. It is an occupied country. They want to defend themselves, and everyday they are killed and attacked. What can they do?

R. If anybody comes to your house and wants to take it by force, what would you do? Would you give it to them and end the war? This is what happened in Palestine. Jews came from America and Europe, settled in it, and occupied it by force. Palestinians have to defend their rights and their land. This is what is happening in Palestine. It is justified even if they kill civilians.

R. Palestine is an exception.

Similarly, in a December 2006 WPO poll, 53 percent of Iranians said that "attacks by Palestinians against Israeli civilians" were sometimes justified, in contrast to their rejection of attacks on civilians in general.

In some cases respondents would invoke a principle of reciprocity in the context of America harming civilians. For example, a Pakistani man said, "If America is bombarding Iraq and civilians die, they say sorry, it was by mistake. But if a jihadi does this, then how can we say that he is wrong? Everything is fair in love and war." But when asked directly whether attacking civilians would be acceptable, he backed away and said it would not be if done intentionally.

Some even claimed that such principles of retribution are rooted in Islam. For example, when the subject of attacks on civilians was raised, a Pakistani man brought up U.S. behavior. He was asked, "So if America, or whoever, does something bad, then you can justify the attacks on civilians?" He replied, "Yes, that is what our Holy Prophet said. That is, whatever you get, do the same things back." There was not complete agreement on this, however, in the group. Another respondent immediately said, "No, he says forgiveness is even greater." And another affirmed that bin Laden's call for attacks on American citizens was "wrong."

For a few, the defense of Islam was such an overriding value that this justified al Qaeda doing whatever is necessary. An Egyptian man explained that this is justified because governments in the Muslim world were failing to defend Islam. "There is a positive point about al Qaeda, but it is due to the negative attitude of the rulers. Al Qaeda granted itself the right to defend Islam. . . . Governments are not doing anything about it, so al Qaeda has to do what it has to do."

Overall, No Single Dominant Feeling toward Al Qaeda

Given all the conflicting views and ambiguities about al Qaeda and its methods, the net effect is that there is no single dominant feeling toward al Qaeda and bin Laden in the Muslim world. Views vary highly between nations. Overall, though, negative views tend to outweigh positive views. Only in Egypt and the Palestinian Territories are views predominantly positive toward al Qaeda, while predominantly negative views are found in Afghanistan, Azerbaijan, Iraq, Saudi Arabia, and Turkey. More mixed views are found in Bangladesh, Indonesia, Jordan, and Pakistan.

Al Qaeda

WPO polling in 2009 in seven nations found majorities in four of them with "negative" views of al Qaeda as opposed to "positive" or "mixed" views—75 percent in Azerbaijan, 71 percent in Iraq, 70 percent in Bangladesh, and 60 percent in Turkey. Indonesians leaned only slightly to the negative (22 percent negative to 17 percent positive), with most saying their views were mixed (35 percent) or not giving an answer (25 percent). Pakistanis leaned more to the negative (27 percent positive, 45 percent negative, 16 percent mixed). Terror Free Tomorrow also found a plurality of unfavorable views of al Qaeda in Pakistan (32 percent favorable, 45 percent unfavorable) in 2008. (See figure 7-7.)

In Saudi Arabia in 2007, Terror Free Tomorrow found a large majority (64 percent) with negative views of al Qaeda. Sixty-one percent said that "defeating al Qaeda and other jihadi groups" is important. But in the same poll the public was divided on whether they supported "the U.S. military working with the Saudi Arabian military and police to pursue al Qaeda fighters inside Saudi Arabia."

Bin Laden

Osama bin Laden is a highly visible figure, even more recognizable than his organization al Qaeda. Views of him are somewhat less negative than of al Qaeda, with large variances between countries. Among ten majority-Muslim nations surveyed by WPO from 2006 to 2009, views were mostly negative in three nations, mostly positive in three, and in four there was not a dominant view. (See figure 7-8.)

Majority negative views were found among Azerbaijanis (84 percent), Iraqis (73 percent), and Turks (60 percent). Also, ABC/BBC found

FIGURE 7-7. Feelings toward al Qaeda

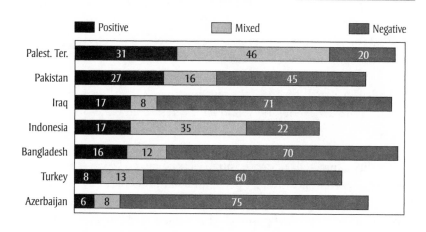

Source: WorldPublicOpinion.org, 2009.

FIGURE 7-8. Feelings toward bin Laden

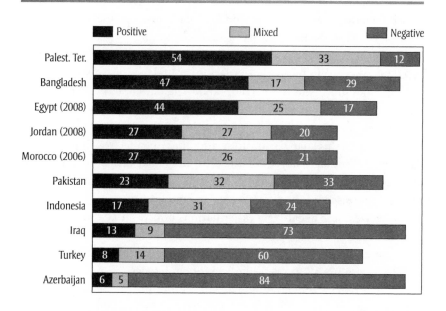

Source: WorldPublicOpinion.org, 2009.

overwhelmingly unfavorable views of Osama bin Laden in Afghanistan (92 percent). In 2007 Terror Free Tomorrow found 64 percent with unfavorable views of bin Laden in Saudi Arabia.

WPO found majorities expressing a favorable view of bin Laden in the Palestinian Territories (54 percent) and Egypt in 2009 (60 percent—up from 44 percent in 2008). Interestingly, views leaned favorable toward bin Laden in Bangladesh (47 percent positive, 29 percent negative, and 17 percent mixed), though seven in ten expressed an unfavorable view of al Qaeda.

In several countries there was no clearly dominant view, but a majority or plurality expressed either a positive view or mixed views. This included Jordan (27 percent positive, 27 percent mixed), Morocco (27 percent positive, 26 percent mixed), Pakistan (23 percent positive, 32 percent mixed), and Indonesia (17 percent positive, 31 percent mixed). In all cases negative views were never higher than one-third, and in many cases large numbers did not answer.

When Pew asked how much confidence respondents had in Osama bin Laden to "do the right thing regarding world affairs," views were more negative—presumably because this raises the question of whether bin Laden behaves morally. As discussed, one can have the view that bin Laden's methods are immoral and still have a favorable view of him because of his goals. In 2010 majorities in Lebanon (98 percent), Turkey (74 percent), Egypt (73 percent), and Indonesia (61 percent) expressed a lack of confidence in bin Laden. A lack of confidence was also expressed by majorities in Kuwait (68 percent) and Bangladesh (52 percent), polled only in 2007.

While a majority in Jordan (60 percent) expressed confidence in bin Laden in 2005, this changed abruptly after thirty people from a Jordanian-Palestinian wedding party were killed by al Qaeda suicide bombers who attacked three hotels in Amman in late 2005. By 2010, 83 percent of Jordanians expressed a lack of confidence in bin Laden.

Views were less negative in other nations polled. In 2010 only pluralities expressed a lack of confidence in bin Laden in Pakistan (45 to 18 percent) and in Malaysia (37 to 32 percent). In Morocco, polled in late 2006, a plurality expressed a lack of confidence (32 to 20 percent), however, a remarkably large 48 percent did not provide an answer, suggesting ambivalence.

As in other polls, the only country to have a majority expressing confidence in bin Laden was in the Palestinian Territories. Polled in 2009, 52 percent expressed confidence, down a bit from 2007, when 57 percent did so.

The United States as a Greater Threat than Radical Islamists

As touched on in chapter 3, the most problematic aspect of Muslim responses to radical Islamists, especially al Qaeda, is that the narrative of the threat from the United States generally supersedes the narrative of the threat from radical Islamists. Because radical Islamists are often seen as a counterforce to the United States, it prompts more positive views of al Qaeda or at least mitigates what negative views might otherwise be present. This response was well articulated in one of the focus groups.

> R1. The Muslims and Arabs feel that America is stealing their resources, and this is not in their favor. The Arab people dislike the American policy, and they find al Qaeda fighting against America. So it is very likely that al Qaeda will have many supporters within the Arab region and the Middle East.
> MODERATOR. Are you among the supporters?
> R2. I don't support al Qaeda itself, but when I see America interfering in Iraq and I find resistance from Al Qaeda, I will be emotionally more drawn towards al Qaeda.

A WPO poll asked Muslims in 2009 to characterize the level of threat in the next ten years they perceive from al Qaeda and U.S. military power (figure 7-9). In three of the four countries, more respondents said U.S. power is a critical threat than said so of al Qaeda (61 to 42 percent in Egypt, 50 to 20 percent in Bangladesh, and 47 to 40 percent in Turkey). The exception was in Indonesia, where 39 percent said the United States is a critical threat and 60 percent said the same of al Qaeda.

In addition to questions about the threat from al Qaeda, respondents in the same countries were asked about local radical Islamist groups. Respondents in two countries judged the local groups as less of a critical threat than U.S. military power (61 percent for the United States and 36 percent for al Gama'a Islamiyya in Egypt, 47 percent for the United States and

FIGURE 7-9.　The U.S. and al Qaeda as Critical Threats

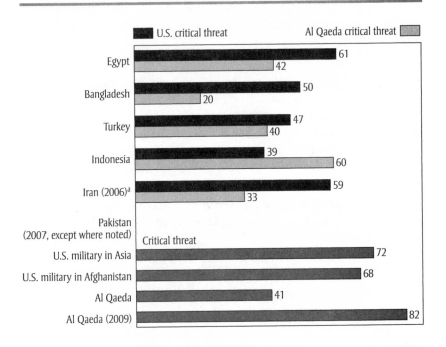

Source: WorldPublicOpinion.org, 2009.
a. Iranians asked to evaluate "U.S. foreign policy" as threat.

32 percent for Islam Buyukdogu Akincilar Cephesi in Turkey). In Indonesia, just as with al Qaeda, more judged that local group Jemaah Islamiah was a critical threat (48 percent) than the United States (39 percent). Bangladeshi opinion on its local radical Islamist group was markedly different than on al Qaeda, as more judged Jama'at-ul Mujahideen Bangladesh (also called Jagrata Muslim Janata Bangladesh) a critical threat (68 percent) than U.S. military power (50 percent).

These perceptions do appear to shift if radical Islamists overplay their hand, as was the case in Pakistan. As was discussed in chapter 3, when Pakistanis were polled in the fall of 2007 about "religious militant groups" and "Islamist militants and local Taliban in Federally Administered Tribal Areas (FATA) and settled areas," 41 percent perceived religious militant groups as a critical threat, and 34 percent perceived militants and Taliban in FATA and settled areas likewise. The U.S. military presence in Asia and the U.S. military presence in Afghanistan were considered critical threats, however, by 72 percent and 68 percent, respectively, in 2007. Then in May 2009, after the Pakistani Taliban advanced into the Swat area, close to the capital, views shifted sharply. Religious militants in general and Islamic militants operating in Pakistan came to be seen as a critical threat by eight in ten. Interestingly, perceptions of al Qaeda as a critical threat also jumped from 41 percent in 2007 to 82 percent in 2009. Thus it appears that when the perceived threat from one Islamic source breaks out of the narrative of the U.S. threat, this effect generalizes to other Islamic threats as well.

With time, though, this effect can diminish. While in 2009 Pew found that a majority of Pakistanis (57 percent) said the Taliban was a "very serious" threat, these numbers drifted down to 34 percent by 2010. Likewise, the perception of al Qaeda as a serious threat dropped from 41 percent in 2009 to 21 percent in 2010.

8 *What Do Muslims Want?*

As has been explored in previous chapters, many Muslims believe that the United States acts to inhibit their nations from becoming what their citizens want them to be. Through explicit or implicit use of coercive threats, America is seen as preventing Muslim nations from acting independently and from finding a social order that is compatible with their Islamic values as well as their interests. U.S. support for governments that suppress Islamist groups has contributed to this perception. As discussed, this perception plays a very important role in feeding anger at America because the internal conflict—between traditional Islamist and liberalizing forces within Muslim society and within many Muslim individuals—becomes externalized in the relationship between the Muslim world and the United States. This dynamic gives al Qaeda more room to maneuver. Rather than representing an extreme end of the spectrum in an internal debate within Muslim society, al Qaeda may be seen as protecting Muslim society from outside forces that seek to undermine the Islamic basis of Muslim society. The perception of the United States as an oppressor also feeds the narrative that the United States promotes the liberal idea of democracy, but then betrays the Muslim people by denying it to them. Others in the world are not seen as betrayed in this way, thus enhancing the perception that the United States has abandoned the principle of religious tolerance when it comes to Islam.

The perception that the United States resists giving the Muslim people full democratic control over their fate is not entirely without foundation. Many American policymakers have expressed concerns about giving the Muslim people full democratic control for fear that they might elect radical Islamist leaders who would phase out democratic institutions and establish a theocratic state. In a Congressional Research Service report, Jeremy Sharp writes of "a long vexing dilemma for U.S. policymakers. . . . Should the United States exert pressure on Arab governments to open their political systems and respect human rights with the knowledge that Islamists, the most popular opposition force in Arab politics, stand to benefit from regional democratization?" He goes on to explain, "Since the 1979 Iranian Revolution, the U.S. government has increasingly believed that, should Islamist groups come to power, they would pursue a more confrontational approach in their foreign policy toward the United States and that key strategic interests would suffer, including access to oil reserves, military cooperation, and the security of Israel, among others.[1]

As mentioned previously, such concerns prompted the United States to quietly acquiesce when the Algerian military in 1991 ignored the results of the election in which an Islamist party appeared to be poised to take control of the government. And more recently, such concerns prompted the Bush administration, in response to electoral successes of Hamas and Egyptian candidates associated with the Muslim Brotherhood, to back away from a renewed commitment to democracy in the region.

Some American analysts have argued that once in power, Islamists would eliminate all liberal concepts of human rights, isolate themselves from and take a hostile stance toward the non-Muslim world, and establish an expansionist revolutionary goal to first restore the *ummah* (a unified world Muslim community) and then to spread Islam around the world. All of these goals have indeed been articulated by radical Islamist leaders. And to the extent that Muslims show some sympathy for such radical Islamist ideas and leaders, it is natural to worry that, over time, they could cede more and more power to a theocratic elite that claims to be the true arbiter of what is truly Islamic. Others, though, have argued that liberal ideas are so well established in Muslim society that it is not feasible for Islamic fundamentalists to impose such an extreme order on the population.

This chapter addresses these issues, answering the broad question of what kind of social order Muslims want by exploring the following specific questions:

—What do Muslims think should be the basis for laws—democracy or Islamic law?

—How do they feel about ostensibly moderate Islamist organizations and parties such as the Muslim Brotherhood, who claim to be democratic as well as Islamist, and how do they perceive the agendas of these organizations?

—Do Muslims support a liberal approach to human rights?

—Do they want to integrate with the larger world or isolate themselves from the non-Muslim world?

—Do they have international Islamic revolutionary aspirations, or do they support a liberal and pluralistic model of world order?

The answers to each of these questions is not simple. Most Muslims endorse both Islamist and liberal principles, even though they may seem contradictory from a Western perspective. The struggle to reconcile these different ideas generates instability within individual Muslims and, at times, seeming confusion.

The responses point to two key conclusions with policy import. One is that in no majority-Muslim country is the general public likely to willingly acquiesce to a totalitarian fundamentalist Islamist government because liberal ideas are too deeply rooted. The other is that in no country are the Muslim people likely to abandon their desire to have Islam be part of the public sphere and accept the Western model of religion as a largely private experience with the public sphere as predominantly secular.

The Basis of Law: Democracy and Islam

Numerous polls have found abundant majorities supporting democracy in majority-Muslim countries, including the broad principle that the will of the people should be the basis for the authority of government. At the same time, most say that democracy and Islam are compatible, even when presented with the radical Islamist argument that they are not. Asked specific questions about the role of sharia and the clergy in government, respondents give complex and sometimes seemingly contradictory responses, suggesting inner conflict.

Support for Democracy

Large majorities say that "a democratic political system" is a good way of governing their own country in a variety of polls. In WorldPublic

Opinion.org (WPO) polling conducted from 2006 to 2007, majorities endorsed this position in Egypt (83 percent), Indonesia (64 percent), Morocco (61 percent), and Pakistan (51 percent). A 2006 Arab Barometer poll found majorities taking this position in Morocco (90 percent), Kuwait (88 percent), the Palestinian Territories (85 percent), Jordan (81 percent), and Algeria (69 percent). In World Values Survey (WVS) polling of eight majority-Muslim countries conducted between 2005 and 2008, overwhelming majorities voiced support for a democratic political system, including 98 percent in Egypt, 92 percent in Malaysia, 91 percent in Indonesia and Iran, 90 percent in Jordan, 84 percent in Morocco, 83 percent in Turkey, and 76 percent in Iraq. While many polls have found majorities endorsing democracy, these numbers for Muslim countries are on the upper end of the spectrum.

Several polls also found large majorities agreeing with the statement, "Democracy may have its problems, but it is better than any other form of government." In WVS surveys of thirteen majority-Muslim countries from 1999 to 2004, majorities in all but one county agreed with the statement. These majorities included 94 percent of Bangladeshis, 91 percent of Egyptians, 89 percent of Albanians, 80 percent of Pakistanis, 79 percent of Turks, 76 percent of Jordanians, 75 percent of Algerians, 74 percent of Kyrgyzstanis, 68 percent of Iraqis, 62 percent of Indonesians and Saudis, and 58 percent of Moroccans. Iran was the exception, where a plurality of 42 percent concurred (though in more recent polls Iranians have expressed strong support for democracy—see below). Majorities in all five of the countries polled by Arab Barometer in 2006 agreed that democracy is better than any other form of government, including in Morocco (85 percent), Kuwait (82 percent), the Palestinian Terroritories (79 percent), Jordan (74 percent), and Algeria (69 percent). Responses to this question in majority-Muslim nations were similar to the responses found in non-Muslim nations.[2]

Similarly, living in a democratically governed country is considered very important to most Muslims. A WVS poll asked respondents in seven majority-Muslim countries to rank the importance of living in a democratically governed country on a scale from 1 ("not at all important") to 10 ("absolutely important"). Majorities in Turkey (55 percent) and Morocco (55 percent) and large majorities in Jordan (75 percent) and Egypt (70 percent) considered living in a democratic country a 10, or "absolutely important." Means in five of the seven countries were 8.5 or higher, with a mean of 7.9 in both Iran and Malaysia.

When a 2007 Pew survey presented two statements about democracy, including that democracy is a "Western way of doing things that would not work here," majorities still opted for the position that "democracy is not just for the West and can work well here." This included majorities in nine of eleven nations polled, including Kuwait (81 percent), Lebanon (79 percent), Jordan (70 percent), Malaysia (69 percent), Bangladesh (67 percent), the Palestinian Territories (60 percent), Egypt (59 percent), Indonesia (58 percent), and Morocco (57 percent). Exceptions were found in Pakistan, where a plurality (48 percent) said democracy could work there, and Turkey, where a plurality (50 percent) said that democracy is a Western way of doing things that could not work in that country.

The 2006 Arab Barometer poll found majorities or pluralities in five majority-Muslim countries rejecting the critiques that "in a democracy, the economy runs badly" and that "democracies are not good at maintaining order." When asked in the same poll, however, whether "democracies are indecisive and have too much quibbling," views were mixed, with a slim majority in the Palestinian Territories (51 percent) and a plurality in Algeria (45 percent) agreeing with the statement while a majority in Morocco (70 percent) and a plurality in Kuwait (48 percent) disagreed. Views were divided in Jordan.

Very large majorities agree with the core democratic principle that "the will of the people should be the basis of the authority of government," even though this phrasing might have elicited the counteridea that Islamic law as revealed to the prophet Muhammad should instead be the basis, as radical Islamists have argued. In a 2008 WPO poll of seven majority-Muslim nations, majorities in all cases agreed with the statement, ranging from 67 percent of Iranians to 98 percent of Egyptians. (See figure 8-1.) Such views are typical around the world. Majorities in all twenty-one nations polled agreed, though Iran was among the lowest.

Similarly, on a question in the same poll asking respondents to rate how much their country should be governed according to the will of the people on a scale of 0 ("not at all") to 10 ("completely"), the mean response was above 5 in all majority-Muslim nations, ranging from 6.6 in Jordan to 8.7 in Indonesia.

Selecting leaders through elections gets very strong support. In the 2008 WPO survey, large majorities in all seven majority-Muslim countries polled said that government leaders should be selected through elections in which all citizens can vote. This ranged from 71 percent in Jor-

FIGURE 8-1. Will of the People

The will of the people should be the basis of the authority of government.

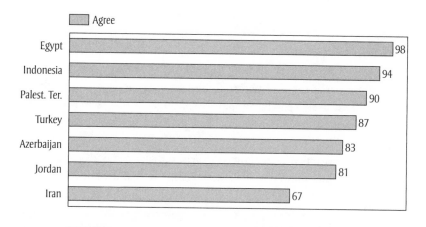

Source: WorldPublicOpinion.org, 2008.

dan to 97 percent in Indonesia. Again, these views were typical of views globally.[3] "Ensuring free elections" was rated as important by 87 percent of Iranians in a 2009 Terror Free Tomorrow poll. In a 2007 Terror Free Tomorrow poll, 79 percent of Saudis rated "ensuring a free press and free elections" as important. WVS polling from 2005 to 2008 that included eight majority-Muslim nations asked respondents to consider the importance of people "choos[ing] their leaders in free elections" on a scale from 1 ("not at all essential") to 10 ("an essential characteristic of democracy"). In seven of the eight nations polled, the mean responses were 8.2 or higher. Malaysia was the exception, with a mean of 7.1. These responses showed little variance with responses in non-Muslim countries.

WPO asked Iranians in December 2006 to rate how important it is to live in a country governed by representatives elected by the people on a scale from 1 ("not at all important") to 10 ("absolutely important"). The mean response was 9.1, with 68 percent of respondents giving a rating of 10.

Muslims also see civil rights as essential to democracy. In the WVS poll of eight majority-Muslim countries from 2005 to 2008, respondents rated "civil rights [to] protect people's liberty against oppression" as essential to democracy. Majorities in Indonesia and Egypt rated such civil rights with a score of 10. Responses in the eight countries together averaged 8.0, with large majorities in most individual nations rating them 8 or higher. Morocco and Malaysia were the two exceptions. In Morocco a slim majority (51 percent) rated civil rights 8 or higher, and in Malaysia, where the mean was 6.5, only 33 percent rated them 8 or more. These were also typical answers globally.

Similarly, a Terror Free Tomorrow poll of Pakistanis in 2008 found an overwhelming majority (94 percent) saying that an independent judiciary was important, and very large majorities underlined the importance of ensuring a free press (83 percent) and protecting civil society groups (68 percent).

When the option of a strong authoritarian leader is also presented, support for democracy is not as strong, but is still a majority in most cases. Asked in a 2007 Pew poll if they would opt for "a democratic form of government" or would rather "rely on a leader with a strong hand," majorities in seven of the ten countries polled preferred a democratic form of government, including large majorities in Bangladesh (79 percent) and Kuwait (65 percent). Majorities in favor of democracy were modest in Malaysia (54 percent) and Jordan (52 percent). A majority of Palestinians (52 percent) and a plurality in Pakistanis (46 percent), however, favored a strong leader, and in Indonesia and Egypt, views were divided. Internationally, majority-Muslim nations, together with former Soviet and Warsaw Pact states, stood out in their relatively higher support for an authoritarian government. Further, when a five-country 2006 Arab Barometer poll asked about "a strong *nondemocratic* leader that does not bother with parliament and elections," (emphasis added) majorities rejected the idea in the Palestinian Territories (83 percent), Kuwait (80 percent), Algeria (75 percent), Morocco (73 percent), and Jordan (63 percent). Though a "strong hand" may be attractive to some, an explicitly nondemocratic leader goes too far.

Are Democracy and Islam Compatible?

For the most part, Muslims tend to say that democracy and Islam are compatible, even when presented with the radical Islamist argument that they are not. Significant minorities, however, disagree, and in Turkey this is sometimes a majority.

In a 2009 WPO poll respondents in four Muslim countries were asked whether they agree with the statement, "Democracy is compatible with

What Do Muslims Want?*   153

Islam." They were also asked whether they agree with arguments made by some radical Islamists that "democracy is not compatible with Islam; it makes people the source of law rather than the Quran" and that "democracy is not compatible with Islam; it makes people the ultimate sovereign rather than God."

In Egypt and Indonesia overwhelming majorities agreed with the statement that democracy is compatible with Islam (91 percent and 83 percent, respectively). In response to the radical Islamist arguments, majorities rejected them, though in somewhat fewer numbers (ranging from 67 to 72 percent). This suggests that the arguments did have traction with some people.

Curiously, among Bangladeshis, relatively large majorities rejected the radical Islamist arguments (59 to 64 percent), but only a bare majority (51 percent) agreed that democracy is compatible with Islam. This suggests that some may have rejected the radical Islamist arguments while still being uncertain as to whether democracy and Islam are compatible. A rather large 45 percent disagreed that they are compatible, with 31 to 38 percent agreeing with the arguments, saying they are incompatible because they make "people" central.

In Turkey more said that democracy and Islam are not compatible. For some Turks this was probably driven more by a secularist view than an Islamist view. When a majority (58 percent) agreed with the argument that democracy is not compatible with Islam because it makes people the source of law, some respondents may have been speaking from a secularist perspective. A plurality (45 percent) also agreed that democracy and Islam are incompatible because democracy makes people the ultimate sovereign.

Arab Barometer in 2006 presented the argument that "democracy is a Western form of government that is not compatible with Islam" in five majority-Muslim nations. Majorities in all cases disagreed with the statement, ranging from 55 percent in Algeria to 75 percent in Kuwait. Nonetheless, substantial minorities agreed in the Palestinian Territories (32 percent), Jordan (27 percent), Algeria (25 percent), Morocco (17 percent), and Kuwait (19 percent).

Should Islam Play a Role in Government?

The question of whether Islam should play a role in government elicits a complex set of responses that are somewhat dissonant, at times even seemingly contradictory. This reflects again the internal conflict between liberalism and Islamism among many Muslims. As discussed in previous chapters, the debate continues between the moderate Islamist view that government should be based on a form of democracy specific to Islam (including, for example, the vetting of laws by Islamic scholars) and the more liberal view that government should be based on a universal form of democracy.

To probe views on this issue, WPO posed these alternatives—as well as the radical option of not having democracy at all—to respondents in seven nations in 2009. Only very small numbers rejected democracy. Views were mixed on the other alternatives. In three countries majorities favored a form of democracy unique to Islamic countries: Egypt (60 percent), Pakistan (54 percent), and Iraq (51 percent). Larger majorities in four nations favored government based on universal principles of democracy: Indonesia (71 percent), Bangladesh (67 percent), Azerbaijan (65 percent), and Turkey (63 percent). Palestinians were divided, with 50 percent favoring a unique system and 47 percent favoring a system based on universal principles.

When Muslims were asked questions about whether religion should be a private matter or play a role in government, responses varied strongly depending on subtle differences in the wording. When WPO in 2009 presented the Islamist argument that "Islam should play a central role in the government," overwhelming majorities agreed in Egypt (92 percent), Indonesia (86 percent), and Bangladesh (82 percent). Even in Turkey a substantial number (37 percent) agreed, though 53 percent disagreed. When the International Republican Institute (IRI) asked Pakistanis in August 2009 to what extent religion should play a role in politics, 86 percent said it should play the dominant role (50 percent) or some role (36 percent). Only 12 percent said it should play no role.

At the same time, Muslims tend to embrace the liberal principle that religion should be a private matter. Asked by Pew in 2007 whether they agreed that "religion is a matter of personal faith and should be kept separate from government policy," large majorities agreed in Lebanon (88 percent), Turkey (86 percent), Pakistan (73 percent), Indonesia (72 percent), Kuwait (72 percent), Morocco (68 percent), and Malaysia (62 percent), along with a significant majority in the Palestinian Territories (56 percent). Only in Jordan did a slight majority disagree (53 percent), and in Egypt views were divided.

A question asked by WPO in 2009 that was worded slightly differently, however, elicited a significantly more varied response. Asked whether they agreed that "religion should be a private matter; it should not play a role in government," majorities agreed in Turkey (77 percent) and Bangladesh (67 percent), but a large majority disagreed in Indonesia (74 percent), as did a majority in Egypt (54 percent).

Views were also mixed, but with lesser variance, when Arab Barometer asked respondents in 2006 whether they agreed that "religious practice is a private matter and should be separated from sociopolitical life." A slim majority of Kuwaitis (51 percent) and Jordanians (51 percent) agreed. Moroccans were divided. Small majorities of Algerians (52 percent) and a plurality of Palestinians (50 percent) disagreed.

Another area of complexity is whether Muslims feel Islam should be the official religion of their country. WPO 2009 polling found very large majorities agreed that it should in Egypt (85 percent), Bangladesh (81 percent), Turkey (69 percent), and Indonesia (58 percent). When presented with the liberal counterargument, however, that "our government should not make Islam the official religion because this would be unfair to citizens of [the country] who are not Muslim," this elicited mixed responses. Majorities disagreed in Bangladesh (80 percent) and Egypt (57 percent), but a majority of Indonesians agreed (56 percent), and Turks were divided.

A related question asked whether non-Muslims should be allowed to run for public office or specifically for president. Allowing non-Muslims to run for any public office was rejected only by Pakistanis (an overwhelming 91 percent) and, surprisingly, Turks (51 percent). Majorities said that non-Muslims should be allowed to run for public office in Bangladesh (87 percent), Indonesia (71 percent), Egypt (66 percent), Azerbaijan (61 percent), Iraq (59 percent), and the Palestinian Territories (57 percent). Support for allowing a non-Muslim to be president, however, was much lower. It was only clearly favored by Bangladeshis (83 percent) and Indonesians (55 percent). In all other six nations support ranged from only 4 percent in Pakistan to 36 percent in Egypt.

The Role of Sharia

Another source of tension is the question of whether sharia or the will of the people should be the basis for law. Radical Islamists insist that sharia should be the sole source and that democracy contradicts Islam because it creates another source of law. Polls reveal that most Muslims want sharia to play a central role in their legal system, while also wanting to pursue liberal democratic principles. As with views on the role of religion, majorities respond affirmatively to poll questions on both sides of the issue, suggesting inner conflict.

When Muslims are presented with the idea of having a strict application of sharia in the context of a radical Islamist agenda, most support it. WPO asked respondents in polling from 2006 to 2009 how they feel about al Qaeda's goal "to require a strict application of sharia law in every country." Large majorities endorsed this view in Bangladesh (81 percent), Morocco (76 percent), Pakistan (76 percent), Egypt (71 percent), and Indonesia (56 percent). A plurality (46 percent) of Turks agreed, while 32 percent disagreed, and many did not take a position.

A more complex response was evident in a series of Arab Barometer questions in 2006 that asked respondents in five nations to evaluate certain "principles as a guide for making the laws of our country." When presented with the strongly stated Islamist argument that "the government should implement *only* the laws of the sharia" (emphasis added), this elicited large majority support (86 percent in Morocco, 80 percent in Algeria, 80 percent in Jordan, 77 percent in Kuwait, and 55 percent in the Palestinian Territories). Yet when the same poll presented the liberal argument that "the government and parliament should make laws according to the wishes of the people," majorities in all five countries also agreed, though in most cases by a lesser margin (82 percent in Morocco, 62 percent in Kuwait, and 59 percent in Algeria, Jordan, and the Palestinian Territories).

When offered the position that "the government and parliament should make laws according to the wishes of the people in some areas and implement sharia in others," this also elicited majority agreement from all nations polled. Majorities ranged from 64 percent of Palestinians to 85 percent of Moroccans. (See figure 8-2.)

While these responses appear to quite contradictory, the idea that democracy and sharia are compatible is a well developed idea in the Islamic world. The Muslim Brotherhood, among other Islamist groups, regularly makes this case. Such groups point to the model of Western democracies, where there is a constitution that puts constraints on what the democratically elected government can do. Sharia, they argue, is simply a more elaborate constitution. Radical Islamists, though, reject this

FIGURE 8-2. Principles Guiding Lawmaking

The government should implement only the laws of the sharia.

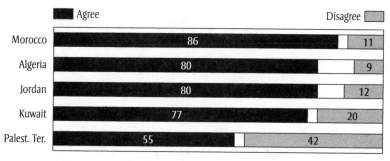

The government and parliament should make laws according to the wishes of the people.

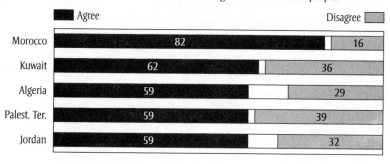

The government and parliament should make laws according to the wishes of the people in some areas and implement sharia in others.

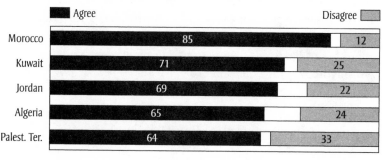

Source: Arab Barometer, 2006.

view in favor of sharia being the sole source, effectively putting the power in the hands of Islamic scholars and the clergy. Yet the fact that majorities embrace all three alternatives—the radical Islamist view that the government should implement *only* the laws of sharia, the liberal view that the wishes of the people should govern, and the moderate view that both should play a role—suggests that many individuals have not really resolved this issue.

In contrast to the Arab Barometer question that asked respondents to evaluate each option in separate questions, Gallup asked respondents in ten nations in 2005 to choose one of three different options for the role of sharia in regard to legislation. The most common position was the moderate view that sharia "must be a source of legislation, but not the only source" (65 percent in Morocco, 63 percent in Iran, 59 percent in Indonesia, and 57 percent in Bangladesh and Lebanon). Only in Turkey did a majority take the purely secular view that sharia "should not be a source of legislation."

Three nations had a majority taking the radical Islamist position that sharia "must be the only source of legislation" (65 percent in Egypt, 59 percent in Pakistan, and 54 percent in Jordan). As noted, however, other polls from these countries reveal support for democratic principles. Thus a positive response to this position does not necessarily mean that majorities are radical Islamists, but, more likely, that their attitudes are not well integrated.

Views are also mixed on the question of whether sharia should play a larger role than it does today, though in no country does a substantial number say it should play a smaller role. Asked by WPO in polling from 2008 to 2009 whether sharia should play "a larger role, a smaller role, or about the same role as it plays today" in the way their country is governed, a majority of Egyptians (57 percent) favored a greater role, as did a plurality of Pakistanis (46 percent). In Bangladesh a majority (52 percent) favored "about the same role," with 14 percent favoring a larger role. "About the same role" was also the favored response in Indonesia (45 percent), with 32 percent favoring a larger role.

Naturally, the question arises of what people mean when they say they favor sharia playing a role in government, and especially when they say they want it to play a greater role. WPO polling in 2008 asked those who wanted a larger role for sharia in the governance of their country what aspects of sharia were important for the government to apply. Respondents were asked four questions about social, moralistic, and punitive aspects of sharia.

In Egypt moralistic and punitive aspects of sharia rated a bit above the social aspect. Larger majorities both wanted a larger role for sharia and rated moralistic and punitive aspects as "very important"—"policing moral behavior" (68 percent), "applying traditional punishments for crimes such as stoning adulterers" (64 percent), and "policing women's dress" (62 percent)—than rated "providing welfare to the poor" (59 percent) as "very important."

In Indonesia, however, where only about one-quarter wanted a larger role for sharia, the social aspect got somewhat more emphasis from this group than the moralistic and punitive aspects. Those that wanted a larger role for sharia and stressed the importance of providing welfare to the poor (24 percent) were greater than those stressing the importance of policing moral behavior (21 percent), policing women's dress (19 percent), and applying traditional punishments (15 percent).

In Pakistan, where a bit under half wanted a larger role for sharia, 36 percent said providing welfare to the poor is a very important aspect of sharia for the government to apply. Thirty-two percent said this about women's dress, 29 percent said this about moral behavior, and 26 percent said this about applying traditional punishments. Regarding punishments, however, when Pakistanis were asked directly about them by Pew in 2010, without the explicit context of sharia, large majorities supported traditional and severe punishments.[4]

In another WPO poll in Iran in 2008, those who supported a larger or about the same role for sharia were asked a follow-up series of questions about the importance of different elements of sharia. Large majorities said five of the six aspects asked about were "very" or "somewhat" important. This included 68 percent for providing welfare to the poor, 68 percent for making health care and education available to all, 67 percent for punishing those who drink alcoholic drinks in public, 67 percent for punishing usury, 65 percent for policing moral behavior such as gambling and prostitution. The only aspect without a majority was applying severe physical punishments to people convicted of certain crimes, though 50 percent still considered this either "very" or "somewhat" important.

On the role of females, a WPO poll of Pakistanis in 2009 found that an overwhelming majority did not think that sharia forbids girls education or women working. Eighty-three percent said sharia allowed for girls going to school, and 75 percent said it allowed for women working.

Polls of Arab countries have found respondents struggling with the challenge of integrating Islamic traditions with modern business. On the one hand, five out of six Arab publics polled in a 2005 Zogby survey favored business operations being governed by sharia law, with Lebanon being the only dissenter. Support ranged from a plurality of 39 percent in Jordan to 82 percent in Saudi Arabia. In Lebanon, however, 67 percent of the overall population was opposed as well as 60 percent of the Muslim population. In addition, large majorities in five Arab nations polled by Arab Barometer in 2006 agreed with the statement, "Banks in Muslim countries must be forbidden from charging even modest interest on loans because this is forbidden by Islam," ranging from 66 percent in Kuwait to 82 percent in the Palestinian Territories.

At the same time, the Zogby poll found that majorities or pluralities in all six countries it polled believed that "sharia law require[s] further interpretation to allow businesses in the Muslim world to integrate into the global economy." These numbers ranged from 40 percent in Egypt to 78 percent in the United Arab Emirates.

The Role of Religious Scholars and the Clergy

Another key debate in the Muslim world centers on the role of religious scholars and the clergy in government. While some take the liberal position that religion and state should be separate, many Islamists, including moderate ones, favor an explicit role for Islam. This necessarily implies the participation of religious scholars and the clergy in government to interpret whether Islam is being properly applied. Such a system is in place in Iran. Some Islamists defend this position as being essentially the same as having a supreme court that has the power to overturn laws that are unconstitutional.

WPO polled this issue in 2009 by asking people in nine nations to choose between the Islamist position that "there should be a body of senior religious scholars that has the power to overturn laws when it believes they are contrary to the Quran" and the liberal position that "if laws are passed by democratically elected officials and are consistent with the constitution, they should not be subject to a veto by religious scholars." Majorities in six of the nine nations polled agreed with the Islamist position, including in Egypt (75 percent), Pakistan (66 percent), Iraq (63 per-

FIGURE 8-3. Islamic Clerics Reviewing Laws

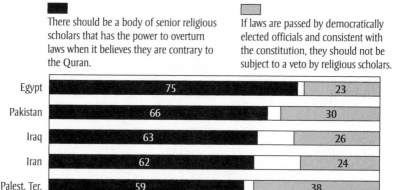

There should be a body of senior religious scholars that has the power to overturn laws when it believes they are contrary to the Quran.

If laws are passed by democratically elected officials and consistent with the constitution, they should not be subject to a veto by religious scholars.

Country	Overturn	Liberal
Egypt	75	23
Pakistan	66	30
Iraq	63	26
Iran	62	24
Palest. Ter.	59	38
Indonesia	54	29
Turkey	35	50
Bangladesh	31	66
Azerbaijan	6	70

Source: WorldPublicOpinion.org, 2009.

cent), Iran (62 percent), the Palestinian Territories (59 percent), and Indonesia (54 percent). Three publics agreed with the liberal position—majorities in Azerbaijan (70 percent) and Bangladesh (66 percent) and a plurality in Turkey (50 percent). (See figure 8-3.)

When WVS presented separately the liberal argument that "religious leaders should not influence government," majorities agreed in Turkey (62 percent), Jordan (59 percent), and Indonesia (54 percent), though not in Malaysia (46 percent), Iran (44 percent), or Morocco (31 percent). Compared to non-majority-Mulim countries where WVS also asked this question, majority-Muslim nations were substantially less likely to agree that religious leaders should not influence government. There were a few notable exceptions, however, including the United States, where views on this question were divided.

When the 2006 Arab Barometer poll presented a similar argument that "men of religion should have no influence over the decisions of government," majorities agreed in Morocco (58 percent) and the Palestinian

Territories (55 percent) as well as a plurality in Algeria (47 percent). Majorities disagreed in Kuwait (56 percent), and views were divided in Jordan.

The Case of Iraq

After the Baathist regime in Iraq was toppled in 2003, the Iraqi people faced the unique circumstance of trying to define what kind of government they wanted. A fairly extensive amount of polling was conducted at the time, providing a unique window on the interplay between Islamist and liberal ideas about governance.

Support for democracy was quite strong. In Gallup's spring 2004 poll, 84 percent said that what Iraq needs is "an Iraqi democracy." In IRI's April 2005 poll, 72 percent said they would prefer that the president be selected by "direct elections by the Iraqi people." Just 13 percent favored the president being appointed "by a national assembly," and only 5 percent "by clerics or religious leaders."

The 2005 IRI poll also asked Iraqis what they thought would be the most appropriate system for a future Iraqi government. Only 22 percent said they would prefer a "religious system" in Iraq. A strong majority of 63 percent said they would prefer either a "parliamentary" (30 percent) or a "mixed parliamentary/presidential" (33 percent) system.

The 2004 Gallup poll asked Iraqis to choose among seven forms of government. A mere 12 percent chose "an Islamic theocracy in which religious leaders or mullahs have a strong influence such as in Iran." Virtually none endorsed the model of the former Taliban regime in Afghanistan. The most popular single model, endorsed by 40 percent, was for "a multiparty democracy such as that in most European and some Asian countries." On a separate question, only 22 percent said that what Iraq needs is a government "made up mostly of religious leaders."

Perhaps most telling, most Iraqis rejected the idea of clerics actually being part of the government. A January 2005 poll by IRI asked Iraqis about "the role of religious leaders in politics and government." Only 28 percent endorsed the view that religious leaders should be "elected to political office and serve in government." The plurality (39 percent) opted for the view that religious leaders may endorse candidates, but not serve in office—not unlike the way the popular and influential Ayatollah Ali al-Sistani of Najaf seems to function today. Twenty-three percent favored religious leaders remaining separate from political life and instead "focusing on spiritual and social life."

Another question in the spring 2004 Gallup poll asked whether "religious leaders themselves—rather than government officials—should be directly in charge" of eight different government functions. For all eight functions only small minorities favored religious leaders being directly in charge of them, including drafting or determining:

—Iraq's next constitution (24 percent)

—National legislation to which all Iraqis would be subject (21 percent)

—Secular family law (17 percent)

—What may be broadcast on television or published in newspapers (15 percent)

—Who may run for elected office (15 percent)

—How women may dress in public (15 percent)

—What will be taught in the country's schools (13 percent)

—Iraq's foreign policy and its relations with other countries (13 percent)

Consistent with this opposition to direct clerical involvement in government, most Iraqis did not feel compelled to follow the views of clerics on political matters. In a December 2004 IRI poll, only 33 percent said they would "follow all decrees issued by clerics concerning the elections."

A majority also supported protection of the rights of non-Muslims. In the spring 2004 Gallup poll, 73 percent said that the Iraqi constitution should guarantee the right of Iraqi citizens to observe any religion of their choice. The April 2005 poll by IRI asked which rights should be part of the constitution. An overwhelming 90 percent said "freedom to practice religion." A remarkable 91 percent also agreed (68 percent "strongly") that "basic human rights" should be part of the constitution.

Concurrent with this widespread support for liberal, democratic principles, most Iraqis also expressed support for religion playing a central role in the Iraqi government. Most rejected the notion of a pure separation of church and state. In the spring 2004 Gallup poll, Iraqis were told that "there is a notion, which calls for the separation of religion from political government." They were then asked whether they supported or opposed this notion. A majority of 58 percent opposed this notion, with 31 percent supporting it.

Overwhelming majorities supported having Islam be the moral basis for the Iraqi legal system. In an August 2004 IRI poll, 84 percent agreed (70 percent "strongly") that "the new Iraqi constitution should take

Islam and the sharia as the sole basis for all laws and legislation." The April 2005 IRI poll found that three out of four Iraqis thought Islam should be "the sole source" (35 percent) or "the main source" (40 percent) in the creation of laws and legislation. Only 12 percent said Islam should be only "one source," and a mere 2 percent said that laws and legislation "should not be based on any religious source."

Overwhelming majorities endorsed the view that Iraq should be an Islamic state. Eighty-eight percent agreed in the August 2004 IRI poll that the "new Iraqi constitution should ensure the Islamic identity of Iraq." In the April poll 92 percent agreed that "the new constitution should make Islam the official religion."

Finally, though Iraqis did not want clerics to serve in government, they did think that clerics should play a key role in shaping outcomes. In March 2005 IRI asked, "In writing the constitution, whose input do you feel should be most important in creating a document that is acceptable to the Iraqi people?" A 59 percent majority of Iraqis chose clerics or religious leaders as their first (47 percent) or second choice (12 percent), outstripping the 30 percent who chose political party representatives (16 percent first choice, 14 percent second choice) and the 26 percent who chose the prime minister (10 percent first choice, 16 percent second choice).

As mentioned above, in the spring 2004 Gallup poll only small minorities favored clerics being directly in charge of eight specified government functions. Very large majorities, however, favored them advising government officials holding these responsibilities.

Also, though most Iraqis said they would not feel compelled to adhere to clerics' decrees on electoral matters, only 13 percent said they would ignore them when polled by IRI in December 2004. Three out of four said they would at least "listen to what clerics have to say" (25 percent), that the "guidance of clerics or religious organizations will be a major factor in their participation in the elections" (16 percent), or that they would "follow all decrees issued by the clerics about elections" (33 percent).

Ostensibly Moderate Islamist Movements and Parties

Throughout the Muslim world there are Islamist parties and movements that claim to be moderate. While they seek to make their societies more Islamic and to have sharia play a central role in the legal structure, they claim they are also democratic and nonviolent. Paramount is the Muslim

Brotherhood, which operates in many Muslim countries. But in most nations there are also local Islamist parties, some of which were originally spawned by the Muslim Brotherhood.

Moderate Islamism is highly controversial. Some argue that the very concept is a misnomer, that Islamism is inherently radical and even revolutionary and that moderate Islamists should not be allowed to participate in elections because their ultimate goals are not democratic. Others argue that such parties are indeed democratic or that they pose no threat and should be allowed to participate. Meanwhile radical Islamists denounce moderate Islamists as having departed from true Islamist principles by agreeing to participate in democratic processes.

As is explored below, polls reveal that majorities in most nations favor allowing Islamist parties to participate in elections. Views of the Muslim Brotherhood and local Islamist parties vary highly between countries, both in terms of their favorability and whether their ultimate goals are indeed democratic. Very few Muslims, however, appear to be looking to Islamist parties as a pathway to a nondemocratic Islamist state.

Democratic Participation of Islamist Parties

It appears that most in the Islamic world support the idea of Islamist parties being free to compete in elections. In WPO polling of eight nations in 2008 to 2009, respondents were reminded that "in some countries there is a debate about whether Islamist political groups should be allowed to organize parties and run candidates in elections." They were then asked to choose between two statements:

—All people should have the right to organize themselves into political parties and run candidates, including Islamist groups.

—Islamist groups should not be allowed to organize and run candidates because their ultimate goals are not consistent with democracy. (See figure 8-4.)

In 2008 an overwhelming 81 percent in Indonesia and 83 percent in Pakistan said Islamist political groups should participate in elections. Re-asked in 2009 in Indonesia, an even larger majority (94 percent) concurred. Indonesia and Pakistan each have numerous legal political parties often described as Islamist.

Even though there is currently no significant Islamist party that is permitted to function in Azerbaijan, three in four Azerbaijanis (75 percent) said Islamist political groups should participate in elections. Twenty-four

FIGURE 8-4. Islamist Participation in Politics

Which view is closer to yours?

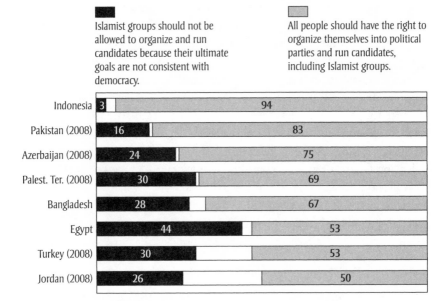

■ Islamist groups should not be allowed to organize and run candidates because their ultimate goals are not consistent with democracy.	□ All people should have the right to organize themselves into political parties and run candidates, including Islamist groups.

Indonesia — 3 / 94
Pakistan (2008) — 16 / 83
Azerbaijan (2008) — 24 / 75
Palest. Ter. (2008) — 30 / 69
Bangladesh — 28 / 67
Egypt — 44 / 53
Turkey (2008) — 30 / 53
Jordan (2008) — 26 / 50

Source: WorldPublicOpinion.org, 2009.

percent said they should not. In the Palestinian Territories, 69 percent agreed with the participation of Islamist parties, while 30 percent disagreed. Hamas—one of the two major political parties there—presents itself as an Islamist party. In Bangladesh 67 percent approved of Islamist participation. The Jamaat-e-Islami Bangladesh party currently has a small number of seats in parliament.

In Turkey a modest majority—53 percent—supported Islamist party participation in elections, with 30 percent disagreeing. As of this writing, the Justice and Development Party (in Turkish, AKP), a moderate Islamist party, is the governing party in Turkey, which is constitutionally a secular state. Turkish polling through 2008 showed the AKP to be the most popular party.

In Egypt a modest 53 percent favored Islamist participation, but an exceptionally large 44 percent opposed it. In Egypt the Muslim Brotherhood is a high-profile Islamist group that has been officially banned. It has sought to participate as a political party, and in 2005, for the first time, individuals associated with the Brotherhood were allowed to run, though as individuals.

Jordanians showed a more tenuous willingness to see Islamist parties contend in elections, with a 50 percent plurality agreeing and 26 percent disagreeing (24 percent did not answer). Jordan has an Islamist party, the Islamic Action Front, which has significant representation in parliament.

The Muslim Brotherhood

The Muslim Brotherhood is arguably the most prominent Islamist organization in the world, with a long and complex history. It was started in Egypt by the schoolteacher Hassan al Banna in 1928 as a peaceful community organization. The Muslim Brotherhood's stated goal has been to instill the Quran and sunnah as the "sole reference point for . . . ordering the life of the Muslim family, individual, community . . . and state." In the 1940s an armed wing was formed that engaged in political violence. In the early 1950s it was implicated in an assassination attempt on Egyptian President Nasser, leading to the imprisonment of its leadership and to a ban on the organization in Egypt.

During this period Sayyid Qutb, a key articulator of the ideas of radical Islamism, was an influential member of the Muslim Brotherhood. Qutb called for the use of violence to bring about fundamentalist Islamic states and was a major influence in the formation of al Qaeda.

The Brotherhood, though, eventually dissociated itself from Qutb and sought to establish itself as a more moderate political force committed to the democratic process. It spawned political parties in various countries, including Hamas in the Palestinian Territories and the Islamic Action Front in Jordan, and operates to some extent in most majority-Muslim countries. In Egypt, while still banned from acting as a party, the Brotherhood ran independent candidates in elections and has become the largest opposition bloc in the parliament.

The Brotherhood continues to be highly controversial. While it has taken great pains to affirm its commitment to democracy and its rejection of violence, including the 9/11 attacks, it is still suspected by some of having a covert radical agenda. The U.S. government refuses to have contacts with the Brotherhood, though it has had some contacts with elected officials with links to the Brotherhood.

Opinion toward the Muslim Brotherhood is varied. In 2009 WPO polling of four majority-Muslim nations, majorities had positive views in

Indonesia (69 percent) and Turkey (52 percent). In the Palestinian Territories only 17 percent had negative views, while most had either positive (43 percent) or mixed views (39 percent). A plurality of Iraqis had negative views (47 percent).

Muslim publics are split on whether the Muslim Brotherhood favors democracy. In the 2009 WPO polling a majority in Indonesia (74 percent) and a plurality in Turkey (41 percent) said the group is democratic (40 percent did not answer in Turkey). Most respondents in the Palestinian Territories and Iraq disagreed, with 69 percent and 52 percent, respectively, saying the group favors some other system of government.

Very few who think the Brotherhood favors a nondemocratic system approve of such a system. Those who both believe that the Brotherhood favors a nondemocratic and that also approve of such a system were 23 percent in the Palestinian Territories, 7 percent in Indonesia, 6 percent in Iraq, and 4 percent in Turkey.

Some who oppose the Muslim Brotherhood participating in the political process fear that it is supported by Muslims who favor the democratic process as a way to elevate the Brotherhood so it could then impose a nondemocratic Islamist system. But WPO polling revealed few such people who support the democratic process but prefer a nondemocratic system. Overall, the percentage that favors democracy, believes that the Muslim Brotherhood favors some system other than democracy, and has a positive view of that system is very small (9 percent on average), but does rise to 21 percent among Palestinians. In short, it appears that few Muslims are looking to the Brotherhood as a path to a nondemocratic state. Should it be elected and begin to move in a nondemocratic direction, it is likely that its support would diminish.

Interestingly, people who think it is "very important" to live in a democracy are far more likely to have positive feelings about the Muslim Brotherhood (48 percent) than people who say it is "not important" (29 percent). Those who say democracy is "very important" are also more likely to have very positive feelings toward the Brotherhood (22 percent) than those who say democracy is "somewhat important" (12 percent).

Local Islamist Parties

In 2009 WPO polled six majority-Muslim nations about ostensibly moderate Islamist parties in their countries. These were

—Azerbaijan—Islamic Party of Azerbaijan (IPA),

—Bangladesh—Jamaat-e-Islami Bangladesh (Jamaat),

—Indonesia—Prosperous Justice Party (PKS),

—Iraq—Islamic Supreme Council of Iraq (ISCI) and Iraqi Islamist Party (IIP),

—Pakistan—Jamaat-e-Islami (JI) and Jamiat Ulema-e-Islam (JUI),

—Turkey—Justice and Development Party (AKP). (The AKP is certainly an Islamic-oriented party, but it is arguably not fully an Islamist party in that it does not explicitly seek to change the secular nature of the Turkish government to one based on sharia.)

Overall, only two of these parties are viewed positively by majorities of respondents in the countries in which they are active (Indonesians for PKS and Pakistanis for JI). Views were mixed regarding the other four parties.

On the question of whether these parties believe that democracy is the best type of system, views varied. Three publics had majorities or pluralities saying their parties have democratic preferences (Indonesians for the PKS, Pakistanis for the JI, and Turks for the AKP). Pakistanis were divided on JUI, while Azerbaijanis were mostly uncertain about the IPA. A plurality of Iraqis said their Islamist parties do not have democratic goals.

Overall, though, it appears that the dominant feeling toward local Islamist parties is one of comfort. Regarding these Islamist groups' participation in elections, respondents in five of the countries (excluding Bangladesh) were asked whether each (1) was still too extreme and not genuinely democratic, (2) has departed too far from its Islamist principles (the radical Islamist critique), (3) has found an acceptable way to blend Islamism and democracy. In every case only small numbers said that the party is too extreme and not genuinely democratic. Curiously, the highest number (26 percent) was for the Turkish AKP, which is arguably the least Islamist of all. At the same time, no more than one in five in any of the five countries supported the radical Islamist critique that these parties have departed too far from Islamist principles, with the curious exception of Iraq on the ISCI (38 percent). By far the most common response was that the parties had found an acceptable way to blend Islamism and democracy. (See figure 8-5.)

Iraq. As indicated, Iraqis were polled about the Shia-aligned Islamic Supreme Council of Iraq (ISCI) as well as the Sunni-aligned Iraqi Islamist Party (IIP). On balance views of the two groups are roughly similar, but views of the ISCI are more polarized.

FIGURE 8-5. Islamist Participation in Elections

Do you think that as [specific group] [has/have] participated in elections:

Country polled	Name of specific group	It is still too extreme and not genuinely democratic	It has found an acceptacble way to blend Islamism and democracy	It has departed too far from its Islamist principles	Don't know
Azerbaijan	Islamic Party of Azerbaijan	15	17	16	52
Iraq	Islamic Supreme Council of Iraq	24	18	38	20
Iraq	Iraqi Islamist Party	20	38	18	24
Turkey	Justice and Develop- ment Party (AKP)	26	48	9	17
Pakistan	Jamiat Ulema-e-Islam (JUI)	10	56	13	22
Pakistan	Jamaat-e-Islam (JI)	5	56	16	23
Indonesia	Prosperous Justice Party (PKS)	6	58	4	33

On the ISCI, 39 percent of Iraqis expressed positive views, 35 percent expressed negative views, and 19 percent expressed mixed views. A plurality (42 percent) said the group does not believe democracy is the best system, though 35 percent said it does. A curiously large number—38 percent—said that in participating in elections "it has departed too far from its Islamist principles," while 24 percent said that "it is still too extreme and not genuinely democratic." An unusually low 18 percent said "it has found an acceptable way to blend Islamism and democracy."

On the IIP, 34 percent said they have positive feelings, 27 percent said negative, and 26 percent said mixed. Roughly four in ten (39 percent) responded that the IIP is not democratic, while 31 percent thought it does believe in democracy (30 percent did not answer). In terms of its participation in elections, 38 percent said it had found a suitable compromise between Islam and democracy, with just 20 percent saying it is too extreme and 18 percent saying it has strayed too far from its principles.

Pakistan. Pakistanis were also polled about two Islamist parties, Jamaat-e-Islam (JI) and Jamiat Ulema-e-Islam (JUI). Unlike Iraq, however, there were significant differences in opinion on the two parties. JI was viewed more favorably and as more democratic. Majorities agreed, however, that both parties have found an acceptable compromise between democracy and Islam.

Two-thirds of Pakistanis (68 percent) had positive feelings toward JI, compared to 15 percent who had negative feelings and 11 percent whose feelings were mixed. A majority (62 percent) expressed confidence that the group believes in the democratic system. Fifty-six percent said the party has found an acceptable way to blend Islamism and democracy, 16 percent said it has departed too far from its principles, and only 5 percent said it is not genuinely democratic.

Opinion toward JUI was more lukewarm, as 47 percent expressed positive views, 30 percent were negative, and 14 percent were mixed. Pakistanis were divided on whether or not JUI is committed to democracy, with 44 percent saying that it is and 41 percent saying that it is not. But more than half (56 percent) said JUI has come to a suitable compromise between its Islamist principles and democracy, with 13 percent believing it has departed too far from those principles and 10 percent saying it is too extreme.

Indonesia. Indonesians are favorable about the Prosperous Justice Party (PKS) and its outlook toward democracy. More than three-fourths (77 percent) had positive feelings toward the group, while 15 percent had mixed feelings and only 1 percent had negative feelings. Fifty-four percent agreed that PKS has a genuine belief in democracy, while 22 percent disagreed. A majority (58 percent) approved of the party's blend of Islamist principles and democracy, while only 6 percent said the party is not legitimately democratic and 4 percent said it has departed too far from its Islamist principles.

Bangladesh. Bangladeshis are divided in their views of Jamaat-e-Islami Bangladeshi. Forty-one percent had negative feelings, 40 percent had positive feelings, and 17 percent had mixed views. Half (50 percent) expressed confidence in Jamaat's belief in democracy, while 46 percent lacked confidence.

Azerbaijan. Azerbaijanis do not have strong views on the Islamic Party of Azerbaijan, with many not taking a position on the questions. The largest number reported having mixed feelings toward the group (37 percent), while 18 percent had negative feelings and 16 percent positive. Roughly one-third (32 percent) said the party is not democratically minded, while 19 percent said it is (49 percent gave no opinion). While the Azerbaijani government has banned it from participating, the party has sought to participate in electoral politics. Azerbaijanis offered no strong opinion on the level of its extremism—52 percent gave no answer. Those who answered the question were divided, with 17 percent saying the group has found a suitable blend between Islamism and democracy, 16 percent saying it has departed from its principles, and 15 percent saying it is still too extreme.

Turkey. Turks are mostly positive about the governing Justice and Development Party (AKP), which is described as mildly Islamist. However, a significant number express negative views and doubts about the party's intentions with regard to democracy.

Approximately half (49 percent) have positive feelings toward the party, 34 percent negative, and 14 percent mixed. Approximately half (47 percent) said they have the impression that AKP "does believe democracy is the best type of political system," while 41 percent do not have that impression. A plurality (48 percent) agreed that the party's participation in elections meant that it has found a suitable blend between Islamism and democracy, while 26 percent said the party is still too extreme and just 9 percent said it has departed too far from its Islamic principles.

Human Rights

On questions of human rights, large majorities in numerous majority-Muslim nations embrace the liberal principles granting freedom of religion, freedom of expression, and equal rights to women. On some questions, however, such as on the right to change one's religion away from Islam (or apostasy), significant numbers adhere to fundamentalist Islamic beliefs that prohibit it. Substantial numbers also oppose the right to read whatever is on the Internet.

Overall, the picture is one of Muslims rather strongly and uniformly absorbing liberal values, but also expressing some trepidation. For example, in a 2006 Arab Barometer poll large majorities in the Palestinian Territories (91 percent), Kuwait (88 percent), Morocco (81 percent), Algeria

(79 percent), and Jordan (76 percent) agreed that "political reform should be introduced little by little."

Freedom of Religion

Radical Islamists have roundly rejected the notion of freedom of religion and embraced the view that those who convert away from Islam should be punished by death. In the words of Abu Musaib al-Zarqawi, bin Laden's authorized chief of Iraq operations until his death in 2006:

> Democracy is based on the principle of freedom of religion and belief. Under democracy, a man can believe anything he wants and choose any religion he wants and convert to any religion whenever he wants, even if this apostasy means abandoning the religion of Allah. . . . This is a matter which is patently perverse and false and contradicts many specific [Muslim] legal texts, since according to Islam, if a Muslim apostatizes from Islam to heresy, he should be killed.[5]

Nevertheless, in numerous polls most Muslims strongly endorse the broad principle of freedom of religion. WPO asked in four majority-Muslim countries in 2006 to 2007 whether in their own country "people of any religion should be free to worship according to their own beliefs." Indonesians were the most emphatic supporters of freedom of religion, with 93 percent supporting the statement (82 percent "strongly"). In Egypt almost nine out of ten (88 percent) agreed, including 78 percent who agreed "strongly." Pakistanis also affirmed freedom of worship, with 75 percent agreeing (53 percent "strongly"). The only country that did not have an overwhelming majority was Morocco, though still a robust 63 percent majority agreed (29 percent "strongly"). In all cases these were *above* the global average among the twenty-two nations in which this question was asked.

Asked by Gallup in 2005 whether "a constitution for a new country should include guarantees for . . . freedom of religion," very large majorities in Bangladesh (98 percent), Indonesia (96 percent), Lebanon (95 percent), Turkey (89 percent), Pakistan (72 percent), and Iran (69 percent) said that it should. Only about half, however, felt this way in Egypt, Jordan, and Morocco.

Large majorities also say that adherents of all religions should be treated equally. WPO asked respondents in 2008 in six majority-Muslim nations, "How important do you think it is for people of different religions to be treated equally?" Majorities in every country polled said that it is "somewhat" or "very important." This ranged from 74 percent in Egypt to 95 percent in Indonesia.

Similarly, in an Arab Barometer poll of five nations in 2006, majorities or pluralities rejected the view that "Islam requires that in a Muslim country the political rights of non-Muslims should be inferior to those of Muslims." The size of the majorities that disagreed with the statement ranged from 54 percent of Moroccans to 72 percent of Palestinians. Only in Algeria was this less than half, with 47 percent disagreeing and 34 percent agreeing.

Concurrent with these large majorities supporting liberal positions on freedom of religion and nondiscrimination are responses to some other questions in which many Muslims agree with positions that impose limits on those freedoms. Slight differences in wording can elicit more restrictive or more liberal attitudes, suggesting that for many Muslims this issue is fraught with inner conflict.

For example, when presented by WPO in 2009 the broader liberal principle that "all people" in their country "should have the right to change their religion if they choose to," large majorities agreed in Bangladesh (67 percent), Turkey (64 percent), and Indonesia (63 percent). Even a plurality of Egyptians agreed (49 to 41 percent).

Asked by Arab Barometer, however, if they agreed that "if a Muslim converts to another religion, he must be punished by execution," majorities agreed in the Palestinian Territories (65 percent) and Jordan (57 percent), as did a plurality in Algeria (45 to 27 percent). Views were divided in Morocco (44 percent agreed, 40 percent disagreed). A plurality (41 percent) disagreed in Kuwait, but a third still agreed (34 percent). As mentioned above, in a 2010 Pew poll of Pakistanis, 76 percent favored the "death penalty for people who leave the Muslim religion."

When a 2009 WPO poll asked people in a different set of countries whether "our government should punish a [country citizen] who changes their religion from Islam to a non-Muslim religion," three out of the four countries disagreed (even with the severity of the punishment not being specified). In just one country (Egypt) did a majority—a large one—agree, with 75 percent saying such a citizen should be punished. In all other cases only minorities agreed: Bangladesh (38 percent), Turkey (18 percent), and Indonesia (10 percent).

In another departure from full freedom of religion, views were mixed on whether it is acceptable to try to convince others to change their religion. WPO asked respondents in 2008 whether they agreed that in their own country "people of any religion should be free to try to convert members of other religions to join theirs." Majorities in all five majority-Muslim nations disagreed. Globally, however, views in non-Muslim nations were divided on the question.

Concurrent with their support for freedom of religion, a substantial number of Muslims accept the notion of having a non-Muslim as a neighbor. Arab Barometer asked Muslims in four countries in 2006 how they feel about having "followers of other religions" as neighbors. Majorities in Jordan (71 percent), Kuwait (71 percent), and Morocco (52 percent) said, "I don't mind," while a plurality of Algerians concurred (48 to 41 percent).

Freedom of Expression

When presented in broad terms, very large majorities support the principle that people should have freedom of expression. Muslims are more likely than people in most other countries, however, to say that governments have the right to impose restrictions on expression that could defame a religion and to control the Internet.

Majorities in all six majority-Muslim nations polled by WPO in 2008 said it is important that people have the right "to express any opinion, including criticisms of the government or religious leaders." This included Indonesia and the Palestinian Territories (94 percent), Jordan (86 percent), Turkey (85 percent), Egypt (80 percent), and Azerbaijan (75 percent). Majorities or pluralities in five of the six nations said it is "very important."

Muslims did not differ much from the average of all nineteen nations polled worldwide on this same question. Worldwide, 88 percent said freedom of expression is important, compared to 85 percent in the average of six majority-Muslim nations. Muslim publics were above or only slightly below the global average except in Egypt and Azerbaijan, where majorities were significantly below the average.

Gallup asked in nine majority-Muslim countries whether the country's constitution should include guarantees for free speech. Large majorities in all cases said that it should, ranging from 82 percent in Pakistan to 98 percent in Lebanon. Other countries with overwhelming majorities included Bangladesh (97 percent), Egypt (94 percent), Iran (93 percent), Indonesia (90 percent), and Morocco (90 percent).

Very large majorities in Iran (polled in 2009) and Saudi Arabia (polled in 2007) responded that freedom of the press is an important goal when asked in separate polls by Terror Free Tomorrow. Eighty-four percent of Iranians said it is either "very important" (62 percent) or "somewhat important" (22 percent). The question asked of Saudis was worded slightly differently (free elections were included as well as freedom of press), but the result was similar, with 79 percent saying it is either a "very important" (60 percent) or "somewhat important" (19 percent) priority.

Closely related to freedom of expression is the right to assemble and to demonstrate. In Gallup's 2005 poll of nine Muslim publics broadly favored a constitutional guarantee for freedom of assembly, with majorities in seven Muslim countries as well as a plurality in Jordan supporting the idea. The highest majorities were found in Bangladesh (87 percent), Iran (73 percent), and Pakistan (69 percent).

The right to demonstrate peacefully to protest against the government is a right supported by majorities in all six majority-Muslim nations in a 2008 WPO poll. In none of the countries polled did a majority think "the government should have the right to ban peaceful demonstrations that it thinks would be destabilizing." The majorities supporting the right to demonstrate ranged from 53 percent in Jordan to 83 percent in Indonesia. On average, 66 percent of respondents in all six majority-Muslim nations supported peaceful demonstrations as a right, slightly lower than the average of 75 percent for all nineteen nations polled worldwide, including the Muslim nations.

For the most part, Muslims express fairly positive attitudes about living in a pluralistic political environment. Asked by WVS in polling from 2005 to 2008 whether they agree that "competition and disagreement among political groups is not a bad thing for our country," half or more said they agree in Kuwait (79 percent), Morocco (67 percent), Algeria (61 percent), Jordan (59 percent), and the Palestinian Territories (50 percent).

Asked by WPO in 2008 whether the government should "have the right to prohibit certain political or religious views from being discussed," majorities in three majority-Muslim nations (64 percent in Azerbaijan, the Palestinian Territories, and Turkey) and a plurality in Jordan said that the government should not have such a right. Egyptians, though, were evenly divided, and a majority of Indonesians (55 percent) supported their government having this right.

In aggregate, the Muslim world was roughly in line with the worldwide average of 57 percent who said the government should not have the right to regulate speech and 36 percent who said it should. Azerbaijan, the Palestinian Territories, and Turkey had above-average percentages opposing government restrictions on certain views, while Egypt, Indonesia, and Jordan were below average.

The rationale most often cited as the basis for limiting freedom of expression is that of security and stability. Muslims, however, resist such an argument. The 2006 Arab Barometer poll asked, "To what degree would you agree that the violation of human rights in [survey country] is justifiable in the name of promoting security and stability?" Majorities in four of the five countries polled said that such violations are not justifiable (ranging from 59 percent among Kuwaitis to 63 percent among Palestinians). The one exception was Morocco, where two-thirds said it is at least "somewhat" justified.

The area where Muslims most diverge from the global norm on freedom of expression is on the subject of defamation of religion. The Organization of the Islamic Conference (OIC), a group of fifty-six Muslim nations, has championed a possible UN resolution that would call on all nations of the world "to effectively combat defamation of all religions and incitement to religious hatred in general and against Islam and Muslims in particular."

In the 2009 WPO survey of seven majority-Muslim nations this topic was polled as part of a larger survey of twenty nations. Respondents were presented with two statements: (1) "People should have the right to publicly criticize a religion because people should have freedom of speech," and (2) "The government should have the right to fine or imprison people who publicly criticize a religion because such criticism could defame the religion." Five out of seven majority-Muslim publics agreed with the second statement, allowing punishment for defamation. The largest support came from Egyptians (71 percent), Pakistanis (62 percent), and Iraqis (57 percent). The dissenting publics were Azerbaijanis and Turks, with 67 percent and 54 percent, respectively, favoring the right to criticize religion. Among the thirteen non-Muslim nations polled, only two agreed with the notion that defamation of religion should be punishable—India and Nigeria.

When WPO also asked whether "people should have the right to read whatever is on the Internet," only two countries out of twenty polled had a majority or plurality saying that the government should have the right to "prevent people from having access to some things on the Internet." These countries were Jordan, where a majority of 63 percent supported limited access, and Iran, where a plurality of 44 percent supported limited access (only 32 percent favored unlimited access). Numbers in the Palestinian Territories were also exceptionally low compared to other nations, with a narrow majority of 52 percent approving of unlimited Internet access. Large majorities in other majority-Muslim nations, however, favored the right to full Internet access, including Azerbaijan (79 percent), Egypt (65 percent), Indonesia (65 percent), and Turkey (60 percent).

Publics in some countries embrace the very non-liberal notion that "people should always support the decisions of their government even if they disagree with these decisions." In 2006 Arab Barometer found majorities believing this in Morocco (58 percent) and the Palestinian Territories (57 percent). Majorities disagreed, however, in Kuwait (69 percent) and Algeria (63 percent), as did a plurality in Jordan (47 to 42 percent).

Attitudes about the United States interact, however, with attitudes about freedom of expression in a way that appears to drive down support for freedom. Despite the positive views of freedom of expression found in other questions, when this notion was associated with the United States, views were much more negative. WPO polling between 2006 and 2008 asked Muslims in four nations their views of "the laws permitting freedom of expression in the United States." A majority of Indonesians (57 percent) said they have unfavorable views of such laws, while pluralities of Egyptians (48 percent) and Pakistanis (44 percent) said the same. Moroccans, however, had a large majority (68 percent) with favorable views.

Women's Rights

Large majorities of Muslims endorse the broad principles of equal rights for women, including the right of women to hold office. On some questions, however, Muslims show more widespread discriminatory attitudes than are found in other parts of the world.

Asked about this issue as part of the larger 2008 WPO poll of twenty nations worldwide, large majorities in seven Muslim-majority nations said that it is either "very" or "somewhat" important for women to have full equality of rights compared to men. Majorities ranged from 78 percent (Iran) to 91 percent (Indonesia and Turkey). Muslim publics were largely in line with the average of all twenty nations polled, in which 86 percent consider equality for women important.

In the same poll WPO also asked respondents whether their governments "should make an effort to prevent discrimination against women" or not. Majorities of all seven majority-Muslim publics favored their governments taking such steps. Favorable responses ranged from 70 percent in Iran to 93 percent in Indonesia. The twenty-nation average was 81 percent. Asked whether their governments are doing enough to prevent discrimination, five out of seven majority-Muslim publics said their governments should do more, including Indonesians (69 percent), Turks (60 percent), Palestinians (56 percent), and pluralities of Azerbaijanis (40 percent), and Iranians (36 percent). Egyptians and Jordanians, however, both said their governments' current efforts are adequate, with 59 and 42 percent, respectively, saying this.

Most Muslims also perceive that women have become more equal. When asked in the same WPO poll if women have achieved more equality in their society during their lifetimes, large majorities said they have in Egypt (94 percent), Indonesia (80 percent), Iran (75 percent), Turkey (69 percent), and Azerbaijan (63 percent). Jordanian views were mixed, but the most common response (43 percent) was that women are more equal. Out of twenty nations, only in the Palestinian Territories did a majority (51 percent) say women are now less equal.

Most Muslims seem to regard women's rights as a fundamental feature of democracy. WVS asked in 2005 to 2008 polling how essential it is to democracy for women to have "the same rights as men." Asked to answer on a scale from 1 to 10, with 1 meaning it is not at all an essential characteristic of democracy and 10 meaning it definitely is, in all cases majorities rate this above 5. Mean responses ranged from 6.4 in Iraq to 8.7 in Turkey.

Support is quite strong for women being able to hold government posts. Gallup asked in 2005 whether "women should be allowed to hold leadership positions in the cabinet or national council" of a country. Large majorities said they should in Lebanon (91 percent), Turkey (86 percent), Iran (78 percent), and Morocco (74 percent) as well as more moderately sized majorities in Pakistan (58 percent) and Egypt (54 percent). The only country that had less than half taking this position was Saudi Arabia (40 percent). An IRI poll in Indonesia in 2009 even found three out of four respondents approving of a quota system in which one out of every three candidates is a woman.

The 2006 Arab Barometer asked a series of questions about the role of women in Algeria, Jordan, Kuwait, Morocco, and the Palestinian Territories. For the most part, majorities expressed fairly liberal attitudes. All five nations had large majorities believing "a married woman can work outside the home if she wishes." These ranged from 71 percent in Algeria to 90 percent in Kuwait. Majorities in all five nations also agreed that "men and women should have equal job opportunities and wages," ranging from 60 percent of Algerians to 82 percent of Kuwaitis. Very large majorities in all nations believed that "men and women should receive equal wages and salaries." These ranged from 78 percent in Jordan and Kuwait to 87 percent in Morocco. Majorities rejected the statement that "a university education is more important for a boy than a girl," ranging from 64 percent in Jordan to 82 percent in Kuwait.

When this last question was asked in eight countries as part of the WVS survey between 2005 and 2008, majorities in six of them also rejected the view that a university education is more important for a boy, ranging from 54 percent in Malaysia to 79 percent in Turkey. There were a few exceptions, however. A majority in Iran (55 percent) gave a higher preference to education for boys, while views in Iraq and Mali were divided.

Even a poll of Afghans found fairly liberal views of the role of women. ABC/BBC asked Afghan respondents in December 2009 whether they support or oppose five different aspects of a woman's role in society. Overwhelming majorities said they support "girls' education" (88 percent) and "women voting" (88 percent). Smaller but still very large majorities also said they support "women holding jobs outside the home" (74 percent) and "women holding government office" (69 percent). At the same time, a January 2009 ABC/BBC poll found a large majority (77 percent) still supporting "women wearing the burqa."

Majorities in four countries polled by Arab Barometer in 2006 agreed that Islam encourages modest dress for women, but does not require they wear the *hijab*. These ranged from 50 percent in the Palestinian Territories to 61 percent in Morocco. Algeria was the lone dissenter, with a plurality (48 percent) disagreeing.

There are, however, some significant exceptions to support for women's rights. WVS polling from 2005 to 2008 found majorities in six out of eight countries surveyed saying men deserve jobs ahead of women when they are scarce. The majorities ranged widely, from 52 percent in Turkey to 89 percent in Egypt. Other countries with very high majorities included Jordan (88 percent) and Iraq (82 percent). The two exceptions were Morocco and Malaysia, and even in these cases half said that men deserve jobs ahead of women. Outside of majority-Muslim countries, only five out of forty-nine countries said men deserve jobs ahead of women (Burkina Faso, Georgia, Ghana, Mali, and India). Arab Barometer in 2006 found majorities in five countries opposing women traveling abroad alone, ranging from 51 percent in Morocco to 70 percent in the Palestinian Territories.

WVS also found majorities in all nine majority-Muslim publics polled between 2005 and 2008 believing that men make better political leaders than women. Numbers ranged from 55 percent in Morocco to 92 percent in Egypt. Arab Barometer found the same result in all five nations it polled on this question. In the WVS poll majorities in nine out of the forty-eight other countries surveyed worldwide agreed that men make better leaders (Burkina Faso, Georgia, Ghana, India, Moldova, Russia, South Korea, Thailand, and Vietnam).

On the other hand, the Arab Barometer poll also found majorities in three nations agreeing that "a woman can be a president or prime minister of a Muslim country," ranging from 56 percent in the Palestinian Territories to 66 percent in Morocco. Kuwaitis were divided, and a majority of Algerians (56 percent) dissented.

Most Saudis did not see "permitting women to drive" as a priority in a 2007 Terror Free Tomorrow poll. Fifty-five percent said it is either "not at all important" (39 percent) or "somewhat unimportant" (16 percent), while 43 percent said it is important.

Concepts of World Order

The liberal model of world order began to emerge after World War I with the development of the League of Nations and various international treaties and conventions such as the Geneva Conventions. It was more fully defined after World War II with the development of the United Nations and other related international institutions such as the International Court of Justice.

A cornerstone of this model is that there should be international laws that govern relations between nations.

This model of world order has been largely denounced by radical Islamists. It is seen as requiring Muslims to subordinate themselves to a system dominated by infidels. Because it seeks to largely preserve the current nation-state system, it is seen as a distraction from the goal of creating a new caliphate and ultimately spreading Islam throughout the world.

As discussed in chapter 7 there is some evidence that the aspiration to create a new caliphate and expand the influence of Islam resonates with many Muslims. There is a surfeit of data, however, showing very strong support for the liberal model of world order based on international law and strong international institutions such as the United Nations. Indeed, an abundance of polling shows robust support for a strong UN. While some polls show mixed or even negative views of the UN, this is mostly for being dominated by the United States and failing to live up to the role it was meant to play in a liberal world order.

The imperative to abide by international law was supported in a 2009 WPO poll of twenty-one nations. Majorities or pluralities in five of the seven majority-Muslim nations polled endorsed the imperative of abiding by international law. Respondents were asked to choose between two statements: (1) "Our nation should consistently follow international laws; it is wrong to violate international laws, just as it is wrong to violate laws within a country," and (2) "If our government thinks it is not in our nation's interest, it should not feel obliged to abide by international laws." Majorities in Egypt (63 percent), Azerbaijan (60 percent), and Indonesia (53 percent) as well as pluralities in the Palestinian Territories (50 to 46 percent) and Iraq (46 to 31 percent) chose the first statement, preferring to consistently follow international laws. Turks were divided, while Pakistanis were the one nation where most (56 percent) said their government should not feel obliged to follow international laws when it is not in their nation's interest. (See figure 8-6.) However, majority Muslim countries were more often below the average (57 percent) of all twenty-one nations polled globally.

Support for Giving the United Nations Greater Powers

Perhaps the most telling indication of support for the liberal world order is the strong support for giving the United Nations greater powers. Between 2006 and 2008 WPO polled five majority-Muslim countries on

FIGURE 8-6. International Law

Which of these two views is closer to yours?

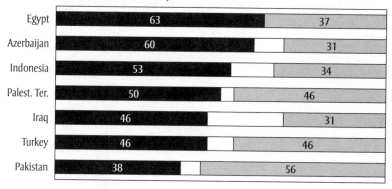

Our nation should consistently follow international laws. It is wrong to violate international laws, just as it is wrong to violate laws within a country.

If our government thinks it is not in our nation's interest, it should not feel obliged to abide by international laws.

	black	gray
Egypt	63	37
Azerbaijan	60	31
Indonesia	53	34
Palest. Ter.	50	46
Iraq	46	31
Turkey	46	46
Pakistan	38	56

Source: WorldPublicOpinion.org, 2009.

four possible new powers for the United Nations as part of a wider survey of twenty-three countries. These possible new powers were (1) the UN having its own standing peacekeeping force, (2) the UN having the power to regulate the international arms trade, (3) the UN having the power to impose a small tax on such things as the international sale of arms or oil, and (4) giving the UN the authority to go into countries in order to investigate violations of human rights. Three out of four of these items received strong support, and the other received modest support.

Publics in five countries polled favored the UN having its own standing peacekeeping force, with majorities ranging from 51 percent of Turks to 74 percent of Indonesians. Nearly as many supported the idea of the UN having the power to regulate the international arms trade. Majorities in four countries approved of the UN having this authority, ranging between 53 percent in Egypt and 64 percent in Indonesia. Turkey was the exception, with a plurality of 39 percent opposing the proposal.

The one area that got more mixed support was giving the UN the power to impose a small tax on such things as the international sale of arms or oil. Still, more leaned toward this idea than leaned against it (42 to 38 percent), with supportive majorities or pluralities in three of the five publics—all three, interestingly enough, in countries that produce some oil or natural gas. Support ranged from 50 percent in Indonesia to 33 percent in Turkey.

Majorities or pluralities in all five countries favored "giving the UN the authority to go into countries in order to investigate violations of human rights," ranging from 47 percent in Turkey to 77 percent in Azerbaijan. The average of all twenty-two countries polled worldwide was 65 percent in favor and 22 percent opposed. Percentages in Azerbaijan and Indonesia were above the average, while those in Egypt, Iran, and Turkey were below the average.

There is strong support for the UN taking a more active role in human rights. Majorities or pluralities in six nations polled by WPO in 2008 said that the United Nations should "actively promote human rights in member states," rejecting the argument that "this is improper interference in a country's internal affairs and human rights should be left to each country." Majorities ranged from 54 percent in the Palestinian Territories to 89 percent in Azerbaijan, while in Jordan support was a plurality (50 percent). (See figure 8-7.) The average of all twenty-one nations in the WPO poll was 70 percent in favor of and 19 percent opposed to an active UN role. Support was below average in four of the majority-Muslim nations, while Azerbaijan was far above average, and Indonesian was exactly average.

There is also support for the United Nations taking a larger role than it presently does. When Muslim publics were asked, "Would you like to see the UN do more, do less, or do about the same as it has been doing to promote human rights principles," majorities in five out of six publics wanted the UN to "do more" (on average 60 percent), ranging from 48 percent of Palestinians to 69 percent of Turks. Of the twenty-one nations surveyed, 65 percent on average favored the United Nations doing more than it does to "promote human rights principles."

UN efforts on behalf of women's rights were favored by four out of six majority-Muslim publics surveyed in the WPO poll. Majorities supporting UN action on the issue ranged from 52 percent in Iran to 74 percent in Indonesia. Egyptians dissented, with 70 percent saying this would be "improper interference in a country's internal affairs." Palestinians were di-

FIGURE 8-7. The UN and Human Rights

As you may know, the members of the UN General Assembly have agreed on a set of principles called the Universal Declaration of Human Rights. Some people say the United Nations should actively promote such human rights principles in member states. Others say this is improper interference in a country's internal affairs and human rights should be left to each country. Do you think the UN should or should not actively promote human rights in member states?

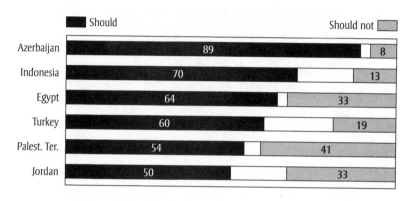

Source: WorldPublicOpinion.org, 2008.

vided. (See figure 8-8.) The average of all nineteen nations surveyed worldwide was 67 percent saying "the UN should make efforts to further the rights of women."

Another possible expansion of the UN's power is to play a larger role in monitoring elections. While radical Islamists would strongly oppose the idea of the UN acting as a judge of elections in a Muslim country, most Muslims show support for the idea. This suggests that many Muslims are not only concerned about the quality of the elections in their countries, but are inclined to look to the international community and the UN specifically to act as a neutral party in the effort to improve the quality of their democracies.

In 2009 WPO asked publics in seven majority-Muslim nations, "Do you think that when there are concerns about the fairness of elections, countries should or should not be willing to have international observers from the United Nations monitor their elections?" Majorities in five said countries should be willing to host observers, ranging from 55 percent of

FIGURE 8-8. UN Efforts to Further Women's Rights

Do you think the UN should make efforts to further the rights of women, or do you think this is improper interference in a country's internal affairs?

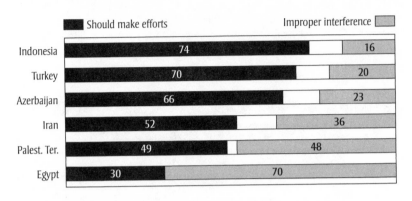

Source: WorldPublicOpinion.org, 2008.

Pakistanis to 83 percent of Azerbaijanis. Turks were divided. Of all eighteen nations surveyed, 64 percent on average said countries should be willing to have international observers from the United Nations monitor their elections when there are concerns, with 30 percent on average opposed.

Respondents in the same nations were then asked whether they think their own country would "benefit from having international observers monitor elections." Majorities or pluralities in five nations believed their countries would benefit, ranging from 49 percent in Pakistan to 71 percent in Azerbaijan. The Turkish public, though, was again divided. Three-fifths (62 percent) of Indonesians believed their country would not benefit. On average, among all seventeen nations surveyed, 55 percent said that their countries would benefit from having international observers monitor their elections, with 37 percent saying that their countries would not.

The UN's Right to Authorize Military Force

Chapter 7 of the UN Charter grants the UN Security Council (UNSC) the right to use military force in response to what it believes is a threat to international security. Consistent with this provision, Muslim publics around the world generally believe that the UNSC should have the right to authorize military force in response to a wide range of situations. While governments regularly invoke the principle of national sovereignty and resist UN intervention in their internal affairs, publics worldwide, including Muslim publics, are strikingly ready to give the United Nations such powers. This is a strong indication that people around the world believe that norms should be applied in a global, not just a national, context.

WPO and the Chicago Council on Global Affairs polled sixteen to eighteen nations on whether the UN Security Council should have the right to authorize military force for a variety of purposes. Support was quite robust in nearly all cases in most Muslim countries, even though many of them would involve actual or possible military action, about which Muslims have shown discomfort.

There was very strong consensus, ranging from 68 percent in Turkey to 82 percent in Azerbaijan, for the UN to conduct its original collective security function of authorizing the use of force "to defend a country that has been attacked." It is interesting that this principle gets such strong support even though it was highly touted as the basis for UN endorsement of the Gulf War, which was not popular among most Muslims. Muslim views correspond roughly to the average of all sixteen nations surveyed (76 percent saying the UN should have this right).

Large numbers agree with the UN having the right to authorize military force to stop a country from supporting terrorist groups (ranging from 61 percent of Palestinians to 81 percent in Egypt). This is especially striking because this could mean the UN using force against some majority-Muslim states that support groups that use terrorist methods. The average of all sixteen nations polled was 73 percent in favor of the UN having this right.

There is significant support for the UN having the right to authorize military force to prevent a country that does not have nuclear weapons from acquiring them. Majorities in four nations approved of the UN having this power, ranging from 58 percent in Turkey to 74 percent in Egypt. Palestinians dissented, with 59 percent saying the UN should not have the right to authorize force in this case. Again, this level of support is interesting given that Iran would be a likely target of such efforts. In various polls Muslims have shown sympathy for Iran's efforts to develop nuclear fuel even though most think that Iran is, in fact, seeking to develop nuclear weapons. Among the seventeen nations polled worldwide on this question, 59 percent on average said the UN should have this power, and 31 percent said it should not.

Relatedly, large numbers endorse the view that the UN has the right to use military force to "prevent a country that does not have nuclear weapons from producing nuclear fuel that could be used for nuclear weapons." WPO found majorities supporting this in four majority-Muslim nations, ranging from 51 percent in Egypt to 62 percent in Indonesia. Again, Palestinians were the only ones to disagree, with 57 percent against. The average of all sixteen nations polled was 56 percent approving the UN having this power and 32 percent disapproving.

Very large majorities of Muslims endorse the UN "having the right to authorize military force or to prevent severe human rights violations such as genocide." All six majority-Muslim publics polled supported this right by majorities, between 64 percent in Turkey and 83 percent in Egypt and Indonesia. Once again, this is striking given the high-profile opposition among the leaders of many Muslim countries to any outside military intervention in the situation in Darfur. On average, the eighteen nations surveyed in total on this question favored the right by 76 to 16 percent.

Further, in all seven nations polled on the question, publics endorsed the controversial view that the UN not only has the right, but the responsibility to authorize military intervention in a country "to protect people from severe human rights violations such as genocide, even against the will of their own government." Majorities or pluralities ranging from 39 percent in Turkey to 82 percent in Indonesia felt this way. In the WPO poll of twenty nations, an average of 61 percent said that the UN has such a responsibility.

The 2009 WPO polling of seven majority-Muslim countries also found strong support for intervening in Sudan for humanitarian purposes against the will of the government. Respondents were told that in response to charges made by the International Criminal Court, the Sudanese president Bashir "has expelled humanitarian groups that have been providing food and other aid to the displaced civilians living in refugee camps." They were then asked, "If, as a result, many people in these camps start dying from hunger and exposure, do you think the UN should bring in food and other aid, escorted by military protection if necessary, even against the will of the government, or do you think this would be too much of a violation of Sudan's sovereignty?" Majorities in Egypt (61 percent), the Palestinian Territories (60 percent), and Turkey (58 percent) approved of such an intervention. A plurality of Iraqis also approved (46 to 29 percent). Only Pakistanis leaned against the idea, with a plurality of 42 percent saying such action would violate Sudan's sovereignty (37 percent thought the UN should intervene).

Similarly, equally robust majorities approve of the UN using military force against the will of governments when their populations are at risk. The 2008 WPO poll posed the question of whether the United Nations should forcibly deliver urgent humanitarian aid if a government refused to allow entry. The question was posed in terms of the events in Burma when the government there refused the delivery of urgently needed aid in the wake of a major cyclone. Respondents were asked, "As a general rule, in such circumstances, should the UN bring in shipments of aid, escorted by military protection if necessary, even against the will of the government, or do you think this would be too much of a violation of a country's sovereignty?" Majorities or pluralities in five out of six majority-Muslim nations polled favored the UN taking action against the will of the government. These ranged from 46 percent of Jordanians to 65 percent of Palestinians. Egyptians had mixed views, with 48 percent taking each position. Of the twenty-one nations polled, an average of 60 percent favored UN action, while 28 percent said it would be too much of a violation of a country's sovereignty.

Finally, publics in five nations polled favored giving the United Nations the power to "restore by force a democratic government that has been overthrown." Majorities or pluralities ranged from 43 percent in Azerbaijan and Turkey to 67 percent in the Palestinian Territories.

Mixed Feelings about the UN's Performance

While Muslims tend to have a positive view of the UN potentially playing a more prominent role in the world, consistent with liberal models of world order, views are more mixed about its performance as an institution per se. It appears that Muslim publics distinguish between a UN that they feel in principle should be a dynamic actor and would naturally take into account the interests of the Muslim, and the existing UN, which they tend to perceive as achieving mixed results in its current efforts and, more importantly, as being dominated by the United States.

Between 2007 and 2009 Pew asked people in eleven Muslim countries whether they have a positive or negative view of the UN. This elicits highly mixed findings. Favorable views were found in Indonesia (87 percent), Bangladesh (80 percent), Lebanon (62 percent), Egypt (56 percent, though not consistently from year to year), and Malaysia (55 percent). Majorities had unfavorable views in the Palestinian Territories (69 percent), Jordan (66 percent), and Turkey (57 percent), while a plurality was negative in Morocco (38 to 20 percent), and views were divided in Pakistan.

Such mixed responses were found in WPO polling from 2006 through 2008 that asked respondents in seven majority-Muslim nations whether it would be positive or negative were the UN to become "significantly more powerful in world affairs." Majorities said it would be mainly positive in Iran (70 percent), Indonesia (53 percent), and Azerbaijan (51 percent), and a plurality said so in Turkey (43 percent). Majorities said it would be mostly negative, however, in the Palestinian Territories (64 percent), Jordan (59 percent), and Egypt (57 percent)—all nations close to the hotbed of the Israel-Palestinian conflict that the UN is perceived as failing to effectively solve. On the other hand, when Lebanese were asked this same question in a 2005 BBC/GlobeScan/PIPA poll, a majority (58 percent) thought a more powerful UN would be positive.

Respondents were also asked in the WPO polling to assess a variety of UN efforts, rating them on a scale from 0 to 10, with 0 meaning "not at all helpful" and 10 meaning "extremely helpful." Ratings were varied and generally lukewarm at best. The lowest ratings were for UN efforts in "working to resolve the Israeli-Palestinian conflict." The mean response was 3.7, with the lowest ratings coming from Jordanians (2.5) and Palestinians (2.6). Only Azerbaijanis were above 5 (5.3). Low ratings of UN performance on the Israeli-Palestinian conflict were highly correlated with the perception that the United States controls the UN. Also, ratings of UN efforts to "resolve the conflict in Darfur" were very low. The mean rating was 3.8. The lowest ratings came from the Jordanians (2.6), and the highest came from Indonesians (5.3). The most positive ratings were for UN performance in "providing humanitarian aid." Ratings ranged from 4.5 (Palestinians) to 7.8 (Indonesians), with a mean of 5.9. Nearly as high were ratings of UN efforts in "running peace-keeping operations," with a mean of 5.3, ranging from 3.5 (Palestinians) to 7.5 (Indonesians). UN efforts to address climate change got mixed reviews, with three nations rating it above 5 and three rating it below 5. The mean was 4.6. (See figure 8-9.)

Respondents in various nations also have highly divergent views on whether "when dealing with international problems, [survey country] should be more willing to make decisions within the United Nations, even

FIGURE 8-9. UN Performance

Averages of six majority-Muslim nations

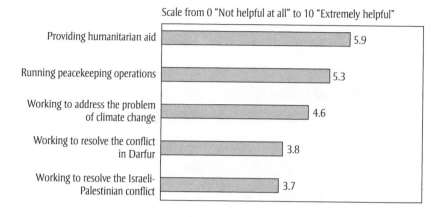

Scale from 0 "Not helpful at all" to 10 "Extremely helpful"

Providing humanitarian aid — 5.9

Running peacekeeping operations — 5.3

Working to address the problem of climate change — 4.6

Working to resolve the conflict in Darfur — 3.8

Working to resolve the Israeli-Palestinian conflict — 3.7

Source: WorldPublicOpinion.org.

if this means that [survey country] will sometimes have to go along with a policy that is not its first choice." When WPO asked this question in polling from 2007 to 2008, more agreed in Egypt (57 percent) and Turkey (39 to 29 percent), while more disagreed among the Palestinians (81 percent), Indonesians (50 percent), and Azerbaijanis (44 to 36 percent).

Trepidation about accepting UN decisions follows logically from concerns that the UN is controlled by the United States. This concern was widely expressed in 2008 WPO polling of six majority-Muslim nations. Respondents were offered two statements. One underscored the limits of U.S power, saying that "through its veto the United States can stop the UN from doing things, but the United States cannot make the UN do things the U.S. wants." This view was endorsed by only one nation (Azerbaijan). Majorities in four nations (Egypt, Jordan, the Palestinian Territories, and Turkey) and a plurality in one (Indonesia) endorsed instead the view that "the United States basically controls the UN and can almost always make the UN do what the United States wants." (See figure 8-10.)

When the subject of the UN was raised in focus groups, concern about the United States dominating the UN was widely expressed, even as people expressed support some of the UN's activities.

FIGURE 8-10.   U.S. Influence on the UN

Which position is closer to yours?

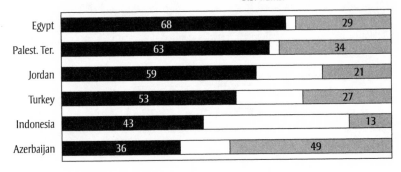

▐ The U.S. basically controls the UN and can almost always make the UN do what the U.S. wants.

▐ Through its veto the U.S. can stop the UN from doing things, but the U.S. cannot make the UN do things the U.S. wants.

Egypt	68	29
Palest. Ter.	63	34
Jordan	59	21
Turkey	53	27
Indonesia	43	13
Azerbaijan	36	49

Source: WorldPublicOpinion.org, 2008.

MODERATOR. How do you feel about the United Nations?

RESPONDENT 1. It is a tool in the hands of America. Its resolutions are fake resolutions that do not serve justice. All resolutions are issued according to the wishes of the American government.

MODERATOR. What about others?

R2. The UN has its positive and negative aspects. Its humanitarian duties are many, and this is really a good thing. . . . But from the political point of view, America is controlling the UN, and I suggest to the UN to nullify the right of veto in order to have equality between all countries.

An Egyptian focus group echoed similar themes, calling for repealing the U.S. power to veto UNSC resolutions.

MODERATOR. Would you like to see the UN more powerful than it is right now?

RESPONDENT 1. For whose interests?

R2. Yes, yes. It should be more powerful, but it should take the weak's side. The UN works only for one nation: the United States.

R1. If a resolution is vetoed, then it won't be implemented. So America is seizing the opinions of others. This veto should be canceled.

MODERATOR. Do the others think canceling the veto would be better?

ALL RESPONDENTS. Yes, of course.

R1. Instead of having one country only controlling the support and the resolutions too.

A recurring theme was that the UN should have the power to impose its will on the United States because of its legitimacy as representing the will of humanity. For example, in a focus group a Jordanian man invoked broad liberal international principles saying, "The UN is supposed to represent the majority of the world." He went on to explain, however, that the United States has betrayed this order by ignoring the UNSC's lack of support for the Iraq war and thus marginalizing the UN: "[The UN] did not approve the war on Iraq. Thus the war was not supposed to happen. When the United States did not take the UN's wish into consideration, it meant that the UN does not matter."

9 What the United States Can Do

On September 11, 2001, the United States was attacked by al Qaeda. The United States declared a war on terrorism, which was the basis for undertaking a major expansion of the U.S. military presence in the Muslim world. Major efforts to undermine the financing of al Qaeda's operations were instituted.

Years later it is unclear how much this effort has achieved. While in the run-up to 9/11 al Qaeda had been waning, it has subsequently renewed its strength and is operating throughout the Muslim world, from North Africa to the Arabian Peninsula to Pakistan to Indonesia.[1] There is no sign that it is reaching the end of its resources. It continues to receive a steady flow of funding. It has been building up new "franchises" in Yemen and in Somalia in the last two to three years. Most significant, it continues to have a steady flow of new recruits ready to commit to jihad and to martyr themselves on command.

This study has explored some of the reasons why. Al Qaeda has succeeded in being the lead formulator of a narrative that has been accepted by a large majority of Muslims. According to this narrative, the United States is oppressing the Muslim people. It dominates and exploits Muslim society and is seeking to undermine Islam. This merges with a broader narrative of Western encroachments into the Muslim world going back to the Crusades. American claims to be governed by universal principles of respect for national sovereignty, international law, and human rights are dismissed as subterfuge.

As previous chapters have shown, many Muslims do not approve of al Qaeda, and large majorities disapprove of such tactics as attacking civilians. As long as the society as a whole, however, embraces the narrative of oppression that fuels anger at America, there is likely to be a steady flow of recruits who are ready to express that anger in violent forms.

Such anger at America is not new. In the post-9/11 period, however, it appears to have worsened. Advancing American military forces into the Muslim world has increased the sense of threat. The perception of the United States as violating international norms by going to war with Iraq and in its treatment of terrorism suspects has amplified the anxiety about the United States as an unconstrained superpower. The discriminatory treatment of Muslims seeking to visit the United States has exacerbated the belief that the United States is hostile to Muslims.

According to al Qaeda's leaders, this was the desired effect of its attacks on America. Frustrated that Muslims were not clearly seeing the insidious nature of America's domination of the Muslim world, they sought to provoke America into revealing its true nature: domineering, violent, and hostile to Islam. This study reveals the success of this effort. The narrative of Muslim oppression by the West has been renewed, and al Qaeda has been elevated as its prime articulator.

This puts the United States in something of a bind. Naturally, it must seek to eliminate the al Qaeda leadership, especially since it plays such a key role in sustaining the narrative. But much of what it has done— expanding it military presence, killing and capturing suspected al Qaeda affiliates, controlling immigration from Muslim countries—has provoked a negative reaction in the Muslim world as a whole, added fodder to the narrative of American oppression, and improved the recruitment environment for al Qaeda. It is not clear that the United States has achieved any net gains, while the costs have been high.

The image of the United States as in conflict with the Muslim world— as seen through the lens of al Qaeda's narrative—also has a harmful consequence at a much more subtle level. As has been shown, most Muslims are drawn toward the idea of greater integration with the West—something potentially beneficial for the West as well for Muslims. At the same time, they fear being overwhelmed by Western influences. This creates an ambivalence, which, as long as it is experienced as an internal conflict, has the potential for being progressively resolved.

However, to the extent the conflict is experienced as an external one—with the United States as an outside force seeking to dominate them—Muslims tend to respond by identifying more closely with the forces within themselves rooted in traditional forms of Islam. Indeed, in the post-9/11 period Muslims have become more traditional, as evidenced, for example, by the more prevalent wearing of headscarves. Such changes have taken on political meaning within the context of Muslim relations with the United States. The changes are clearly desirable from the perspective of al Qaeda because they suppress the underlying attraction among Muslims to connect with the West and subvert the process of integration of liberal and Islamic values both within Muslims and between Islam and the West.

Besides increasing the sense of threat from American military power, in the post-9/11 period the Bush administration used rhetoric that contributed to the polarizing narrative that al Qaeda sought to further. Most notable was the unfortunate use of the term "crusade" to describe America's response to the 9/11 attacks. While it was presumably an honest mistake, it has to go down as one of the greatest public diplomacy errors in history. As mentioned, it was repeatedly cited in the focus groups as evidence that the United States seeks to undermine Islam.

More fundamental was the categorical statement to the world after 9/11 that "either you are with us or with the terrorists."[2] While most Muslims were repelled by the attacks of 9/11, few were ready to align themselves with the United States. Pressed to choose, they were more likely to choose the terrorists. The net effect was to push them closer to al Qaeda.

President Obama has been more effective in his rhetoric. In his speeches in Ankara and Cairo he made great efforts to communicate his respect for Islam. Polls at the time showed that he made some progress on this front and even helped soften some views of the United States. Pundits throughout the region, however, said they were looking to see if "actions" would follow, without necessarily defining which actions were meant. Most important, polls now show that the fundamental elements of the narrative of American oppression and betrayal—that the United States dominates the Muslim world and seeks to undermine Islam—are still firmly in place and are associated with Obama himself as well as the United States.

To truly counter the narrative of American oppression requires that the United States do more than communicate that the United States respects Islam. It requires that the American leadership answer two questions that it has not yet answered: (1) Is the United States ready to relinquish the image that America dominates the Muslim world? (2) Is the United States ready to actively trust the Muslim people to govern their societies?

Relinquishing the Image of American Domination

As has been shown, most Muslims perceive that the United States has extraordinary power over the Muslim world. The United States is seen as having a large military presence in Muslim regions of the world, extraordinary economic leverage, and huge influence over the media worldwide. Events are perceived as tending to go the way the United States wants. Ergo, it is assumed the United States is largely in control, and certainly far more than the United States will admit. The leaders of most Muslim countries are perceived as being to a large extent under the control of the United States.

The perception of the United States as being extraordinarily dominant, often in nontransparent ways, leads many Muslims to respond with a hypervigilance that spawns extreme beliefs about American power and control that border on the fantastical. When the United States is called "the Great Satan," it is more than an epithet, capturing the superhuman character of America's perceived power. Not all Muslims share these extreme views, but nearly all perceive America's power as vast, and a failure to perceive it as such is dismissed as naïve.

As Egyptian human rights activist Saad Ibrahim has commented, many Arabs today do not believe that they have "genuine sovereignty." Rather, they believe that "their national assets—including some foreign policy decisions—are not totally under their own control, but rather reflect foreign priorities," implicitly American ones.[3]

The felt imperative to resist American power has roots in religious identity and thus has a unique intensity. The United States is seen as seeking to undermine Islam and to impose a new order that removes religion from the public realm, while also having an underlying goal of furthering Christianity.

The need to resist American power also arises from the liberal values of freedom, national sovereignty, and people's right to self-determination. Interestingly, the irony that the United States is seen as a major purveyor of such values is not lost on most Muslims and is even a source of enhanced outrage that America does not live up to its values.

Within the West there is some debate about how much power the United States does and should have over the Muslim world. Some argue from both Marxist and realist perspectives that the United States is indeed an imperial power. Of those who believe this, some argue that such an outcome is simply inevitable, others that it is a moral travesty, and others that it is an unrecognized blessing to the Muslim people.

Others, however, argue that America's influence is really quite limited and is generally benign. According to this view, rather than being a threatening military power, America is a stabilizing force whose military presence is sanctioned by host governments. American diplomats could, no doubt, tick off a long list of changes they have tried and failed to bring about in Muslim countries. The effect of American popular media, it can be argued, is simply the result of Muslims choosing to consume it.

But the question of how much power the United States actually has is not the central issue. The fact is that Muslims believe the United States is dominant. They believe that the United States is controlling them. The question, then, is whether the United States wants to try to change that perception.

It is not self-evident that the United States would want to change it. Some American leaders may well believe that such a belief is an asset, that it serves U.S. interests. Whether the perception that America is controlling the Muslim world is accurate or not, the perceived potential for America to punish Muslims appears to make them, by their own account, more acquiescent to American wishes. In the current situation the United States can officially deny that it is controlling the Muslim world, but still elicit acquiescent behavior. To disabuse Muslims of the belief that the United States controls them may make them less acquiescent.

Yet as we have seen, the belief that the United States is controlling the Muslim world fuels a dangerous level of anger toward the United States, creating an environment that breeds a readiness to use violence against America and making it easier for anti-American groups such as al Qaeda to thrive. Simply eliminating these problematic manifestations while maintaining the broader status quo is not a real option. As we have seen, efforts to forcefully eliminate these hostile forces have bred more hostility. After nearly a decade of concerted efforts, there is no clear evidence of a net gain on this front. In short, the United States cannot have it both ways. It cannot sustain the benefits of Muslims believing the United States is in control but not have the blowback.

The idea that the United States, through effective communications, can persuade Muslims that the status quo, however defined, is indeed in their interest, thereby eliminating the blowback, is probably fatuous. Because they perceive the United States as having extensive control of their media and great influence over their governments, Muslims readily dismiss any such arguments as mere rhetoric. When such arguments were put forth in the focus groups, respondents reacted as if these were tired and disingenuous explanations.

Living with the status quo, including ongoing attacks on U.S. interests, is clearly an option. But it is also worthwhile to consider relinquishing the image of American control. This may well disrupt the status quo, but it may also diminish anger at America, including some of its virulent manifestations.

So how could this be done? What could the United States do to mitigate the perception that it controls the Muslim world? As mentioned, a strategy based entirely on rhetoric is unlikely to be effective. Persuading someone who believes that you are controlling them that you are not is itself an effort at control and is likely to be perceived as such. And like the perceived control, the effort to persuade them is likely to be seen as serving nefarious purposes.

Yet there are at least four other approaches that would likely be effective. These are as follows:

—Lighten the U.S. military footprint in the Muslim world.
—Minimize actual and implied threats.
—State that the United States does not have a right to Middle East oil.
—Differentiate the United States from Israel.

Naturally, other foreign policy considerations would have to be taken into account in the specifics of pursuing such approaches. But the significant potential benefits of mitigating Muslim anger at America and reducing the likelihood of the pernicious manifestations of such anger through these approaches should be recognized.

Lightening the U.S. Military Footprint

As has been shown, Muslims perceive the U.S. military presence in the Muslim world as threatening and coercive. All other things being equal, to mitigate the perception that the United States is dominating the Muslim world, the United States could seek opportunities to minimize this presence.

Quite apart from the effect the U.S. military presence has on Muslim public opinion, some analysts make the case for reducing this presence on purely strategic grounds, particularly in light of its potential for affecting recruitment. One of the major recommendations of the Afghanistan Study Group, an ad hoc group of policy analysts, was to "reduce the U.S. military footprint" in southern Afghanistan. According to this study group, the U.S. military presence "radicalizes many Pashtuns and is an important aid to Taliban recruitment."[4] More broadly, a RAND Corporation study by Seth Jones and Martin Libicki that examined terrorist groups concluded that in regions where such groups are operating, the United States should have a "light military footprint or none at all" and that military presence "is likely to increase terrorist recruitment."[5]

As the polls and focus groups have shown, Muslims are quite unequivocal in their opposition to U.S. military forces in Muslim countries. Very large majorities approve of al Qaeda's goal of getting U.S. forces out of all Muslim countries. Most believe that the U.S. military presence justifies attacks on American forces. And, as has been shown, large numbers—in some nations majorities—approve of attacks on U.S. troops in Afghanistan, Iraq, and the Persian Gulf.

Muslims also said in the polls that if the United States were to withdraw its forces from Muslim countries, it would have a positive effect on their views of the United States. As stated in chapter 3, the 2009 Sadat Chair poll of six Arab countries found that the two steps by the United States that would most improve respondents' views of the United States—out of seven options—were both related to the withdrawal of U.S. military forces from the region: U.S. withdrawal from Iraq and U.S. withdrawal from the Arabian Peninsula.[6] These even superseded the assumed effect of the United States brokering an Israeli-Palestinian peace agreement. Terror Free Tomorrow also found large majorities of Iranians, Pakistanis, and Saudis saying it would improve their opinion of the United States if it were to withdraw forces from Iraq.

The United States, of course, has now withdrawn its "combat forces" from Iraq. There is, however, a residual unresolved question about U.S. forces in Iraq. U.S. intervention in Iraq is widely seen as having been motivated by a desire to expand America's military footprint in the region. Even though the United States has withdrawn the bulk of its combat forces from Iraq, there is still uncertainty about whether the United States plans to maintain some kind of permanent military base there. WorldPublicOpinion.org (WPO) polling of Iraqis over the last few years has found that most Iraqis assume that the United States does plan to retain permanent bases, with 55 percent assuming this in the most recent poll in 2009.

The assumption that a U.S. military presence will remain in Iraq appears to play a key role in persisting support among Iraqis for attacks on U.S. troops there. Even though in 2009 WPO found only 44 percent of Iraqis wanting U.S. forces to leave sooner than the established timetable, 50 percent still approved of such attacks. Support for such attacks is strongly correlated with the belief that the U.S. plans to retain permanent bases. Thus it appears that support for attacks is prompted by a desire to ensure that the United States does not retain permanent bases.

Naturally, U.S. decisions about whether to retain such bases in Iraq should take into account the likelihood that the bases will be seen throughout the Muslim world as serving U.S. efforts at domination. Thus they will likely contribute to hostility toward the United States. As the polls have shown, large numbers of Muslims, in some countries majorities, approve of attacks on U.S. troops in Iraq, and this is likely to continue.

Reducing the U.S. military presence in the Persian Gulf would be another significant step. Large majorities disapprove of U.S. bases there. They reject the argument that these bases are stabilizing, saying they provoke more conflict than they prevent. Rather, they perceive them as part of America's coercive and threatening presence in the region. Most also believe, correctly, that the people living in the Gulf also oppose them, adding to the sense of their illegitimacy.

It is normal and appropriate to say that U.S. military planning should be run according to strategic objectives, not by concern for political optics. It appears, however, that the primary purpose of the forces in the Gulf, including the expanded presence after 9/11, is already prompted by its desired effect on political optics—to project power as a show of resolve—more than military requirements.

The question, then, is whether the effects of having those forces there are optimal. Intimidation through a military presence can have desirable effects. But reassurance through the lessening of a military presence can also have desirable effects. The challenge is to find the proper balance. The findings of this study suggest that the effect of recent U.S. actions has been to tip the balance in the direction of intimidation. This has stimulated a backlash throughout the Muslim world, with U.S. forces seen as part of America's war on Islam in response to 9/11 as well as part of its ongoing effort to exploit Middle East oil. The fact that Arab governments in the region have officially invited the United States to have bases there is not highly relevant. As we have seen, majorities disapprove of the presence of Western troops even when a Muslim government requests it.

Reducing the U.S. military presence in the Gulf may actually be one of the least difficult steps to take. It is not entirely clear how much the U.S. presence there is critical from a military point of view. Until the early 1980s the United States had a very small presence there. This did not appear to have major consequences for U.S. capabilities. Even the most drastic scenario—a power such as Iran blocking the Strait of Hormuz—can be addressed by forces based in Diego Garcia as well as other over-the-horizon capabilities. The proximity of forces in the Gulf is unlikely to play a critical role.

Reducing the current magnitude of the forces in the Gulf is complicated, however, by ongoing operations in Iraq and Afghanistan. Nevertheless, these forces are expected to be drawn down over the next few years. As this happens the United States should reassess the costs and benefits of different levels of U.S. presence there.

In regard to all aspects of U.S. involvement in the Muslim world as well as the Gulf, the United States could look for ways to multilateralize its methods for pursuing its objectives, including the protection of sea lanes. As has been shown, Muslims perceive multilateral efforts, especially those associated with the UN, as having more legitimacy. Such efforts are less apt to be perceived as a means for the United States to expand its dominance. This perception is predicated on the assumption that multilateralization imposes some constraints on the United States. It may indeed impose some constraints, but the costs of any such constraints would need to be weighed against the potential benefits of the greater perceived legitimacy of such multilateral approaches.

In the focus groups respondents were fairly unequivocal about their preference for U.S. dominance to be replaced by a multilateral system, and there was optimism that a transition to such a system is possible.

> MODERATOR. OK, so let's imagine that the United States pulled out all the bases [in the Persian Gulf], stopped giving aid, just basically disengaged from the region, saying we're not going to be involved here anymore. What would happen?
>
> RESPONDENT 1. The United Nations can replace the law of the policeman played by the United States.
>
> R2. In a hypothetical situation, if the United States would withdraw, I think another system would replace it, and I think the United Nations can play a role to stabilize areas like Darfur, Israel, Palestine, Iraq.
>
> R3. Every country can play this role [of policeman], but within the framework of the UN.
>
> R4. I think the scenario would go like this: If America disappears from the area, there will a state of chaos. The reason is that the power balance would be different then. But this won't last forever. It would only continue for a period of time, after which there will be stability.

A more difficult challenge is how the United States can minimize its military footprint relative to the operation in Afghanistan. Opposition to the U.S. presence there is strong throughout most of the Muslim world. Majorities in most, though not all, Muslim nations polled disapproved of the decision in February 2009 to increase the number of American troops in Afghanistan.

The Obama administration has stated that drawdowns will begin in 2011, though their pace has not been specified. Reiterating the intention to draw down troops can be helpful. It is likely, however, that Afghanistan will be the arena in which the United States will have the most direct confrontations with Muslims over the next few years.

To mitigate the effect of the U.S. presence, the administration can draw on several aspects of the situation in Afghanistan. First, there is some sympathy for the goal of keeping the Taliban from regaining power. As mentioned in chapter 3, in 2009 WPO found majorities in five of seven majority-Muslim nations polled saying it would be bad if the Taliban regained power in Afghanistan. Also, as discussed, many Muslims incorrectly assume that most Afghans want NATO forces out. The 2009 WPO poll found that majorities or pluralities in six of seven nations polled believe the people of Afghanistan want NATO forces to leave immediately. The Afghan public, however, has consistently expressed support for the presence of U.S. forces there. A December 2009 ABC/BBC poll found 68 percent approving of the presence of "U.S. military forces," an increase from 63 percent in January of that year, and three-quarters said that attacks on U.S. or NATO forces cannot be justified. Sixty-one percent approved of Obama's increase of troops levels.

These opinions are an important public diplomacy asset that the United States is clearly not capitalizing on. WPO found that among Muslims who believe that most Afghans approve of the NATO presence there, large majorities in every nation—on average eight in ten—said they favor its continued presence. Conversely, among those who believe that most Afghans oppose the NATO presence, an average of eight in ten said it should be ended. Thus increasing awareness of Afghan support is likely to have a positive effect on attitudes toward the U.S. presence there.

One reason that so many Muslims assume that Afghans oppose the U.S. presence in their country is that much reporting has focused on Afghans' frustration with the way the U.S. forces have operated in Afghanistan. Polls show that this is quite real. As discussed in chapter 3, the ABC/BBC poll found that majorities are generally critical of U.S. forces and are especially unhappy with the U.S.-caused civilian casualties.

All this points to the need to put a greater priority on avoiding Afghan civilian casualties. Naturally, when the focus is on achieving military gains against the Taliban, many of whom are difficult to distinguish from the general population, prioritizing the avoidance of civilian casualties may seem like an onerous restraint. Nevertheless, civilian casualties have a direct impact on the recruiting environment for anti-American forces not only in Afghanistan, but in the wider Muslim world. Also, were frustration about the conduct of American forces to subside in Afghanistan, this would likely increase support for the presence of U.S. forces among the Afghan people and help improve perceptions throughout the Muslim world.

Pakistan also poses a conundrum for the United States. As has been shown, for some time Pakistanis have strongly opposed any U.S. military presence in Pakistan and perceive the U.S. military as a greater threat to Pakistan than Islamist militants operating there. Pakistanis have also shown reluctance to support an aggressive campaign by its military to root out Pakistani Taliban, Afghan Taliban, and al Qaeda forces in their country, apparently in significant part because this would effectively align them with U.S. goals.

After the Pakistani Taliban advanced into the Swat Valley in 2009, however, attitudes shifted. Concern about these fighters grew, and majorities supported a more aggressive campaign by Pakistani government forces. Large majorities, however, have continued to oppose U.S. military involvement in fighting the Pakistani Taliban and strikes on Afghan Taliban and al Qaeda forces operating there, including with Predator drones. Animosity about such actions is, of course, enhanced when U.S. strikes kill Pakistani civilians.

Within Pakistan there are high-value targets, especially al Qaeda leadership, whose elimination would be valuable in terms of the ideological battle with al Qaeda in addition to being militarily significant. American military planners, however, in making the cost-benefit analysis of any particular military action, need to consider the high cost of its impact on attitudes toward the United States and the potential for undermining support for Pakistani government action against militants.

The United States should also reevaluate the trend toward increasing use of the military in humanitarian activities and economic development. Prompted by the recognition that U.S. military forces are not viewed favorably in the Muslim world, there has been an effort to "win hearts and minds" by having the U.S. military, rather than civilian nongovernmental organizations (NGOs), carry out such programs. Such efforts are not likely to affect the core perception that U.S. military forces perform a fundamentally coercive function. Instead, by displacing American civilian programs that are of a more explicitly humanitarian nature, it is likely to increase the perception that the role of the United States in Muslim countries is fundamentally a military one. The goal should be to diminish the military aspect of America's relationship with the Muslim world, not to expand it.

Finally, the question arises about whether it is politically feasible for the United States to lighten its military footprint in the Muslim world. Polls of the American public suggest that such a move is unlikely to encounter majority resistance. Support for bases in Muslim countries is already quite soft. Asked by the Chicago Council on Global Affairs in 2010 whether the United State should have long-term military bases in a list of countries that included four majority-Muslim countries, respondents showed modest support for bases in Afghanistan (52 percent) and Iraq (50 percent), while majorities were opposed to bases in Turkey (53 percent opposed to 43 percent in favor) and Pakistan (52 percent opposed to 45 percent in favor).

Americans have expressed serious doubts about the value of the U.S. military presence in the Middle East. Asked in a BBC/GlobeScan/PIPA poll in December 2006 whether the U.S. military presence in the Middle East is a "stabilizing force" or "provokes more conflict than it prevents," a majority of Americans (53 percent) said that it provokes more conflict. Only 33 percent saw it as a stabilizing force. In a November 2006 WPO poll, 68 percent of Americans said they were opposed to having "permanent military bases in Iraq."

Americans also show a readiness to be responsive to the preferences of the people in the region. When asked in a 2004 Chicago Council poll what the United States should do if "a majority of people in the Middle East want the U.S. to remove its military presence there," a strong majority of 59 percent said the United States should remove it (37 percent said it should not). And asked by WPO in November 2006 how the United States should respond if the Iraqi government were to oppose permanent U.S. bases there, 85 percent of Americans said the United States should comply with this preference.

More generally, Americans express some discomfort with the United States playing a policing role. In the 2010 Chicago Council poll, 79 percent agreed that "the U.S. is playing the role of world policeman more than it should be."

Minimizing the Use of Implied Threats

Clearly, the United States is not going to abandon the option of making implied threats to use military force. It should be recognized, however, that in the context of the U.S. relationship with the Muslim world, making such threats—especially to use force outside of the constraints of international law—is costly. The costs are not simply in terms of public diplomacy and a less positive image of the United States, or the long-term concern about the erosion of the international norms against the unilateral use of military force for nondefensive purposes. Such implied threats enhance the image of the United States as an unconstrained military power, which has been shown to increase support for and the recruitment potential of radical Islamist groups hostile to the United States. Such costs are significant, and American policymakers should make certain that they are not incurred inadvertently. It should be realistically recognized that certain actions may be perceived as threatening even if they can be justified on other grounds. Above all, the costs of making implied threats should be incurred judiciously.

A key example of such an implied threat is the use of the phrase that "all options are on the table" in the effort to dissuade a Muslim country, most recently Iran, from taking action opposed by the United States. Clearly, this signals the readiness to use military force. Most problematic is that it signals a readiness to take military action unilaterally, without UN Security Council approval, as the United States did against Iraq in 2003. As has been shown, the intensely negative reaction to the Iraq war stemmed more from the concern that it signaled American readiness to use military force outside of the bounds of international law more than concern about the toppling of the government of Saddam Hussein.

Another type of implied threat is the conduct of war games. Arguably, these are simply necessary for training purposes and can be conducted quietly. They are often conducted, however, in a way that is meant to be an implied threat to use such force. For example, when British sailors were captured by Iran in 2007 and diplomatic efforts were under way to free them, the United States conducted a very large war game involving more than 10,000 U.S. personnel that lasted for several days and simulated attacks on enemy aircraft and ships. In an Associated Press article titled "U.S. Navy Flexes Muscles in Persian Gulf," one of the commanders of the operation explained, "If there is strong presence, then it sends a clear message that you better be careful about trying to intimidate others," clearly linking this to Iran's actions. A Pentagon spokesman also tried to put the war games in a broader context, explaining that "the exercise should reassure our friends and allies of our commitment to security and stability in the region." Such statements confirm Muslim perceptions that the United States is ready to use military force to maintain the type of order in the region that serves its interests.

Stating that it is or might be a U.S. goal to bring about regime change is also an implied threat to use military force. This language was used in the run-up to the overthrow of the Saddam Hussein, and thus when it is used in relation to Iran, it is read as an implied threat to undertake a similar action against the government in Tehran. Furthermore, the intimidation resulting from the threat is not simply felt by the people in the country whose government the United States is targeting. People in all countries perceive that they too could be subject to such threats if their governments were to depart too far from policies preferred by the United States, and, as has been shown, this provokes a strong reaction.

Yet one more implied threat, once again aimed at Iran as well as North Korea, was embedded in the 2010 Nuclear Posture Review. While the United States committed to not use its nuclear weapons against non-nuclear states, it carved out an exception for countries that are not in good standing in regard to the Nuclear Non-Proliferation Treaty (NPT)—an unambiguous reference to Iran and North Korea. Such a statement is, of course, perceived—and is presumably meant to be perceived—as a possible threat to use nuclear weapons if the target country does not comply with American demands. The deterrent benefits of intensifying the threat against Iran by implying that the United States might not just use its conventional forces, but nuclear weapons as well, needs to be weighed against the costs incurred by the image of the United States implicitly brandishing the first-use of nuclear weapons against a Muslim state. Such an implied threat is inconsistent with the intent of the Non-Proliferation Treaty, which delegitimates the use of nuclear weapons except, temporarily, for deterrent purposes. Thus threats of this sort are perceived as consistent with the image of the United States as pressing other nations to abide by the constraints of a liberal international order while refusing to accept those constraints itself.

The American public is also unlikely to oppose refraining from using threats of military force, at least in regard to Iran. In 2006 WPO asked Americans, "Do you think the U.S. should deal with the government of Iran primarily by trying to build better relations, or pressuring it with implied threats that the U.S. may use military force against it?" A 75 percent majority rejected the option of pressuring Iran with implied threats and preferred to try to build better relations. Consistent with this preference for building better relations, in the more recent 2010 Chicago Council poll, 65 percent of Americans said that the United States should be ready to meet and talk with the leaders of Iran.

Renouncing a Right to Middle East Oil

The U.S. government has never made the statement that it has a right to Middle East oil irrespective of the wishes of the sovereign rights of the governments there. Nonetheless, Muslims clearly perceive that the United States has granted itself such a right. When, as has been shown, very large majorities say it is a U.S. goal "to maintain control over the oil resources of the Middle East," most respondents assume they are stating the obvious. As a member of a Pakistani focus group said, the United States has "this point of view that the oil and gas is ours." U.S. military forces in the Gulf are seen as a means to ensure that right, by threatening or, if necessary, actually using force to gain such access. Not surprisingly, Muslims find this offensive, humiliating, a violation of their sovereignty, and a betrayal of the principles of international law that the United States purports to stand for.

Something that has contributed to Muslims' impression that the United States claims such a right is the Carter Doctrine. After the Soviets invaded Afghanistan in 1979, President Jimmy Carter issued the following statement: "Let our position be absolutely clear. An attempt by any outside force to gain control of the Persian Gulf region will be regarded as an assault on the vital interests of the United States of America, and such an assault will be repelled by any means necessary, including military force."

Even though this statement was targeted at the Soviet Union, it was widely read as the United States giving notice to the world that it regards the countries of the Gulf as having limited sovereignty, that these countries' interests are subordinate to America's interests, and that the United States has assigned itself the right to take whatever action is needed to preserve its access to Middle East oil. This was seen as continuous with a variety of U.S. actions perceived as removing threats to that access, including participation in the overthrow of Iranian president Mossadegh in the early 1950s in response to his popularly supported nationalization of Iran's oil industry. It was also seen as part of America's extensive economic role in the development of the oil industry in the Gulf, such that the United States could think of these assets as belonging to the United States irrespective of the views of the host government.

One may claim that this is all a big misunderstanding, that the United States has not accorded itself this unique right. But arguing over the historical record is unlikely to be effective. American leaders could, however, mitigate this perception by periodically making statements to the effect that Persian Gulf governments have sovereignty over their territory, including the oil there. Reducing America's military footprint in the Gulf and/or multilateralizing the policing of the Gulf would further contribute to the impression that the United States does not lay claim to such access.

Some may argue that this would send the wrong signal—that the United States can have it both ways by never claiming the right to access, but not countering the belief that the United States *has* effectively laid claim to Middle East oil. Some may argue that this ambiguity serves U.S. interests by having an intimidating effect while preserving deniability. From the perspective of the Muslim people, however, there does not appear to be much ambiguity. The United States is simply perceived as laying claim to Middle East oil. And Muslims are largely correct that the United States has not tried to disabuse them of this perception.

Thus U.S. policymakers need to decide whether having Muslims continue to believe that the United States has made a claim to Middle East oil—along with all the anger it generates—produces a net benefit for U.S. foreign policy. While it may intimidate people in the region and elicit acquiescence, it also elicits a belief that defiance—even in violent forms— serves Muslim interests (by affirming national sovereignty and restoring Muslim pride) and is justified by international law.

Differentiating the United States from Israel

Muslims tend to see the United States and Israel as largely continuous. Some view Israel as controlling the United States through pro-Israel lobbying organizations. The high visibility of Jews in America's foreign policy establishment is seen as further evidence of a kind of infiltration. But the more common view is that the United States controls Israel. U.S. aid to Israel, especially its military aid and security guarantees, are seen as purchasing American influence. Others perceive the influence as flowing in both directions in a symbiotic relationship.

This perception of the United States and Israel as so deeply interconnected creates complications for the United States, in that Muslims perceive the United States as effectively responsible for Israel's behavior. This leads them to look to the United States to press Israel to be more accommodating in its relations with the Palestinians and the Arab world in general, with a high level of confidence that the United States could do so if it wished. Ironically, the kind of control they look to the United States to exert over Israel is just the kind of hegemonic domination that they complain the United States imposes on them.

In terms of the American public, the executive branch does have the option of playing a more even-handed role in the conflict between Israel and its neighbors and even pressuring Israel harder to be more accommodating. A large majority of Americans have consistently favored the United States not taking sides in the Middle East conflict, most recently in a 2010 Chicago Council on Global Affairs poll in which 66 percent favored the United States not taking sides in the Middle East conflict (28 percent favored taking Israel's side). Some older polls have found a readiness to put greater pressure on Israel. In a 2002 CNN poll 74 percent said they would support "apply[ing] economic and diplomatic pressure to Israelis to try to reach a peaceful solution." In 2003 PIPA found 63 percent in favor of reducing aid to Israel as a way of pressuring it to move toward a peace agreement. More recent polling does not indicate any change in this attitude. A 2009 PIPA poll found that opposition to Israel building settlements in the Palestinian Territories had increased from 52 percent in 2002 to 75 percent in 2009.

The United States could also invest more capital in trying to broker an Israeli-Palestinian peace agreement. Polls of Muslims show that they would like the United States to do so and that this would improve their feelings toward the United States. Indeed, brokering such an agreement would probably be the most powerful game changer in the relationship with the Muslim world, and it behooves the United States to continue to make such efforts. The Obama administration's efforts to revive talks in September 2010 and reach an agreement within one year are certainly being watched closely. Letting the peace process languish, however, would surely be read as an acceptance of the status quo, which is perceived as favoring Israel.

As is well known, there are many complex forces inside and outside the United States arrayed against the realization of a peace agreement between Israel and the Palestinians. Though polls indicate that a majority of the people in Israel and the Palestinian Territories believe the two can find common ground, powerful political forces on both sides regularly stymie the realization of this possibility. And it is not clear that this situation will change anytime soon, even with a renewed American commitment. Polls show Arabs are also quite pessimistic about the prospect of ever achieving peace between Israel and the Palestinians.

Al Qaeda has capitalized on this impasse by making part of its core narrative the argument that the United States is rightfully subject to terrorist attacks as long as the Palestinian people are suffering. By making a hurdle that the United States cannot jump over even if it wanted to, al Qaeda ensures that the conflict with the United States will be legitimated indefinitely.

Thus the United States needs to assess options for mitigating the effect of Israel's conflicts with the Palestinians—and the Arab world in general—short of achieving a peace agreement. The challenge is to find ways to differentiate the United States and Israel in the minds of Muslims. The goal is to reduce the perceptions that America is effectively responsible for Israel's behavior and that America is under the control of Israel.

Recent efforts by the Obama administration to get Israel to stop building settlements in East Jerusalem have some modest potential to succeed in unblocking the peace process. But even if they do not succeed, these efforts help weaken the perception of the United States and Israel as one and the same.

Showing humanitarian concern for the Palestinians' plight helps form an emotional bond between the United States and Palestinians that is not mediated by Israel. Obama pursued this approach when, during the election, he cited the suffering of the Palestinian people. To this end, humanitarian aid to Palestinians should be clearly differentiated from any effort to influence Palestinian behavior relative to Israel.

One of the key ways for the United States to differentiate itself from Israel is to refrain from framing Israel's conflict with Hamas and other Palestinian groups that use terrorism as being continuous with America's conflict with al Qaeda. The whole notion of a "war on terrorism" lends itself to such conflation. The United States can condemn Hamas' refusal to accept Israel's right to exist and its terrorist methods without portraying the United States as being at war with Hamas.

The United States also needs to take into account the consequences of U.S. complicity—since 1969—in Israel's refusal to acknowledge its nuclear weapons as part of its policy of "nuclear ambiguity." This posture is fraught with problems for U.S. relations with the Muslim world. Since the United States has taken the position that all nations should participate in the NPT, refusing to recognize Israel's nuclear weapons implicitly affirms the illegitimacy of Israel's possessing nuclear weapons. At the same time, by refusing to acknowledge them, the United States is perceived as party to Israel's nuclear weapons program.

It does appear that the Obama administration has recently taken an incremental step away from this position by stating that it is a U.S. goal for Israel to be part of the NPT. In May 2009 assistant secretary of state Rose Gottemoeller, speaking at a UN meeting on the NPT, said Israel should join the treaty: "Universal adherence to the NPT itself, including by India, Israel, Pakistan, and North Korea . . . remains a fundamental objective of the United States."[7]

More broadly, the United States can look for subtle opportunities to differentiate U.S. national interests from those of Israel. Even the choice of words in diplomatic language can help make this distinction. Differentiating the United States from Israel may actually have a positive effect on the Middle East peace process. It would likely increase America's credibility as playing an even handed role (a role the American public favors). It may also put forward a model that would encourage major Arab countries to feel less of a need to keep such close ranks with the Palestinians and freer to press them to be accommodating.

Naturally, any such steps will raise alarms that the United States may be withdrawing its security commitment to Israel. Such a perception would indeed be destabilizing were it to lead any actors in the Arab world to assume that America is not committed to ensuring the territorial integrity of Israel. Thus the United States would need to regularly reaffirm its commitment to Israel.

Ironically, to facilitate the differentiation of the United States from Israel, it may be useful for the United States to formalize America's security commitment to Israel in the form of a treaty (which it has not done). This could provide reassurance to Israel, but could also normalize the nature of America's commitment to Israel. It could help clarify that, as with other allies, such a security commitment does not make the United States an effective party to whatever actions Israel takes.

Trusting the Muslim People with Democracy

As has been shown, a major source of Muslim anger at America is its perceived opposition to democracy in the Muslim world. Because the United States supports democracy virtually everywhere else, Muslims conclude that this is driven by a mistrust of what the Muslim people might decide, in particular the decision to create an Islamist state that, among other things, might try to manipulate its power over the oil supply to achieve an ideological end. It is not hard to see how this is perceived as an expression of fundamentally anti-Islamic attitudes in the U.S. leadership.

One can debate what U.S. motives truly are. At times the United States has tried to promote democracy, even pressing governments to be more democratic. At other times it has turned a blind eye and implicitly supported the suppression of democracy in Algeria, Egypt, and Jordan. It has accepted Pakistan as an officially Islamist state and even accepted certain Islamist principles being written into the Iraqi constitution. But it has been cool, if not hostile, to Islamist groups that call for making sharia the basis of law and has been unambiguously hostile to Iran's system, even though Iran is actually one of the most democratic Muslim countries. While the United States has called for democracy at times, many Muslims are quite aware of how George W. Bush's renewed commitment to democracy in 2005 quickly evaporated once the candidates affiliated with the Muslim Brotherhood and Hamas did well at the ballot box.

This perception of America as not trusting the Muslim people is the flip side of the perception that the United States is seeking to control the Muslim world. A failure to trust the Muslim people is perceived as, and logically leads to, an effort to control. To convince Muslims that it is not trying to control them, the United States must convince them that it trusts them. This is not something that can be faked. Ultimately, the United States must make a decision about whether to trust the Muslim people to determine their fate—a decision that has not been clearly made.

One may argue that the Muslim people have to earn America's trust. But this is not likely to happen under the current circumstances. Muslims find this notion both insulting and inconsistent with liberal principles, just as Americans would. They believe that self-determination is their right, not something they must earn. When the U.S. projects a message that Muslims' right to self-determination is conditional on America's judgment, this produces an angry backlash, not a desire to prove their trustworthiness to the United States.

Still, one may ask whether trusting the Muslim people to determine their fate might not lead to something worse. The greatest concern is that allowing self-determination and democracy will lead to the election of Islamists who will then use their positions to reverse democracy and impose an authoritarian theocratic order—the fear embodied in the presumed Islamist aspiration of "one man, one vote, one time" formulated by Bernard Lewis and subsequently echoed by many others.

The probability of such an outcome is not zero; neither is it certain. Scholars argue at length about how probable it is. The findings of this study, especially those in chapter 8, suggest that Muslims are receptive to some Islamist ideas, but they are also quite wedded to liberal ideas of democracy, human rights, and even pluralism. Thus an elected Islamist party with authoritarian aspirations would likely face stiff resistance from the population.

Deciding to trust the Muslim people is a difficult issue, and, as with all difficult decisions, is a gamble that comes with some degree of uncertainty and anxiety. It is understandable that one could conclude that the present tensions between the United States and the Muslim world are preferable to the uncertainties that would come with trusting the Muslim people to decide their fate. It should be recognized, though, that there is little reason to expect relations to improve within the present structure.

So what would it mean to trust the Muslim people? First, it would not mean abandoning the fight with al Qaeda. Al Qaeda effectively declared war on the United States, and the United States must defend itself. As long as the al Qaeda leadership has the intention and the means to attack Americans, the United States must continue to seek to eliminate the al Qaeda leadership. Indeed, one of the main reasons for the United States to shift its stance toward the Muslim people is that it would change the conditions in the Muslim world that help sustain al Qaeda.

Trusting the Muslim people would also not mean abandoning Israel to the tender mercies of the Arab world. The United States has made a security commitment to Israel, and there is no reason why it should reverse this.

Probably the most important change the United States could make is one that could be communicated in subtle ways. Lacing diplomatic communications with references to the rights of Muslim people to democracy and self-determination is paramount. As noted, when George W. Bush spoke of a renewed commitment to democracy, it had strong repercussions throughout the Muslim world. As Saad Ibrahim has noted, "In the twelve months that followed, an unprecedented number of elections and referenda took place, namely in Iraq, Palestine, Egypt, Lebanon, Kuwait, Bahran, Qatar, and even Saudi Arabia. . . . Even Islamists, despite their long-standing belief that democracy is a repugnant Western importation, changed their mind and joined the bandwagon." A renewed emphasis may well have a similar effect.

As mentioned, affirming that Middle East nations have a sovereign right to the oil on their territory would also help to remove a key ambiguity. America's refusal to trust Muslims is widely seen as a subordination of Muslims' right to self-determination to America's need for access to oil.

Providing financial support for democracy promotion would also send an important signal. Some of this aid should naturally flow to governments, especially for proving technical assistance in conducting elections. Only sending aid to governments, however, suggests that the United States is only interested in appearances, continuing to sustain a fundamentally undemocratic order that happens to serve U.S. interests without truly seeking to support democracy. Truly promoting democracy means helping to develop civil society. This requires the creation of NGOs that help give voice to the values and concerns of the general public that are not being adequately reflected in government policy. Of particular value are organizations that explicitly align themselves with the will of the people.

This may seem to pose a conundrum for the United States. Promoting civil society would in all probability lead to tensions with existing authoritarian governments. The United States would no doubt be accused of trying to impose its will and its efforts would be cast as part of the narrative of American domination. (This may be one reason why the Obama administration has moved away from providing such support.) The term "democracy promotion" also comes with some negative baggage since it was used as a rationale for the Iraq war. In Iran it is likely that the general public would view such efforts with suspicion.

But in focus groups elsewhere in the Muslim world, respondents expressed support for American efforts at democracy promotion through developing civil society, even if such efforts might not be welcomed by their governments. Indeed, the tension that it could create between the United States and authoritarian governments would likely add to the credibility of American commitments to democracy.

Finally, there is the issue of how the American public would react over time if U.S. policy shifted toward trusting the Muslim people with democracy. Americans tend to think that Islam and democracy are compatible and that the possible difficulties for the United States in the process are worth risking. When given two alternatives in a 2005 WPO poll, only 34 percent said that "democracy and Islam are incompatible," while a clear majority of 55 percent said "it is possible for Islamic countries to be democratic."

Americans show a modest tendency toward supporting democracy in Muslim countries even if this might mean that the elected government might be less friendly to the United States. In the same 2005 WPO poll a 48 percent plurality still said they would want to see an Islamic country become more democratic "even if this resulted in the country being more likely to oppose U.S. policies" (39 percent disagreed). Asked specifically about Saudi Arabia, 54 percent thought the United States should support free elections there even if it is likely that the elected government would be unfriendly.

When the Chicago Council in 2010 presented a scenario in which a Muslim country "would probably elect an Islamist fundamentalist leader" once it became democratic, only 5 percent said that the United States should discourage democracy there. Just 25 percent said that the United States should encourage it, while 68 percent said it should not take a position either way.

Taking a Friendlier Stance toward Moderate Islamists

Perhaps the most concrete change that could help improve relations with the Muslim world would be for America to change its stance toward moderate Islamist parties. While Islamist parties get mixed reviews among Muslim publics, they are, nonetheless, widely seen as being legitimate players in the political process. America's suspicious and standoffish stance toward many of them, especially the Muslim Brotherhood, has contributed significantly to the perception that the United States is anti-Islamic and denies Muslims the right to self-determination. Refusing to grant visas to highly regarded scholars who endorse Islamist ideas, even when they are also explicitly prodemocratic and antiterrorist, is seen as discriminatory. When Islamism, not radicalism, is targeted, then Islam itself appears to be the real target.

Naturally, the United States must clearly the draw the line at Islamist groups that are not moderate, in other words, those that call for the use of violence—especially violence against civilians—as a means of bringing about the Islamicization of society. But regarding parties that aspire to make sharia the basis of law as outside the pale puts the United States at odds with the majority of the Muslim people who regard such a position as legitimate and as not contradictory with democracy. The key factor for most Muslim people is whether such groups pursue these goals through legitimate, nonviolent political means.

The Muslim Brotherhood has made great efforts to persuade American leaders of its democratic and peaceful intentions. Brotherhood leaders have, at times, endorsed the use of violence, most notably when Sayyid Qutb was highly influential in the 1950s and 1960s. And as mentioned previously, a member of the Brotherhood did attempt to assassinate Egyptian President Gamal Abdel Nasser in 1954. For some time now, however, the Brotherhood has distanced itself from the ideas of Qutb and has been quite consistent in its rejection of the use of violence to bring about political change.

The Brotherhood is still committed to bringing about Islamic states in Muslim countries, with sharia being the cornerstone of the legal system. Its party platform, however, is replete with references to democratic principles and human rights.[8] To Western ears this clearly seems like a contradiction. How can the people rule, as in a democracy, and at the same time have sharia dictate laws? Islamist scholars are quick to argue that this is not fundamentally different than a traditional constitutional democracy, whose constitution limits what the popular will can decide.

This defense is similar to the defense of the Islamist idea of having an ulema—a body of religious scholars who would have the power to veto laws it determines to be contrary to Islamic law. Islamists point out that this is essentially the same as the power of the supreme judicial body in liberal democracies to overturn laws deemed to be contrary to the nation's constitution.

In response to Western criticism, the Muslim Brotherhood has attempted to soften aspects of its platform. While it has endorsed the idea of the ulema, more recently it backed away from giving it binding power to veto laws, giving it, instead, an advisory role. While the Brotherhood has said that only Muslim men can hold office in an Islamist state, more recently it has said that this limit only applies to the office of the president.

Nonetheless, the Obama administration has largely continued the cool posture toward the Muslim Brotherhood of earlier administrations. The State Department has continued the policy of not having direct contact with the Muslim Brotherhood, though there have been contacts with some parliamentarians affiliated with the Brotherhood explicitly in their capacity as parliamentarians. When Obama spoke in Cairo in June 2009, he reportedly invited members of the Muslim Brotherhood to the speech.[9]

In the speech itself, however, he implicitly reiterated the long-standing suspicion that Islamist groups attempting to participate in the democratic political process, once in office, would revert to authoritarianism. He said, "There are some who advocate for democracy only when they are out of power. Once in power, they are ruthless in suppressing the rights of others. No matter where it takes hold, government of the people and by the people sets a single standard for all who hold power." Obama then, curiously, shifted to speaking in the second person, as if he were addressing specific individuals in the lecture hall: "You must maintain your power through consent, not coercion. You must respect the rights of minorities and participate with a spirit of tolerance and compromise."[10]

Many Muslims—as well as members of the Muslim Brotherhood—find such comments frustrating and even insulting. There are no cases when an Islamist party was elected through a democratic process and then became undemocratic. Thus it is heard as simply a fear held by Americans that tends to be specifically directed at Muslims. Despite the protestations of the Brotherhood that it is indeed democratic, the United States has taken a position that it is not yet convinced. Islamists may well feel that they are being treated as guilty until proven innocent. And what would prove this innocence is not entirely clear, short of simply abandoning Islamist principles.

Principles aside, from the U.S. perspective, taking a friendly stance toward moderate Islamists does entail a degree of risk. It therefore makes sense to try to determine as far as possible the intentions of these ostensibly moderate Islamists and assess the viability of an alternative stance toward them. Various scholars and policy analysts have attempted such an assessment. To a striking extent the conclusions of these assessments have been largely convergent, providing reassurance and encouragement for more engagement.

A leading example is the assessment of Emile Nakleh, the recently retired CIA officer who directed its Political Islam Strategic Analysis Program. In that role he undertook a major effort to understand Islamists, conducting extensive interviews as well as tracking their formal statements. He writes:

The leaders of mainstream Islamic political parties and movements—such as the Muslim Brotherhood (MB) in Egypt and elsewhere, elements of Hamas in Palestine and Hizballah in Lebanon, the Islamic Action Front in Jordan, the Islamic Constitutional Movement in Kuwait, the Wifaq in Bahrain, the Islamic Party of Malaysia, the Prosperous Justice Party in Indonesia, and Justice and Development Party (AKP) in Turkey—they advocate a centrist (*wasatiyya*) politico-religious ideology and are committed to nonviolence and gradual change.[11]

He largely dismisses the concern that Islamists will turn radical once in office, arguing that based on the historical record they are more apt to become less radical.

Once these parties became part of the political process, they competed for votes, moderated their message, cooperated with other, mostly secular groups to pass legislation, and generally adopted a pragmatic attitude toward governance. . . . The "parties of God" have at long last decided to set aside their commitment to "divine rule" (*hukm*) and play in the sandbox of the "democracy of man.[12]

He also expresses confidence in the Muslim public.

The electorates in many Muslim countries are becoming more sophisticated and discriminating and generally do not vote for radical parties and their candidates. Islamic political parties that tend to overemphasize their Islamic credentials have not done well in national elections.[13]

Ultimately, he comes to the unequivocal conclusion that engaging moderate nationalist Islamists is the best way to isolate and weaken radical Islamists such as al Qaeda.

The ideological divide that separates nationalist Islamic parties from al-Qa'ida and other radical groups is at the center of an ongoing debate within Islam and could be exploited to involve these parties in the political process. Al-Qa'ida's strenuous and shrill objections to the participation of Islamic parties in elections, as demonstrated in several statements by Bin Ladin's deputy al-Zawahiri, has failed to dissuade these parties from participating in national elections, indicating that nationalist Islamic activism remains a potent force. . . . Not dealing with these parties is no longer tenable and in the long run will be harmful to American national security. As several of these parties have made a serious commitment to democracy and have shown a high degree of pragmatism and willingness to compromise with other centrist and secular groups, they should be welcomed as potentially credible partners in the political transformation of their societies.[14]

A group of scholars at the Carnegie Endowment for International Peace who have undertaken an ongoing effort to study and directly engage moderate Islamists in the Middle East have come to similar conclusions. Nathan Brown, Amr Hamzawy, and Marina Ottaway write:

> The evidence suggests that in most Arab countries there is no possibility of encouraging a process of democratization or at least liberalization, without seeing at the same time the increased influence of Islamist movements. We can only conclude that a policy of engagement with Islamist organizations, particularly with their reformist wings, is the only constructive option open to organizations and governments that believe democratic development in the Middle East is in everybody's interest.[15]

A failure to engage moderate Islamists, they warn, is likely to strengthen radical Islamists.

> While the outcome of participation [by Islamists] is not invariably a process of further democratization and moderation, it is also clear that nonparticipation . . . is a guarantee that a process of moderation will not take place. This is a sobering thought for those . . . that would like to set the bar for participation by Islamists extremely high. The choice is not between allowing the somewhat risky participation by Islamists in politics and their disappearance from the political scene. It is between allowing their participation . . . [and] ensuring the growing influence of hard-liners inside those movements.[16]

Robert S. Leiken and Steven Brooke of the Nixon Center met with dozens of leaders and activists of the Muslim Brotherhood in numerous countries and summarized their conclusions in an article titled "The Moderate Muslim Brotherhood" in *Foreign Affairs*.

The Brotherhood is a collection of national groups with differing outlooks, and the various factions disagree about how best to advance its mission. But all reject global jihad while embracing elections and other features of democracy. There is also a current within the Brotherhood willing to engage with the United States. In the past several decades, this current—along with the realities of practical politics—has pushed much of the Brotherhood toward moderation.

U.S. policymaking has been handicapped by Washington's tendency to see the Muslim Brotherhood—and the Islamist movement as a whole—as a monolith. Policymakers should instead analyze each national and local group independently and seek out those that are open to engagement. In the anxious and often fruitless search for Muslim moderates, policymakers should recognize that the Muslim Brotherhood presents a notable opportunity.[17]

Similar themes have been echoed by Mona Yacoubian in a report for the U.S. Institute of Peace, by Khalil Al-Anani in an article published by the Saban Center of the Brookings Institution, and Juan Cole.[18]

Finally, it appears that America's European allies are moving in the direction of greater engagement with moderate Islamists. In May 2007 the European Parliament announced that it would provide support for "moderate Islamists" and unambiguously opposed the limits on political activity that have been applied to Islamists in Egypt. In March 2009 the U.K. government announced its intention to talk to members of Hezbollah's political branch, which elicited an angry response from the United States.[19] The U.K. foreign secretary argued in a speech on relations between the West and the Muslim world also in March of that year that peace and security requires building the broadest political coalition possible. He said that this will sometimes include "groups whose aims we do not share, whose values we find deplorable, whose methods we think dubious."[20]

All this is not to say that the United States would need to step back from its readiness to express its liberal values. To the extent that Islamist groups express ideas or take actions at odds with American values, the United States should freely express its views. As long as it is not implied that such disapproval might lead the United States to take some coercive action, the United States would simply be participating in just the kind of dialectical discourse that is natural in a liberal public sphere.

As we have seen, the most central drama in the Muslim world is not the conflict between Islamist and liberal groups, but the conflict between Islamist and liberal values within most Muslims. To the extent that the United States is perceived as using its inordinate leverage against Islamist groups, this has a destabilizing effect on the process of integrating these two sets of values. It actually drives Muslims closer to Islamists—violently radical ones as well as moderate ones—because Muslims perceive U.S. efforts as seeking to undermine Islam itself. People generally tend to identify more strongly with something they feel they need to defend.

To the extent that the United States is seen as entering the discourse on a purely conceptual level, though, there is evidence that this can be helpful. Muslims are quite receptive to liberal ideas. As long as the United States is not seen as trying to impose its will and is respectful of the process that Muslims are going through, Muslims have proven to be interested in what Americans have to say.

Renewing the Image of America as Committed to Liberal Principles

As has been discussed, deeper than the narrative that portrays the United States as a classical imperial and oppressive hegemon is the narrative of the United States as a lapsed idealist that has strayed from the liberal principles that have made many Muslims, at some level, admire the United States. Any effort the United States can make to renew this image of the United States as a power that acts according to the liberal principles it professes will incrementally diffuse the image of the United States as an oppressor and renew the underlying feelings that draw Muslims closer to the United States.

This is not to say that the United States should or can completely abandon its role as a global hegemon. The fact that the United States controls approximately half of all the military power in the world and a quarter of the global economy assures that the United States will continue to play that role no matter how much it reins itself in at the margins. Because the United States is so much the "fat boy in the canoe," all countries watch it warily. Thus it is especially important that the United States avoid being unpredictable in its actions.

All hegemons effectively proffer an order that the hegemon is willing to sustain and that weaker states will, arguably, see as in their interest to follow.

Within such an order, the hegemon inherently accepts certain constraints in exchange for the cooperation of weaker states within that system. The U.S. version is the liberal order spelled out in the period after World War II. As we have seen, this order is well regarded by most Muslims, and to the extent that the United States is seen as abiding by its stated role, especially by being constrained, they tend to have a more relaxed and trusting response toward the United States.

Conversely, any U.S. action inconsistent with this image—that shows the United States to be unconstrained by the liberal order—will have a deleterious effect. It will enhance the perceived legitimacy of the efforts of al Qaeda and others to constrain the United States through violence. It will also weaken the position of those in Muslim society that favor participation in the liberal world order. When assessing the costs and benefits of any particular action, U.S. policymakers should include an assessment of the action's impact on this image.

The central problematic image is that the United States seeks to impose a constraining international legal order on others while regarding itself as uniquely unconstrained by it. Statements made in American policy circles—such as that the United States does not need a "permission slip" from the UN to use military force to protect its (nonterritorial) interests—certainly contribute to that impression, especially when the proposed military action is also legitimated by the charge that an offending party is in violation of international law or UN resolutions.

To defuse this image, it behooves American leaders, in public discussions of American options, to reference international law as a significant factor constraining American action, above all in regard to military force. American leaders should appear fully cognizant that Article 51 of the UN Charter abjures the use of unilateral military force except in self-defense and that the only exception, under Chapter 7, permits the UN Security Council to authorize the use of force if it deems that there is a threat to international peace.

American leaders do not necessarily have to say that they would never, under any circumstances, consider stretching or breaking such rules. But they should also implicitly communicate that it would only be done in extreme cases, with full recognition of the corrosive effects it would have on the international order.

Naturally, some will argue that projecting an image of being constrained undermines the deterrence of actors who might harm U.S. interests by making them think the United States would fail to forcefully defend its interests. As has been shown, however, this is hardly a real problem for the United States. Indeed, Muslims perceive the United States as so unconstrained that many are ready to support or at least accept al Qaeda and other groups, violating Islamic norms in the effort to punish the United States for its forcefulness. Support for punishing the United States, such as through attacks on U.S. troops, is not only an expression of anger, but is intended to incentivize the United States to recommit to being constrained. The greater threat to U.S. interests arises from people acting on the assumption that the United States is not constrained enough, not that it is too constrained.

Another set of norms the United States has been perceived as violating is in the treatment of detainees (detention is effectively a use of force). Obama has no doubt made gains for the American image by reaffirming the U.S. commitment to the Geneva Conventions and unambiguously rejecting the use of torture. While there are continuing issues about the treatment of combatants that do not fall neatly into the categories established by the conventions—some would say the United States continues to act improperly—at least the Obama administration appears to be genuinely concerned about what is consistent with the conventions. By initially deciding to try 9/11 mastermind Khalid Sheikh Mohammed in a civilian court in Manhattan, the administration was communicating to the Muslim world that the United States is fair and plays by the rules.

Some have argued that such constraints, while appropriate in America's relations with other states that might show reciprocal restraint, should not apply when dealing with terrorist groups that will surely be unconstrained themselves. In fact, al Qaeda and other such groups have not been known to torture Americans or other fighters—perhaps because they are concerned about their reputation among the Muslim people. The key audience, however, is the Muslim people, not terrorist groups. Renewing America's reputation as a nation constrained by international law is critical in diminishing the Muslim people's readiness to support terrorist groups.

While the standard approaches of public diplomacy—the effort to communicate in a polite, respectful, and "diplomatic" fashion—are not by themselves adequate to America's present diplomatic challenge in the Muslim world, they can play an important role in renewing America's image as committed to acting according to liberal principles. Implicit in the polite respectfulness of diplomatic language is an affirmation of the underlying liberal principles of international relations. The United States may well benefit from looking for opportunities to implicitly and explicitly affirm such principles—that all nations are equally sovereign, that they have the right to self-determination, that no nation should coerce another, and that relations should be based on principles of reciprocity.

Finally, American leaders should remember the words of William Faulkner: "The past is never dead. It's not even past." At numerous times in the postwar period the United States has acted in ways that fell short of its liberal ideals and that continue to fester in the minds of Muslims. Examples are the United States failing to recognize that Iraq violated international law by attacking Iran in 1980 and then subsequently providing support to Iraq in its war with Iran, the United States quietly going along when the Algerian military refused to recognize the outcome of the election in 1991 when an Islamist party won, and the United States attacking Iraq in 2003 without UN Security Council approval. It is not necessary for the United States to issue a raw mea culpa. American leaders have at times, however, subtly expressed reservations about past U.S. actions, often by simply reaffirming its principles and recognizing the negative consequences of failing to uphold them at an earlier time. Such communication does help heal past wounds and renew the image of America as committed to being constrained as a global power by its liberal ideals.

The Possibility for Change

Naturally, one may ask whether Muslim views of the United States are so entrenched that there is little the United States can do to affect them. This is an important question because the steps the United States could take to mitigate Muslim hostility may incur costs in other dimensions.

As evidenced in chapter 1, negative views of the United States have not been static. They worsened after the Iraq war. They showed some modest signs of improvement with the election of Barack Obama and following his speeches in Ankara and Cairo in which he reached out to the Muslim people—changes that were short-lived in most nations, but persisted in some.

In February 2008 Pakistanis appeared to be going through a process of reassessment. In several focus groups conducted just a few days after the Pakistani general election in which America's preferred candidate, Pervez

Musharraf, was unseated, the negativity toward the United States was noticeably lower than in previous focus groups. Respondents were apparently reevaluating America's role in the democratic process in Pakistan in light of the fact that the United States was perceived as not having gotten its way.

There was also an interesting exchange in which other members of the focus group uncharacteristically challenged respondents who were describing how America dominates Pakistan. One explained how America controls how people vote in Pakistan through threats, even asserting that "they are so powerful that they can enforce or threaten people into voting for Musharraf." Another joined in echoing his position, "America wants their chosen government to come into power in Pakistan because they view Pakistan as a sensitive area." The rest of the discussion went as follows.

> MODERATOR. Do you think the outcome of the elections is what America wanted?"
> RESPONDENT. [*pugnaciously*] Yes, it's possible.
> MODERATOR. Do all of you feel that way?
> R. [*serious and measured, after an awkward pause*] No, I don't feel that way. Previously, I thought that all the elections were influenced by America. However, this time around I was in charge of one of the polling stations and discovered that what America wants doesn't necessarily always happen, and in fact what the people want happens. The policy should be according to the needs of the people.
> MODERATOR. [*after an uncomfortable silence*] How many of you think that the outcome of the elections was something that America wanted? Please raise your hands. [*Only two respondents raised their hands.*]
> R. America wants that democracy in Pakistan should be strong and the people should progress. America doesn't want that the people should come and attack them, or we should have to fight against them.

In another focus group later that day respondents also showed a greater readiness to critically assess their assumptions about whether the United States has pervasive control over events in Pakistan and to assume greater responsibility for outcomes. One respondent made a common, bitter statement that the United States "just issues orders and we follow them." Once again, there was an awkward pause, as the charge seemed to ring a bit hollow. Then another respondent said thoughtfully, "We only know of these developments through the media, so there is a possibility that the Pakistani government may be trying to blame someone else to cover its own shortcomings." Another nodded and added, "We normally blame others for our mistakes."

Underlying Desire for Engagement with America

While the view that the United States is an unreconstructed imperial hegemon that should simply disengage from the Muslim world is loudly and widely articulated in the Muslim world, the deeper feeling of disappointment that the United States is not living up to the positive ideals it has projected provides some hope for changing perceptions. At this deeper level there are positive feelings toward the United States and a desire for it to engage with the Muslim world in ways that are consistent with liberal ideals. Were the United States to reduce the role of coercion in its relations with the Muslim world, it is likely that incipient desires for engagement with America would surface. Indeed, both the focus groups and some poll questions revealed such desires.

For example, a group of Pakistani women were asked whether the United States should totally disengage with Pakistan. Even as they continued to express their concern about U.S. domination, they clearly expressed a desire for U.S. engagement. They used a metaphor for the desired relationship that implied a certain level of dependency, while also preserving autonomy.

> MODERATOR. Do you think America's influence on Pakistan is mostly good or mostly bad?
> RESPONDENT 1. Mostly bad.
> MODERATOR. So would you like America to be less involved?
> R2. They should do things, but not in a manner that would bring us completely under their control. . . . We should work together, but not in a manner whereby America completely controls the actions of our government.
> R3. Our government should be in control.

R2. We want them to work together with our government for the betterment of our country.

R3. We should have independence, just like in a house where there are two sisters and the younger one is not working. Then the elder one should support her and then work together.

MODERATOR. Do you want America to play a bigger role or a smaller role in Pakistani affairs?

R2. If it's for the good of our own country, then they should do more.

As discussed in chapter 5, a key role that many Muslims want the United States to play is to be a broker in the Israeli-Palestinian conflict. While at times comments were made that implied the United States and Israel are virtually a singular entity that inevitably pursues America's imperial interests, at other times respondents implored the United States to recall its higher nature and play a more active and neutral role in mediating the conflict.

In general, rather than simply disengaging, there seemed to be a call for the United States to be a better hegemon. Interestingly, some comments implied that there was an earlier time when the United States generally played a more neutral role. For example, a Moroccan said, "Nowadays we can clearly see that the U.S. government is no longer neutral. It takes sides." Bill Clinton was also extolled, because of his efforts in the Middle East, for having been "a man of peace."

The idea that the United States should play a mediating role in the Israeli-Palestinian conflict came up in regard to other regions as well. For example, an Egyptian man initially complained that "America is insisting on going into Darfur," as another example of American domination. But he also would not say that the United States should simply disengage, and instead prescribed a mediating role.

RESPONDENT. It is better that interference be fair.

MODERATOR. And what does fair interference mean in your opinion?

R. They should sit with everyone, listen to all opinions, listen to neighboring countries, and see what the right thing to do is. It shouldn't force any solution.

Pakistanis also looked to the United States to help in resolving the conflict in Kashmir. Interestingly, in a focus group one woman even called for the United States to play a coercive role (presumably toward India), while others called for the United States to simply play a mediating role. When the subject of Kashmir came up, there was some implied criticism of the United States. The discussion went as follows.

MODERATOR. Can the U.S. government help in this matter?
RESPONDENT 1. They can in a friendly way.
R2. Yes, it can.
MODERATOR. How?
R1. They are a superpower. They are in a position to coerce
    governments. So they should come to a decision, and we too
    want them to come with a decision to end this war.
R3. They should make them sit together and listen to both sides
    and come to a joint decision.
R4. They could do this if they wanted.
R2. If they don't want, then . . . look at that place, entire
    generations have been wiped out.
R5. Everyone deserves freedom.
R6. And we want America to resolve this issue.
R7. After Pakistan's independence, many issues have been dealt
    with. Why can't this one be resolved?

Polls of publics in three of Iraq's neighbors—Iran, Saudi Arabia, and Syria—also found support for their governments cooperating with the United States to help resolve the conflict and stabilize Iraq. In a 2009 Terror Free Tomorrow (TFT) poll, two-thirds of Iranians (68 percent) favored their government working with the United States to help resolve the Iraq war. Similarly, in WPO polling in 2008, 69 percent of Iranians approved of their government having talks with the United States on Iraq. In Saudi Arabia, surveyed by TFT in late 2007, 69 percent of Saudis agreed with their government working with the United States on Iraq. Among Syrians polled by the same organization in 2007, 64 percent favored such cooperation.

Other polls of Iranians, though, have found more mixed results on the prospect of cooperation with the United States, especially when there is any suggestion of military cooperation. In a 2009 University of Tehran poll, Iranians were divided on working with the United States to bring stability to Iraq and Afghanistan. The 2009 WPO poll found a divided result on "Iran cooperating with the United States to combat the Taliban operating in Afghanistan near Iran's border." The University of Tehran poll found a majority (66 percent) disagreeing with a proposal "for Iran to militarily cooperate with the United States to fight terrorist organizations such as the Taliban."

More broadly, though, Iranians do support diplomatic engagement with the United States. In the 2009 WPO poll, 60 percent favored "full, unconditional negotiations between the government of the Islamic Republic of Iran and the government of the United States." When TFT asked the same question in 2008 and 2009, the level of support was roughly the same. GlobeScan in June 2009 found that 58 percent agreed with "pursuing direct talks with the United States to resolve problems between the two countries." In WPO polling in 2008, 57 percent of Iranians favored the United States and Iranian governments having "direct talks on issues of mutual concern," an increase from late 2006, when 48 percent favored this.

Iranians also go further than their government in calling for restoring diplomatic relations with the United States. Sixty-three percent favored the two countries restoring diplomatic relations in the 2009 WPO poll. Additionally, when presented with a battery of proposals by TFT in 2009 for improving their opinion of the United States, 52 percent of Iranians said that the United States "reopening its embassy in Tehran and engaging in comprehensive negotiations with Iran" would at least somewhat improve their opinion.

Very large majorities of both Iranians and Syrians supported their governments "seeking trade and political relations with Western countries," according to polling done by TFT. Among Iranians polled in 2009, 75 percent favored such efforts. Among Syrians polled in 2007, 87 percent were in favor.

Various Muslim publics view the possibility of increased economic relations with the United States favorably. TFT has found majorities saying that having a free trade treaty with the United States would better their opinions toward the United States: Saudi Arabia (72 percent in 2007), Iran (70 percent in 2008), and Pakistan (64 percent in 2008). WPO also found in 2008 that two-thirds of Iranians supported greater trade between the United States and Iran. In 2008 TFT polling 69 percent of Pakistanis said more business investment would improve their views of the United States and seven in ten Iranians favored Western investment in Iran to create more jobs. In Syria, however, majorities opposed "American investment in energy refineries to lower the price of gasoline" (71 percent in 2007) and "American trade and investment to create more jobs" (70 percent).

According to polling by TFT, Muslims have a positive view of the United States providing aid and say that the United States doing so has improved or would improve their opinion of the United States. For example, eight in ten Iranians in 2008 favored "medical, education, and humanitarian aid from Western countries to Iranian people in need." Majorities of Pakistanis also said in 2008 that their views of the United States would be improved by U.S. support for medical care and training (68 percent), school construction and teacher training (67 percent), and increasing scholarships for Pakistani students to study in the United States (59 percent). In 2005 and 2006 two-thirds of Indonesians and more than three-quarters of Pakistanis said that U.S. humanitarian aid following the Indonesian tsunami and the Pakistani earthquake made their attitudes more favorable toward the United States. While views of the United States in these countries did improve following humanitarian interventions, the effects were not long lasting, as intervening events, apparently, gained greater influence. Positive views of U.S. humanitarian aid were reiterated in Pakistan in 2008.

Three-quarters of Afghans polled in 2009 approved of the presence of foreign aid organizations operating in Afghanistan—the lion's share of which are supported with U.S. government money. Majorities of Saudis (63 percent) and Pakistanis (53 percent), polled in 2007 and 2008, said that the United States providing "military equipment and training" for their country's armed forces would make their opinion of the United States more favorable. Six in ten Syrians polled in 2007, however, opposed medical and educational aid for Syrians and housing assistance for Iraqi refugees in Syria.

Muslims also express support for greater personal engagement with the United States. In TFT polling in 2007 and 2008, large majorities in three countries said that the United States increasing visas for people to come study or work would ameliorate opinion toward the United States. This included three-quarters of Saudis, six in ten Iranians, and six in ten Pakistanis.

The possibility of greater educational and cultural exchanges with the United States has also elicited positive responses among Iranians. In a 2008 WPO poll, 71 percent supported "having more Americans and Iranians visit each other's countries as tourists," 70 percent supported "providing more access to each other's journalists," and 63 percent supported "having greater cultural, educational, and sporting exchanges." When WPO asked Americans the same questions in 2008, views were similar. Seventy percent supported "providing more access to each other's journalists," and 63 percent supported "having greater cultural, educational, and sporting exchanges." Only 43 percent, however, supported exchanging more tourists—perhaps due to concerns about terrorism.

Conclusion

The goal of this study has been to understand the roots of Muslim hostility toward America. It has come to the disconcerting conclusion that America and the Muslim world are caught in a vicious cycle. Decades ago the United States extended its economic and military presence into much of the Muslim world, most notably the Middle East. This thrust the United States into the midst of a broader cultural conflict within the Muslim world—between those responding favorably to the liberalizing forces of Western influences most visibly associated with the United States, and those wanting to preserve the traditional forms of Islamic society.

While the conflict between these forces occurs most fundamentally within individual Muslims, the conflict has also been externalized in the form of competing parties and organizations. With limited awareness of the consequences of its actions, the United States has become a major factor in this struggle. While it is debatable how central a role the United States has actually played, Muslims have come to perceive the United States, with its overwhelming power, as upholding anti-Islamic structures in the Muslim world, including secular governments and the state of Israel.

This has created a unique opportunity for radical Islamist organizations, most notably al Qaeda, to promulgate a narrative within which the struggle between traditional Islam and liberalizing forces is played out as a struggle between the United States and al Qaeda. While this narrative is not original to al Qaeda, it has been uniquely potent at employing it.

Most Muslims have many reservations about al Qaeda. They do not respond positively to its extreme form of Islamism and disapprove of its use of violence against civilians. The narrative that al Qaeda has propagated, however, does exert a powerful influence on most Muslims. It complements and enhances the larger, long-standing narrative of Western, most recently American, oppression. Though al Qaeda very much rejects the principles of liberalism, the al Qaeda narrative also complements and enhances the underlying theme that the United States has enticed Muslims with the principles of democracy, the constraints of international law, and religious tolerance and then violated them. Even al Qaeda points to America's hypocrisy on these issues. Thus al Qaeda's narrative draws on and in many ways blends together with the larger narrative of oppression that is endorsed by the majority of Muslims even though there are aspects of al Qaeda's narrative that are not endorsed by the majority.

Once attacked by al Qaeda, the United States had little choice but to respond militarily. And yet nearly a decade later there is little sign that the threat from al Qaeda has abated. Indeed, the expansion of the U.S. military role in the Muslim world has enhanced the power of al Qaeda's narrative of the United States as an oppressor and a latter-day Crusader.

Angry about its use of violence against Muslims, many have turned against al Qaeda, most notably in Iraq, Jordan, and Pakistan. But the power of al Qaeda's narrative is still potent enough that it continues to attract a seemingly endless flow of new recruits to participate in violent jihad, to destabilize many parts of the Muslim world, and to threaten U.S. interests. Equally important, the narrative of the United States as oppressing the Muslim world continues to exert a strong hold on the whole of Muslim society, creating problems for the United States in multiple dimensions.

When the United States is attacked, it is normal to see the hard power, military response as central. Efforts at public diplomacy, while valued, are nonetheless on the margins and play a subordinate role relative to the use of force. But broad-scale military efforts to eliminate those infected by al Qaeda's narrative are widely interpreted throughout the Muslim world in a way that feeds the narrative and facilitates recruitment. Thus it is not clear that they achieve any net gain and may at times even do more harm than good.

The challenge for the United States, then, is how to fight a narrative. Eliminating the al Qaeda leadership would have an important effect. But once the narrative takes hold in the culture, it has the capacity to spread virally well beyond the direct control of its progenitors. The shootings at Fort Hood in the United States by an Arab-American soldier were not under the operational control of any particular organization. They were, however, a direct consequence of the narrative of U.S. oppression.

Given that the roots of the narrative are psychological, it must be addressed as such. A key principle in psychotherapy is that many interpersonal conflicts are rooted in inner conflicts. As long as the conflict is externalized, it cannot be resolved. Only when it is experienced as an inner conflict can the competing forces achieve a more integrated relationship.

This means that the goal for the United States should be to extract itself from the externalized conflict as much as possible. As we have discussed, this can be pursued through gradually lightening America's military footprint, minimizing the use of threats, renouncing a right to oil, seeking to differentiate the United States from Israel, and trusting the Muslim people with democracy.

The United States will not and should not suddenly withdraw all its forces from the Muslim world. The gradual drawdown of forces in Iraq has been endorsed by the Iraqi people as well as the government, and the Afghan people want U.S. forces to remain awhile longer. Efforts to kill or capture the al Qaeda leadership will no doubt continue. What is most important is for the United States to be seen as not threatening, as predictable, and as constrained by international norms.

Within this context there are a variety of ways that Muslims would like to see the United States continue to be engaged with the Muslim world. Besides economic forms of engagement, these include playing a role in furthering democracy and, certainly, educating Muslims with the knowledge and even ideas that the West has developed.

Some may worry that reducing the role of hard power in America's relation to the Muslim world is not politically feasible given American domestic politics. Certainly, some American commentators would seek to portray it as a sign of American weakness that will embolden al Qaeda and its like and make them appear stronger in the eyes of the Muslim world.

But this is unlikely to be a majority view in the American public. For some time, polls have shown that the American public believes there is a need for a new approach to the problem of terrorism and that there has been too much emphasis on the use of American hard power. In a 2008

GlobeScan/PIPA poll for BBC, only 31 percent of Americans said that the United States is winning the war on terror.[21] When asked whether the war on terror has made al Qaeda stronger or weaker, just 34 percent of Americans said it has made al Qaeda weaker, while six in ten said that it has had no effect (26 percent) or even strengthened al Qaeda (33 percent).

Earlier PIPA polling found majorities saying that the United States had put too much emphasis on the use of military force. Two-thirds said that countries around the world have grown more afraid in recent years that the United States might use force against them. Asked whether it is good for U.S. security if the leaders of some countries grow more afraid of the United States because it makes foreign governments "more likely to refrain from doing things the United States does not want them to do," or bad because it makes them "seek out new means of protecting themselves," Americans said it is bad by a two-to-one margin. Specifically, in the effort to fight terrorism, 67 percent said that the Bush administration at that time should have been putting more emphasis on diplomatic and economic methods rather than military methods.

It is unlikely that a less forceful U.S. approach would embolden al Qaeda. In the past when the United States has increased its military presence, the al Qaeda leadership has tauntingly expressed glee that this will help their recruitment efforts. More significant, shortly after Obama was elected, the prospect of a more moderate U.S. approach made the al Qaeda leadership clearly worried and disoriented, almost as if it was stumbling from a tug-of-war adversary having loosened the rope. Far from gloating that the election of a potentially less aggressive leader was some kind of victory, they made substantial efforts to convince the Muslim people that while Obama may talk a good line, he represented no real change in U.S. foreign policy.[22]

The findings of this study suggest that al Qaeda's worries are warranted. Should the Muslim people perceive the United States as less threatening, this would likely weaken al Qaeda's position in the Muslim world. By weakening the narrative of American oppression, objectionable features of al Qaeda would likely become more salient. The defensive tendency to turn a blind eye to its violations of Islamic strictures against attacking civilians would likely weaken, and reservations about its extreme form of Islamism would likely become stronger.

Perhaps most important, the widely experienced tension between the attraction to liberal ideas and engagement with the larger world on the one hand and the desire to retain a sense of Islamic identity on the other would be experienced less as conflict between the Muslim world and the United States and more as a conflict internal to the Muslim world and to Muslim individuals. As this tension becomes increasingly internalized, the potential for Muslims to find a new equilibrium and an integration of these powerful streams in their psyches and their culture becomes increasingly likely.

As Muslims internalize this conflict, they are more apt to see America with new eyes. The complexity of America is likely to come into greater focus. America is not simply the force of modernity any more than the Muslim world is simply the force of Islam. Most Americans share with Muslims a uniquely strong desire to stay rooted in their traditional sense of religiosity, even as they engage modernity. While there are forces in America that seek to exert control over other nations, there are other forces that are committed to abiding by permissive liberal principles. With more differentiated awareness, they are likely to be less reactive to American political rhetoric and also to be more effective in dealing with America.

The complex set of feelings that underlies the narrative of U.S. oppression for most Muslims includes an attraction to many things associated with America, especially liberal principles of tolerance, democracy, human rights, and international law. Yet they have felt betrayed by the United States for failing to live up to these principles, especially in regard to the Muslim world. The blunt narrative of the United States as simply an oppressor suppresses the complexity of these feelings. Were this narrative to be loosened by mitigating the sense of threat, it is more likely that these feelings would come to the surface. These include feelings of resentment and disappointment. But at an even deeper level, these feelings flow from a desire for and a belief in the possibility of the United States and the Muslim world having a shared set of norms within which Muslims can feel accepted and safe—and maybe even amicable toward America.

Notes

Introduction

1. Alan B. Krueger and Jitka Maleckova, "Attitudes and Action: Public Opinion and the Occurrence of International Terrorism," *Science*, September 18, 2009, pp. 1534–36.

2. Ibid., p. 1536.

3. Ethan Bueno de Mesquita, "Correlates of Public Support for Terrorism in the Muslim World," United States Institute of Peace Working Paper, May 17, 2007, especially pp. 2, 4, 41 (www.usip.org/pubs/working_papers/wp1.pdf).

4. Mark Tessler and Michael D. H. Robbins, "What Leads Some Ordinary Arab Men and Women to Approve of Terrorist Acts against the United States?" *Journal of Conflict Resolution* 51, no. 2 (April 2007): 305.

5. Audrey Cronin, "How al-Qaeda Ends: The Decline and Demise of Terrorist Groups," *International Security* 31, no. 1 (Summer 2006): 27.

6. De Mesquita, "Correlates of Public Support for Terrorism in the Muslim World," p. 3.

7. Daniel L. Byman, "The War on Terror Requires Subtler Weapons," Brookings Institution, May 27, 2003 (www.brookings.edu/opinions/2003/0527terrorism_by man.aspx).

8. David Petraeus. "Petraeus on Afghanistan, Taliban" interview by John Hockenberry, *Public Radio International,* February 1, 2010 (www.pri.org/world/middle-east/petraeus-on-taliban-reintegration-in-afghanistan1857.html).

9. Stanley A. McChrystal, "News Transcript: Press Roundtable with Gen. McChrystal in Istanbul, Turkey," NATO International Security Assistance Force, February 4, 2010 (www.isaf.nato.int/en/article/transcripts/news-transcript-press-round table-with-gen.-mcchrystal-in-istanbul-turkey.html).

10. Robert A. Pape, *Dying to Win: The Strategic Logic of Suicide Terrorism* (New York: Random House, 2005).

Chapter One

1. Clark McCauley, "The Psychology of Terrorism," *After September 11 Archive,* Social Science Research Council (http://essays.ssrc.org/sept11/essays/mccauley.htm).

Chapter Two

1. Sayyid Qutb, *Milestones* (Cedar Rapids, Iowa: Mother Mosque Foundation, 1981), pp. 159–60.
2. Osama bin Laden, interview, January 4, 2004, in *Compilation of Usama Bin Laden Statements, 1994–January 2004,* Foreign Broadcast Information Service, January 2004, p. 273 (www.fas.org/irp/world/para/ubl-fbis.pdf).
3. Bernard Lewis, "The Roots of Muslim Rage," *Atlantic Monthly*, September 1990.
4. Samuel Huntington, *The Clash of Civilizations and the Remaking of the World Order* (New York: Simon & Schuster, 1996).
5. For a fuller development of the idea that Islamism represents a resistance to Western culture, see Alastair Crooke, *Resistance: The Essence of the Islamist Revolution* (New York: Pluto Press, 2009).
6. Sayyid Qutb, "The America I Have Seen," in *American in an Arab Mirror*, edited by Kamal Abdel-Malek (Palgrave Macmillan, 2000).
7. In the 2006 BBC/GlobeScan/PIPA survey, the average among countries polled around the world was 56 percent saying that common ground is possible and 28 percent saying that violent conflict is inevitable. This included 64 percent of Americans saying common ground is possible as well as large majorities in most European countries. However, in 2010 the Chicago Council on Global Affairs found that the number saying common ground is possible had dropped to 51 percent.
8. Survey nations in Asia and Africa were the most favorable toward globalization when asked in this formulation, while responses in the United States and Europe were more lukewarm. Among majority-Muslim nations, Azerbaijan, Pakistan, and Turkey were comparable to European nations. Mexicans joined the Palestinians and Indonesians as the only publics with majorities or pluralities considering globalization "mostly bad."
9. Majorities in forty-three of the forty-six countries surveyed agreed that they see themselves as a citizen of the world. African countries were more likely to agree than majority-Muslim countries, while eastern European countries and Germany tended to agree less.
10. Among all nations surveyed, only Kenya, Nigeria, and the United States had majorities who believed that the United States sets a good example by abiding by international law. Non-Muslim nations that were very critical of the United States included China, France, Russia, and South Korea.

11. Many countries, especially in Europe, both prior to and under the Obama administration, have agreed with the assessment that the United States does not take their interests into account. Indonesia's more favorable attitude—that the United States does take their interests into account either "a great deal" or a "fair amount"—however, was similar to other Asian powers, including India (83 percent) and China (76 percent) as well as Kenya (75 percent), Nigeria (66 percent), and Brazil (56 percent).

Chapter Three

1. Majorities or pluralities in Chile, Germany, Kenya, and Nigeria said the United States treats their countries fairly. In most of the countries surveyed, though, majorities or pluralities said the United States "abuses its greater power."

2. Every nation surveyed had a majority or a plurality saying the United States uses the threat of force to gain advantages. The countries taking this view most strongly were China, Mexico, and South Korea.

3. Majorities in eighteen of twenty non-Muslim-majority countries, including the United States, agreed that the U.S. military presence in the Middle East provokes more conflict than it prevents. The only majority-Muslim countries in which substantially larger numbers did not agree were Nigeria, where a plurality said the U.S. presence is a stabilizing force, and the Philippines, where opinion was mixed.

Chapter Four

1. Sayyid Qutb, *Milestones* (Cedar Rapids, Iowa: Mother Mosque Foundation, 1981), p.116.

Chapter Six

1. Ussama Makdisi, "Anti-Americanism in the Arab World: An Interpretation of a Brief History," in "History and September 11," special issue, *Journal of American History* 89, no. 2 (September 2002): 548.

2. Muqtedar Khan, as quoted in David Smock, "Islamic Perspectives on Peace and Violence," *Special Report* 82, United States Institute of Peace (January 2002): 3 (www.usip.org/resources/islamic-perspectives-peace-and-violence). See also comments by Richard Haass on the impact of the Second Gulf War on views of American nation building: "Throughout much of the region, democracy has become associated with the loss of order. . . . Anti-American sentiment, already considerable, has been reinforced." In Richard Haass, "The New Middle East," *Foreign Affairs* 85, no. 6 (November/December 2006): 3.

3. Mark Tessler and Michael D. H. Robbins, "What Leads Some Ordinary Arab Men and Women to Approve of Terrorist Acts against the United States?" *Journal of Conflict Resolution* 51, no. 2 (April 2007): 305–28.

4. Globally, the 2007 Pew survey found majorities in forty-three out of forty-seven nations polled agreeing that the United States promotes democracy mostly where it

serves its interests. This included 63 percent of Americans. Outside the Muslim world such views were strongest in Europe, while Africans tended to be more divided.

Chapter Seven

1. Quoted in Anthony Oberschall, "Explaining Terrorism: The Contribution of Collective Action Theory," *Sociological Theory* 22, no. 1 (March 2004): 34.

Chapter Eight

1. Jeremy M. Sharp, "U.S. Democracy Promotion Policy in the Middle East: The Islamist Dilemma," Congressional Research Service, June 15, 2006 (www.fas.org/sgp/crs/mideast/RL33486.pdf).

2. Opinion in the fifty-five other countries surveyed by World Values Survey between 1999 and 2004 was consistent with the views of majority-Muslim publics, with majorities agreeing that democracy was the best form of government in all but two countries. The exceptions were Russia, where only a plurality agreed, and Nigeria, where a majority disagreed. Bangladesh and Egypt were among the largest majorities agreeing, along with European countries, while Morocco, together with Asian countries, was at the lower end of the range. All, though, were clear majorities.

3. All twenty-one nations polled globally favored government leaders being selected through elections in which citizens can vote. More Indonesians took this position than any other public polled. Egyptians, Iranians, and Jordanians, while still large majorities, were on the lower end of the range, with only Indians having a smaller majority.

4. Large majorities favored making each of the following law in Pakistan: "punishments like whipping and cutting off of hands for crimes like theft and robbery" (82 percent), "stoning people who commit adultery" (82 percent), and "death penalty for people who leave the Muslim religion" (76 percent). The "segregation of men and women in the workplace" was also supported by 85 percent.

5. Abu Musaib al-Zarqawi, "Zarqawi and Other Islamists to the Iraqi People: Elections and Democracy Are Heresy," Special Dispatch 856, Middle East Media Research Institute, February 1, 2005 (www.memri.org/report/en/0/0/0/0/0/0/1308.htm).

Chapter Nine

1. *Hearing on al Qaeda in 2010: How Should the U.S. Respond? Before the House Armed Services Committee*, 111th Cong. (January 27, 2010) (statement of Steve Coll, President of the New America Foundation) (www.newyorker.com/online/blogs/stevecoll/2010/01/).

2. Transcript of President Bush's Address to a Joint Session of Congress, September 20, 2001, CNN.com (http://archives.cnn.com/2001/US/09/20/gen.bush.transcript/).

3. Saad Eddin Ibrahim, "Remarks on Stephen D. Krasner's 'Sovereignty and Democracy Promotion,'" in *Reform in the Muslim World: The Role of Islamist and*

Outside Powers, Doha Discussion Papers (Project on U.S. Relations with the Islamic World, Saban Center, Brookings, 2008): 30.

4. Steve Clemons, William Goodfellow, and Matthew Hoh, *A New Way Forward: Rethinking U.S. Strategy in Afghanistan,* Report of the Afghanistan Study Group, September 8, 2010 (www.afghanistanstudygroup.org/NewWayForward_report.pdf).

5. Seth G. Jones and Martin C Libicki, *How Terrorist Groups End: Lessons for Countering Al Qa'ida* (Santa Monica, Calif.: RAND Corporation, 2008) (www.rand. org/pubs/monographs/2008/RAND_MG741-1.pdf).

6. These responses were selected by the largest numbers in the six countries as a whole based on a population-weighted average across the six countries.

7. Eli Lake, "Secret U.S.-Israel Nuclear Accord in Jeopardy," *Washington Times,* May 6, 2009 (www.washingtontimes.com/news/2009/may/06/us-weighs-forcing-israel-to-disclose-nukes/).

8. Mohamed Fayez Farahat summarizes this as follows: "In the 2007 electoral platform, the Brotherhood also went out of its way to emphasize three other important guarantees: that Islam by nature rejects religious authority, 'since the state in Islam is a civil state with its systems and institutions put in place by the umma, and in which the umma represents the source of authority,' and human ijtihad [independent reasoning] within the framework of the immutable points of Islamic Shariah is not forbidden. The second guarantee is that 'Islam does not have religious authority for anyone.' Finally, the third is that 'the ruler's authority is derived from the social contract between the ruler and subject, enacted by the umma.' In addition to the draft party platform reasserting these guarantees, the draft also promised that the application of Islamic Shariah itself would take place through 'the vision which the umma agrees upon, through a parliamentary majority in the freely elected legislative authority.'" Mohamed Fayez Farahat, "Liberalizing the Muslim Brotherhood: Can It Be Done?" *Arab Insight* 2, no. 6 (Winter 2009): 15. Tamara Wittes also notes, "The [2007 Muslim Brotherhood draft] Platform endorses in no uncertain terms virtually every aspect of Western-style democracy: citizenship (2.1.a), separation of powers (2.2.2), a civil and technocratic state (2.2.1.e), political pluralism (2.2.5), civil society (2.2.1.c), human rights, constitutionalism (2.1.b), rule of law (2.1.d), mass political participation (2.2.1.a), transparency and freedom of information (2.2.3), and free and fair elections (2.2.7)." Tamara Cofman Wittes, "Remarks on Stephen D. Krasner's 'Sovereignty and Democracy Promotion,'" in *Reform in the Muslim World: The Role of Islamist and Outside Powers,* Doha Discussion Papers (Project on U.S. Relations with the Islamic World, Saban Center, Brookings, 2008): 43.

9. Max, "Muslim Brotherhood to Attend Obama's Speech in Cairo," POMED Wire, June 2, 2009 (http://pomed.org/blog/2009/06/obama-to-meet-with-muslim-brotherhood.html/).

10. Barack Obama, "Remarks by the President on a New Beginning," June 4, 2009, Cairo, Egypt (www.whitehouse.gov/the_press_office/Remarks-by-the-President -at-Cairo-University-6-04-09/).

11. Emile Nakhleh, *A Necessary Engagement* (Princeton University Press, 2009), xvii.

12. Ibid., p. 33.

13. Ibid., p. 64.

14. Ibid., p. 94.

15. Marina Ottaway and Amr Hamzawy, *Islamist Movements and the Democratic Process in the Arab World: Exploring the Gray Zones*, Carnegie Paper 67 (Washington: Carnegie Endowment for International Peace, March 2006): 19.

16. Marina Ottaway and Amr Hamzawy, *Islamists in Politics: The Dynamics of Participation*, Carnegie Paper 98 (Washington: Carnegie Endowment for International Peace, November 2008): 22.

17. Robert S. Leiken and Steven Brooke, "The Moderate Muslim Brotherhood," *Foreign Affairs* 86 no. 2 (March/April 2007): 107–08.

18. Yacoubian writes, "Moderate Islamist parties that reject violence and practice democratic ideals are an important counterweight to Islamist extremism, and their work should be encouraged. . . . In every case, U.S.-funded efforts to engage moderate Islamists resulted in strong working relationships, featuring regular contact between democracy promoters and Islamist-party partners and a strong reservoir of trust. . . . Moderate Islamist parties are crucial to the U.S. strategy to promote democracy in the Arab World. The parties have proven their popular strength, ability to win free elections, and capacity to moderate. Such evolution requires close scrutiny, but fears of Islamist parties run amok, and a repeat of an Iranian-style revolution elsewhere appear to be exaggerated. Instead, we should ask whether we could have democracy in the Arab world without Islamists. The arguments for engaging with them are powerful, as meaningful political participation appears to exert a moderating influence on Islamist parties." Mona Yacoubian, *Engaging Islamists and Promoting Democracy* (Washington: United States Institute of Peace, August 2007): 14–15.

Khalil Al-Anani argues that the United States has wrongly conflated moderate Islamists and radical Salafists (who are ideologically opposed to democracy) and that by tacitly supporting the exclusion of moderate Islamists from government, it has strengthened the Salafists. He writes, "There are benefits in engaging with moderate Islamists. Islamists have a wider appeal across the Arab and Islamic world than radicals and are well positioned to challenge Islamic extremism. In addition, dialogue with Islamists would bolster public opinion of the United States." Khalil Al-Anani, *The Myth of Excluding Moderate Islamists in the Arab World* (Saban Center, Brookings, March 2010).

Cole writes, "A Muslim Brotherhood willing to participate in civil politics and to foreswear violence is an asset, not a danger. It has been convincingly argued that where a country has a significant party dedicated to political Islam, it takes up the space that al-Qaeda might otherwise fill, and so acts as a barrier to radicalism. . . . If this theory is correct, recent U.S. State Department and congressional contacts with Muslim Brotherhood parliamentarians, condemned by the American right and by the Mubarak government alike, may be the healthiest way forward for American policy. . . . The Brotherhood could, if the right policies are adopted in Egypt, come to play a role analogous to the Christian Democrat parties in Germany and other nations of Europe." Juan Cole, *Engaging the Muslim World* (New York: Palgrave Macmillan, 2009): 78, 81.

19. Alex Glennie, *Building Bridges, Not Walls: Engaging with Political Islamists in the Middle East and North Africa* (London: IPPR, September 2009).

20. Ibid., p. 44.

21. Asked whether the United States or al Qaeda is winning in the war on terror, a substantial majority (56 percent) of U.S. respondents said that neither side is winning, while 31 percent said the United States is winning and 8 percent said al-Qaeda is winning. These opinions were similar to the global average of the twenty-three countries polled by BBC/GlobeScan/PIPA in 2008, with 47 percent of respondents believing that neither side is winning, 22 percent saying the United States is winning, and 10 percent saying that al Qaeda is winning. A CNN poll found similar results in 2007, with a plurality of 46 percent saying neither side is winning, 32 percent saying the United States is winning, and 21 percent saying the terrorists are winning.

22. In August 2009 al Qaeda's second in command, Ayman al-Zawahiri, commented, "Obama tries to sell illusions to the delusional and weakened people, as he realized that the anger of the weakened and especially in the Islamic World over America, and their hatred towards its policies, has caused it disasters and plagues and broke[n] its back, and now he is trying to say: 'Do not hate us, we do not have hostility towards you, but we will continue killing your people in Afghanistan and Iraq and Palestine and Somalia, and we will continue the occupation of Muslim lands, and our military existence will remain in the Gulf to secure the robbery and thievery of petroleum with the prices we agree on, and we will continue supporting Israel and protect its Jewishness, and consider Jerusalem a united indefinite capital for Israel, and we will continue assuring its military dominion, and we will continue supporting the oppressive, torturous, and thievery regimes in your countries, but do not hate us.'" Ayman al-Zawahiri, "Shaykh Dr. Ayman al-Zawahiri: The Facts of Jihad and the Lies of the Hypocrites," interview by NEFA Foundation, August 5, 2009, NEFA Foundation (www.nefafoundation.org/miscellaneous/Featured Docs/nefa_zawahiri0809.pdf).

Index

Personal names starting with al are alphabetized by the following part of the name.

Education
    differences in Muslim views on U.S. due
        to level of, 17
    sex discrimination in, 180
    in U.S., as desirable by Muslims, 33
Egypt
    1999–2004 poll on democracy as desir-
        able, 149
    2002 poll on views on U.S., 10
    2005 poll
        on freedom of expression, 176
        on freedom of religion, 173
        on sharia role, 160
        on U.S. support for democracy in
            Middle East, 111
        on women's rights, 180
    2005–08 poll
        on democracy as desirable, 149,
            151–52
        on employment of women, 181
    2005–09 poll on Muslim identity, 33
    2006 poll
        on anti-Muslim bias of U.S., 83
        on democracy as desirable as priority
            for U.S., 105
        on September 11 attacks responsibil-
            ity, 129
    2006–07 poll
        on civilian attacks as justified, 125
        on democracy as desirable, 149
        on freedom of religion, 173
        on inevitability of conflict between
            Western and Muslim cultures, 29
        on oil as U.S. right, 46
        on U.S. trying to weaken Islam's
            growth, 86
        on war on terrorism, 71
    2006–08 poll
        on Muslim views on U.S., 12
        on terrorism, 125
        on UN powers, 183–84, 190
        on U.S. control of world events, 60
        on U.S. freedom of expression laws,
            178
        on U.S. goal to prevent extremist
            groups from taking control of
            Islamic countries, 108

2006–09 poll
    on al Qaeda attacks on civilians,
        120–21
    on al Qaeda goal to end U.S. bias for
        Israel over Palestinians, 93
    on bin Laden, 20, 142
    on Israeli expansionism supported by
        U.S., 91
    on Palestinian state and U.S. role in
        creating, 94
    on sharia as official law, 156
    on suicide bombings, 126, 127
2007 poll
    on Darfur situation, 57
    on democracy as desirable, 150, 152
    on separation of religion and state,
        154
    on U.S. promotion of democracy in
        Middle East, 107
2007–08 poll
    on civilian attacks as effective,
        124–25
    on September 11 attacks responsibil-
        ity, 129, 131
    on UN deference, 191
2007–09 poll
    on al Qaeda support, 116, 117
    on UN role, 189–90
2007–10 poll on Muslim views on U.S.
    foreign policy, 40
2008 poll
    on Christian expansion as U.S. goal,
        81
    on civilian attacks on Europeans, 123
    on democracy as desirable, 150
    on freedom of expression, 175, 177
    on freedom of religion, 174
    on humanitarian intervention in
        Burma, 189
    on Israeli-Palestinian conflict and U.S.
        role in resolving, 99
    on likelihood of al Qaeda attacks in
        U.S. if U.S. withdrew from Iraq, 71
    on moderate governments' legitimacy,
        120
    on Muslim opinion on U.S. culture,
        34

Iran (cont.)
2006–09 poll on al Qaeda attacks on civilians, 120
2007 poll on U.S. withdrawal of troops from Iraq, 62
2007–08 poll on visas for travel to U.S., 232
2008 poll
on democracy as desirable, 150
on educational and cultural exchanges, 233
on inevitability of conflict between Western and Muslim cultures, 29
on Iran-U.S. relations, 231
on Iraq war resolution, 230
on sex discrimination, 179
on sharia role, 159
on UN powers, 184
on women's rights, 179
2008–09 poll
on competing images of fundamental U.S. intentions, 87
on trade relations with U.S., 231–32
on U.S. hostility toward Islam, 73
2009 poll
on Afghanistan and Iraq stability, 230–31
on attacks on U.S. civilians, 121
on freedom of expression, 176
on Internet access, 178
on Iran-U.S. relations, 231
on Iran working with U.S., 231
on Iraq war resolution, 230
on Obama, 15, 74
on religious scholars' and clergy's role, 161
on trade and political relations with Western countries, 231
on UN use of military force to stop terrorism, 187
on U.S. foreign policy, 14
2010 poll on Obama as world leader, 16
focus groups
on abuse of U.S. global power, 45
on Christian expansion as U.S. goal, 81–82
on dictatorships supported by U.S., 104

on domination as global goal of U.S., 48–49
on domination of Muslim countries by U.S., 57
on oil as U.S. right, 48
on U.S. bias in applying liberal ideals to Israel and Arabs, 97
on U.S. conflict with, 69
implied threats by U.S. against, 207
and nuclear weapons, 98
as study participant, 6
U.S. relations with, 216
Iraq
1999–2008 poll on democracy as desirable, 149
2005–08 poll on women's rights, 179–81
2006–08 poll on radical groups attacking Americans, 19
2006–09 poll
on bin Laden, 140–41
on Palestinian state and U.S. role in creating, 94
2008–09 poll on U.S. hostility toward Islam, 73
2009 poll
on Afghanistan war, 64–65
on al Qaeda support, 140, 234
on attacks on U.S. civilians, 121
on attacks on U.S. troops, 21
on defamation of religion, 177
on democracy's compatibility with Islam, 154
on humanitarian intervention in Sudan, 188
on international law as governing, 182
on Muslim Brotherhood, 168
on non-Muslims allowed to hold public office, 155
on Obama, 15, 74
on religious scholars' and clergy's role, 160–61
2010 poll on Muslim views on U.S., 15
Muslim goals for, 162–64, 230
as study participant, 6
withdrawal of U.S. troops from, improving U.S. image by, 62–63, 200–01, 235

self-defense as sole grounds to use, 35, 224

threat of, 5, 50–55, 199, 202, 206–08, 228, 234

withdrawal of U.S. forces from Muslim countries, 199, 200–06

Missionaries from U.S., 28

Moderate Islamist movements and parties

al Qaeda's and radicals' rejection of moderate governments as illegitimate, 120, 165

controversial nature of, 164–72

and democracy, 154, 217–23

Mohammed, Khalid Sheikh, 225

Morocco

1999–2004 poll on democracy as desirable, 149

2001 and 2005 polls on September 11 attacks as justified, 122

2004 poll

on Iraq War as indicating U.S. pursuit of Middle East dominance, 107

on war on terrorism as justification for U.S. presence in Muslim countries, 70

2004–05 poll on U.S. intentions regarding democracy promotion, 110

2005 poll

on freedom of expression, 176

on freedom of religion, 173

on sharia as official law, 158

on U.S. as seeking to weaken and divide Islam, 75

on U.S. support for democracy in Middle East, 111

on women's rights, 179–80

2005–08 poll

on democracy as desirable, 149, 152

on pluralistic political environment, 176

on women's rights, 181

2005–09 poll on Muslim identity, 33

2006 poll

on al Qaeda support, 116, 117

on Arab rejection of existence of Israel, 90

on Christian expansion as U.S. goal, 81

on democracy as desirable, 105, 149, 150, 152

on democracy's compatibility with Islam, 153

on freedom of expression, 178

on freedom of religion, 174, 175

on human rights, 172–73, 177

on Muslim identity, 34

on Muslim views on U.S., 12

on positive attributes of U.S. and Western culture, 31

on radical groups attacking Americans, 17

on religious scholars' and clergy's role, 161–62

on separation of religion and state, 155

on sharia as official law, 156

on support for civilian attacks in Iraq to resist U.S. occupation, 123

on U.S. culture, 34

on women's rights, 180, 181

2006–07 poll

on civilian attacks as justified, 125

on democracy as desirable, 149

on freedom of religion, 173

on inevitability of conflict between Western and Muslim cultures, 29

on oil as U.S. right, 46

on U.S. trying to weaken Islam's growth, 86

on war on terrorism, 71

2006–08 poll

on radical groups attacking Americans, 19

on terrorism, 126

on U.S. control of world events, 60

on U.S. freedom of expression laws, 178

on U.S. goal to stop extremist control of Islamic countries, 108

2006–09 poll

on al Qaeda attacks on civilians, 120

on al Qaeda goal to end U.S. bias for Israel over Palestinians, 93

on bin Laden, 20, 142

on Israeli expansionism supported by U.S., 91

WPO polls, 2006–07 (cont.)
  on inevitability of conflict between Western and Muslim cultures, 29
  on U.S. trying to weaken Islam's growth, 86
  on war on terrorism, 71
2006–08
  on Muslim views of U.S., 12
  on terrorism, 125–26
  on UN powers, 182–83, 190
  on U.S. control of world events, 60
  on U.S. freedom of expression laws, 178
  on U.S. goal to stop extremist control of Islamic countries, 108
2006–09
  on al Qaeda attacks on civilians, 17–18, 20, 120–22
  on al Qaeda goals and methods, 20–21, 93–94, 127–28
  on bin Laden, 140–42
  on Israeli expansionism supported by U.S., 91–92
  on oil as U.S. right, 46–47
  on Palestinian state and U.S. role in creating, 93–95
  on sharia as official law, 156
  on suicide bombings, 126–27
  on U.S. working to weaken and divide Muslim world, 73–74
2007
  on justification for U.S. to bomb al Qaeda training sites, 67
  on trade and business ties between Muslim and Western countries, 32–33
2007–08
  on civilian attacks as effective, 124–25
  on September 11 attacks responsibility, 129–31
  on UN deference, 191
2007–09 on al Qaeda support, 116
2008
  on civilian attacks on Europeans, 123
  on democracy as desirable, 150–51
  on educational and cultural exchanges, 233
  on freedom of expression, 175
  on freedom of religion, 174, 176–77
  in Iran on Iraq war resolution, 230
  on Iran-U.S. relations, 231
  on Israeli-Palestinian conflict and U.S. role in resolving, 99
  on likelihood of al Qaeda attacks in U.S. if U.S. withdrew from Iraq, 71
  on military presence of U.S. in Muslim countries, 69–70
  on moderate governments as legitimate, 120
  on peaceful demonstrations against government, 176
  on religious proselytizing, 81, 175
  on September 11 attacks' consequences for Islamic world, 122
  on sex discrimination, 179
  on threat of military force from U.S., 52–53
  on U.S. control of UN, 191–92
  on U.S. culture, 34
  on women's rights, 179
2008–09
  on abuse of U.S. global power, 43
  on competing images of fundamental U.S. intentions, 87–88
  on humanitarian aid, 188–89
  on Islamist political parties' participation, 165–66
  on military presence of U.S. in Persian Gulf, 62–63
  on sharia role, 158–59
  on U.S. failure to live up to its ideals, 36–37
  on U.S. promotion of democracy in Middle East, 106–07
2009
  on Afghanistan situation, 64, 203–04
  on al Qaeda support, 140
  on attacks on U.S. troops, 21–22
  on Christian expansion as U.S. goal, 81
  on civilian attacks, 22–23, 136–37
  on defamation of religion, 177–78
  on democracy's compatibility with Islam, 152–53, 154
  on election fairness, 185–86
  on freedom of religion, 174